TIME'S SUBJECTS

TIME'S SUBJECTS

Horology and Literature in the Later Middle Ages and Renaissance

JOHN SCATTERGOOD

FOUR COURTS PRESS

Typeset in 10.5pt on 13.5pt CaslonPro by
Carrigboy Typesetting Services for
FOUR COURTS PRESS LTD
7 Malpas Street, Dublin 8, Ireland
www.fourcourtspress.ie
and in North America for
FOUR COURTS PRESS
c/o IPG, 814 N Franklin St, Chicago, IL 60610.

© John Scattergood and Four Courts Press 2022

A catalogue record for this title is available
from the British Library.

ISBN 978-1-80151-020-2

All rights reserved.
Without limiting the rights under copyright
reserved alone, no part of this publication may be
reproduced, stored in or introduced into a retrieval system,
or transmitted, in any form or by any means (electronic, mechanical,
photocopying, recording or otherwise), without the prior
written permission of both the copyright owner and
publisher of this book.

Printed in England,
by CPI Antony Rowe Ltd, Chippenham, Wilts.

in memoriam

Professor Eric Gerald Stanley
(1923–2018)

my teacher and my friend

Contents

LIST OF ILLUSTRATIONS		8
LIST OF ABBREVIATIONS		10
PREFACE		12
INTRODUCTION		15
1	The shape of time: history and the life of man	18
2	Living in time: years, months, weeks and days	50
3	Measuring time in the Middle Ages and Renaissance	80
4	The development of the mechanical clock	99
5	The use of time: some social and moral implications of the mechanical clock	120
6	Clocks, order and anxiety in some Renaissance texts	147
7	Some conclusions	164
NOTES		176
FURTHER READING		191
INDEX OF MANUSCRIPTS		193
GENERAL INDEX		195

Illustrations

FIGURES

1. The four ages of man: Byrhtferth's *Manual*; Oxford, Bodleian Library MS Ashmole 328. — 43
2. The seven ages of man: Langthorpe Tower, Northamptonshire, photograph by Julie Potton. — 47
3. The labours of the months: Oxford, Bodleian Library MS Digby 88. — 53
4. Town hall clock in Clusone, Lombardy. — 82
5. Sundial, St Gregory's Minster, Kirkdale, Yorkshire. — 85
6. Astrolabe with Arabic markings: Jean Fusoris, *c.*1430. — 89
7. Clepsydra or water-clock: Dar-al-Magana, Fez (Morocco). — 95
8. The mechanism of the Salisbury Cathedral clock. — 100
9. The verge and foliot escapement mechanism. — 101
10. Giovanni de' Dondi's Astrarium, Museo della Scienza e della Tecnologia 'Leonardo da Vinci'. — 105
11. The Hampton Court clock. — 107
12. The Strasbourg Cathedral clock. — 108
13. The Bourges Cathedral clock. — 110
14. Jacquemarts on the Cathedral of Notre Dame, Dijon. — 125
15. Pierre Moysant's skull watch. — 152

PLATES
appear between pages 96 and 97.

1. Four Monarchies: BL MS Additional 11695, the Silos Apocalypse.
2. Joachim da Fiore: Oxford Corpus Christi College MS 225a, fol. 10r.
3. Giorgione, *The Three Ages of Man*.
4a. January: Trento, Torre d'Aquila.
4b. April: Trento, Torre d'Aquila.

LIST OF ILLUSTRATIONS

5   August from *Les Très Riches Heures du Duc de Berri*.
6   Lady Eleanor Welles kneeling before the Virgin and Child: Dublin, Royal Irish Academy MS 12 R 31, fol. 196v.
7   January: BL MS Additional 18851, fol. 1v.
8   Ambrogio Lorenzetti, 'Fresco of good government', Palazzo Pubblico, Siena.
9   Richard of Wallingford and his clock. BL Cotton Nero D. VII, fol. 20.
10a The Wells Cathedral clock: Jack Blandiver.
10b The Wells Cathedral clock: the black and white knights.
11 The Prague town-square clock.
12 Heinrich Suso's *Horloge de Sapience*: Bruxelles Bibliothèque Royale MS IV. 111.
13 Abraham Mignon, *Stilleven met Bloemen en een Horloge, Still life with flowers and a watch*, c.1660.
14 Pieter Claesz, *Vanitas: still life 1630*.
15 *Nicholas Kratzer*, after Hans Holbein the Younger.
16 Charter of the Worshipful Clockmakers of London MS 6430.

Abbreviations

PRIMARY TEXTS

Chaucer — Quoted and referred to from the texts in *The Riverside Chaucer*, ed. Larry D. Benson, et al., 3rd edn (Boston, 1987)

Dante — Quoted and referred to from the texts in *The Divine Comedy of Dante Alighieri, Italian text with translation and comment* by John D. Sinclair, rev. edn, 3 vols (Oxford, 1948)

Donne's *Poems* — Quoted and referred to from the texts in *John Donne, the complete English poems*, ed. A.J. Smith (London, 1971)

Greene, *Carols* — *The early English carols*, ed. Richard Leighton Greene, 2nd edn, rev. and enlarged (Oxford, 1977)

Lydgate, *Minor poems* — Quoted and referred to from the texts in *The minor poems of John Lydgate*, 2 vols, ed. Henry Noble MacCracken, vol. I (EETS ES, 1962), vol. II (EETS OS 192, 1961)

Pepys's Diary — Quoted and referred to from the text in *Pepys's Diary*, selected and edited by Robert Latham, 3 vols (London, 1996)

Robbins, *Secular lyrics* — *Secular lyrics of the fourteenth and fifteenth centuries*, ed. Rossell Hope Robbins, 2nd edn (Oxford, 1964)

Shakespeare — The plays are quoted and referred to from the texts in *William Shakespeare, the complete works*, ed. Stanley Wells and Gary Taylor (Oxford, 1986)

Shakespeare, *Sonnets* — Quoted and referred to from the texts in William Shakespeare, *The Sonnets and a Lover's Complaint*, ed. John Kerrigan (London, 1995)

Skelton, *English poems* — Quoted and referred to from the texts in *The complete English poems of John Skelton*, ed. John Scattergood, rev. edn (Liverpool, 2015)

SCHOLARLY LITERATURE

Britten, *Old clocks* — F.J. Britten, *Old clocks and watches & their makers* (Antique Collectors Club, 1994)

Burrow, *Ages of man*	J.A. Burrow, *The ages of man: a study in medieval writing and thought* (Oxford, 1988)
Cipolla, *Clocks*	Carlo M. Cipolla, *Clocks and culture, 1300–1700* (New York and London, 2003)
Duncan, *Calendar*	David Ewing Duncan, *The calendar: the 5000-year struggle to align the heavens – and what happened to the ten missing days* (London, 1998)
Gimpel, *Medieval machine*	Jean Gimpel, *The medieval machine: the industrial revolution of the Middle Ages* (London, 1977)
Landes, *Revolution*	David S. Landes, *Revolution in time: clocks and the making of the modern world*, rev. and enlarged edn (Cambridge, MA, 2000)
Le Goff, *Time, work and culture*	Jacques Le Goff, *Time, work and culture in the Middle Ages*, translated by Arthur Goldhammer (Chicago, 1980)
North, *God's clockmaker*	John North, *God's clockmaker: Richard of Wallingford and the invention of time* (London, 2005)
Robertson, *Evolution*	J. Drummond Robertson, *The evolution of clockwork* (London, 1931)
Symonds, *English clocks*	R.W. Symonds, *A book of English clocks*, rev. edn (London, 1950)
Tait, *Clocks and watches*	Hugh Tait, *Clocks and watches* (British Museum, London, 1990)
Tilley	Morris Palmer Tilley, *A dictionary of the proverbs in England in the sixteenth and seventeenth centuries* (Ann Arbor, MI, 1950)
Turner, *Time*	*Time*, ed. A.J. Turner (The Hague, Tijd voor Tijd Foundation Amsterdam, 1990).
White, *Clockmakers*	Sir George White, *The clockmakers of London* (London, 1998)
Whiting	Bartlett Jere Whiting and Helen Scott Whiting, *Proverbs, sentences and proverbial sayings from English writings mainly before 1500* (Cambridge, MA, 1968)
Whitrow, *History*	G.J. Whitrow, *Time in history: views of time from prehistory to the present day* (Oxford, 1989)

Preface

THIS IS A BOOK ABOUT HOROLOGY and literature, particularly about how the development of the mechanical clock, and subsequently watches, was addressed by writers; what concepts emerged about the shape and construction of the universe, the ways in which society organized itself, what moral issues came to the fore and what anxieties. It makes no claim to be comprehensive, though it focusses mainly on England and English texts, it ranges over several centuries and a number of European languages; ideas about time were not confined to any one culture, nor were the instruments which were developed to measure it. Nor does this book claim to be definitive: anyone addressing these subjects needs to have limited aims. For one thing, the basic material of this study, early clocks, often went wrong, had to be repaired and upgraded, and so it is difficult sometimes, as in the case of the famous and elaborate Strasbourg clock (see p. 109), or the astronomical clock in Bourges (see p. 109), to know how much early work one is dealing with. The literature is also, sometimes, highly problematic in its allegorical and metaphorical manifestations.

I should like to thank the librarians and staff of the British Library London, the Bodleian Library Oxford, Cambridge University Library and the Library of Trinity College Dublin who have facilitated my researches over many years. I have also availed of the collection of Clocks in the British Museum London, the Victoria and Albert Museum London, the Museum of the Worshipful Company of Clockmakers of London, housed in the Guildhall, and the Museum of the History of Science Oxford, for its wonderful collection of astrolabes. I also owe an immense amount to scholars who have previously written on the topics addressed in this book and I hope I have given full recognition to them in what follows. I am particularly indebted to the work of, amongst others, Drummond Robertson, Carlo Cipolla, Jean Gimpel, David S. Landes, John North, and, for his many books on the subject of time, G.J. Whitrow – all of whom have guided me, by their writings, through this difficult and complex subject. But I have also used extensively the work of local historians – of clockmakers guilds, of cathedrals and towns and their clocks, and of individual testimonies both in print and verbally transmitted: I hope I have remembered and recorded and acknowledged what I owe to them.

But not all of this research is bookish or library based or museum based or based on verbal testimony, and cannot be so: some of what remains of early timekeepers and mechanical clocks has to be looked at, *in situ*. Consequently, I have a number of more practical and personal debts: overwhelmingly to my wife Alexandra Anderson, who has accompanied me on many informative and sometimes adventurous trips in Ireland, England, France and northern Italy looking for early clocks and time-measuring devices; to Iris Bedford, for some fine photos particularly of the Hampton Court clock; to Valérie Gallmard for an instructive visit to the astronomical clock at the cathedral of St Etienne, Bourges; to Karen Hodder, for a visit to look at the sun-dial on the south porch of St Gregory's Minster in Kirkdale (Yorks.) and for other information on Yorkshire clocks; and to my brother, Michael Scattergood, particularly for discussions on the mechanical workings and configurations of early clocks and especially of the *fusee*. My Trinity College friend of many years Tommy Murtagh has kindly read through the book and made various suggestions as to its structure and in relation to specific details: it is much the better for his help.

I also owe an immense debt to the late Dr Jan Jaap Haspels (1940–2016), curator for many years of the 'Museum Speelklok' in Utrecht. On one memorable afternoon, in 2007, when I was a Visiting Professor at the University of Utrecht, he showed me his collection of early clocks, and explained the technological workings of them, with examples which could be closely observed, accompanied by a detailed commentary of more clarity and more specificity than I had ever known. I am also grateful to his friend, and my long-time friend, Dr Erik Kooper, of the University of Utrecht, who, in the same year, accompanied me on an informative walk around Utrecht, an incomparable city of clocks and carillons.

This book has been a long time in the making, and my interest in horology and literature dates from many years back: it was initially a hobby which turned into an academic subject for research and greater development. I have already published two substantial essays on the subject – 'Writing the clock: the reconstruction of time in the late Middle Ages'[1] and 'A pocketful of death: horology and literature in Renaissance England'.[2] I have drawn freely on these essays in the pages which follow. But much of this book, particularly the closing chapters, has been written in the last two years – when I have largely, for reasons wholly apparent, been confined to my study. Consequently, access to public libraries has been limited and I have had to rely on my own personal collection of books, from correspondence and from what I could glean from the internet and from digitized collections. This is not how I might have wished rhe book to be, but in the circumstances of lockdown it is the best I can do. As always, I am grateful to Four Courts Presss for agreeing to publish this book and, especially, to Martin Fanning, for acquiring and organizing the illustrations for me – though I have chosen them.

Trinity College Dublin,
December 2021

Introduction

ANYBODY WHO SEEKS TO COME to terms with the idea of time engages in a difficult set of problems which, over a long historical sequence, have puzzled and frustrated some of the most eminent of thinkers. There are those, like the fifth-century Greek thinker Antiphon (c.480–411 BC), who asserted that time had no substantive existence but was an invented mental concept convenient for measurement, 'a point of view', writes one modern historian, 'that strikes us today as being remarkably modern'.[1] But time is a compelling subject and impossible to ignore because everybody is conscious, at an existential level, of living in time. The sequence of years, the turning of the seasons, the regular but uneven circular succession of the months, the weeks, the days all suggest the existence of a temporal continuum in the natural world. The sequence of human life – birth, infancy, childhood, adolescence, maturity, senescence, death – testifies to another trajectory, this time a linear one. 'We are time's subjects', as Shakespeare put it (2 *Henry IV*, I. iii. 110).

There is ample evidence, from the earliest periods, that men have sought to measure and organize temporal movement by means of calendars and a variety of timekeeping devices, often of great ingenuity and complexity, both at a public and at a private level. Most cities and towns, most organizations and businesses display public clocks. The domestic clock, the pocket watch, the wristwatch, the alarm-clock, the time signal on a computer or mobile telephone are among the latest personalized timekeepers, the omnipresent reminders of a revolution in timekeeping that took place between the thirteenth and the seventeenth centuries in Europe, a revolution which was gradual and hesitant, but which has, nevertheless, shaped many modern conceptions of time, creating a deep and lasting influence on behaviour at both a religious, political, social and personal level.

The basis of this horological revolution was scientific and technological: it depended on developments in physics and mechanics which were exploited so that it became possible to produce timekeeping machines independent of natural phenomena, sun and moon, daylight and darkness, and which were alternatives to fire-clocks, sand-clocks, water clocks and the like. Medieval society – especially the building, metalworking and cloth-making trades – was highly mechanized, but David S. Landes has proposed that the use of 'oscillatory motion to divide time into countable beats' was the 'great invention' of the age.² For Jean Gimpel, the most important machine developed in the late Middle Ages was the mechanical clock,³ and Jacques le Goff, addressing a shift in culture that he perceived in the fourteenth century, parodied Protagoras's famous humanist maxim and asserted that 'Henceforth the clock was to be the measure of all things.'⁴ In line with all this, Lewis Mumford argued that the mechanical clock was the most important instrument of change in early modern Europe:

> The clock, not the steam engine, is the key machine of the modern industrial age ... In its relationship to determinable quantities of energy, to standardization, to automatic action, and finally its own special product, accurate timing, the clock has been the foremost machine of modern technics.⁵

These positions, though very positively expressed, are clearly arguable. But whether they are true or not, they represent a progressivist attitude towards the evidence, a reading back in terms of what subsequently happened, and do not represent a view that prevailed in the later Middle Ages and the early modern period. With a few notable exceptions, early mechanical clocks were crudely designed and clumsily constructed, difficult to maintain and repair, inaccurate for the most part. And, though they were gradually improved and refined, they were used for a long time in conjunction with other methods of timekeeping and were not seen initially as devices that might displace other methods. There were, particularly on a social level, all sorts of ways of calculating time, and in many ways mechanical clocks were perceived to be inferior instruments: they frequently had to be reset by reference to sundials. One boastful motto on a sundial makes the contrast starkly:

> Je marque le temps vrai
> L'horloge marque le temps moyen.⁶
>
> [I mark true time; the clock marks mean time]

In the later Middle Ages and the early modern period it was their utility and convenience that largely ensured the success and spread of mechanical clocks rather than their mechanical accuracy.

What follows is concerned with the measurement of time and the development of the mechanical clock, and is especially about the impact of this new machine on society and on writing. It is not essentially an account of philosophical ideas about time, which are to some degree peripheral to the subject. A.J. Turner, writing about the origins of modern time, addressed the problem as follows:

> Time, as it is lived and used, and time as it is discussed by philosophers and theologians seem to have rather little to do with each other. In part this is the result of a preoccupation with different time-scales, in part because different kinds of time are being discussed. The time in which daily life is lived is felt to be qualitatively different from the time of the gods, and this again is different from the ritual time in which man attempts to approach his god, or the time in which he divides up and orders his past …[7]

It is, however, one of the most common paradoxes about time that it is easier to measure than to define and broader philosophical and theological questions about the nature of time, particularly those which are concerned with its shape and structure, had some influence, limited though real, on the way in which mechanical clocks were constructed and used. Most early mechanical clocks, it has to be remembered, were developed to serve the needs of religious houses, and latterly to serve the needs of political institutions, towns and cities, and, only after that, to serve the needs of individuals.

In the pages that follow I seek to address the ways in which, in the later Middle Ages and Renaissance, the invention and development of the mechanical clock competed with other methods of timekeeping and time calculation, and, gradually but inexorably, displaced them. The mechanical clock also changed the ways in which people thought about subjects such as time, the structure of their universe, the nature of their daily world, their political systems and society, their own moral and personal behaviour. The mechanical clock became, inevitably, particularly important in relation to subjects like transience and death. In general, I am concerned with the way writers reflected on these changes and came to terms with them – either through acceptance or by offering critical reservations, open or veiled.[8] All the evidence suggests that the mechanical clock immediately imposed itself on the imagination. It is adverted to not only in scientific and technological writings, but also in religious, devotional and political texts. More specifically, I seek to explore the ways in which writers incorporated the mechanical clock into their imaginative worlds and tried to address some of the issues it raised by way of using it as a focus and eliciting meaning from it – either as an emblem, or allegorically, or less directly through metaphor, or simile or allusion, or simply by description. However, it was not only writers who responded to the changes occasioned by the mechanical clock, but also those who designed the clocks and those who depicted them in art – hence the references to manuscript illustrations and paintings.

CHAPTER 1

The shape of time: history and the life of man

IT IS CLEAR THAT THOSE philosophers and theologians who addressed issues relating to time recognized only too well the difficulties of the subject. At the beginning of his *Enneads* in which he discusses problems relating to time and eternity Plotinus says that we think we 'have a clear and distinct experience of them' and are 'always speaking of them' but 'when we try to concentrate on them and, so to speak, get close to them, we find again that our thought runs into difficulties ...' (III. 7. 1).[1] And later, St Augustine famously wrote in his *Confessions* that he knew what time was well enough provided nobody questioned him on the subject, and admitted that if he tried to explain, 'I am baffled' (XI. 14).[2]

But despite their puzzlement, or perhaps because of it, both men and other early thinkers, such as Aristotle and Plato in Western Europe, addressed various aspects of the subject from various points of view. Questions were raised as to whether time had any real existence, and did it depend merely on motion and change as Aristotle in his *Physics* had proposed: 'not only do we measure the length of uniform movement by time, but also the length of time by movement, since they mutually define each other'. But, if so, what was time's relationship to rest? Did concepts like 'past', 'present' and 'future' have any validity, and did time pass always at the same speed? (IV. x–xii)[3] Questions were also asked about the relationship between the passage of time on earth and the turning of the heavens, the succession of the seasons, and the alternation between day and night. Larger questions were also raised as to whether time existed before the creation of the world and the relationship between time and history and time and eternity. Was time, as Plato proposed in his *Timaeus*, 'a movable image of eternity' (37A),[4] shown in the movement of the heavenly bodies, generated by the turning of the celestial sphere and so not existing in its own right but as something inherent in the make-up of the universe?

These and other issues impacted, sporadically and in individual cases, on subsequent discussions of time and on time measurement and the development of the mechanical clock. But perhaps the most important problem – one that divided the Christian St Augustine from the classical predecessors whose ideas he had used – involved the concept of the shape of universal time, its circularity or its linearity. Is time a circle or is it a line?[5]

The question, as posed thus, has more to do with metaphysics and religious belief than with the measurement of time, but beliefs generate crucial differences here. The belief in the circular nature of universal history and of time is perhaps best known through the concept of the Great Year, when the sun, moon and planets return to the positions they had when they were first created and set in time. Plato's understanding of this, as set down in the *Timaeus*, was highly influential. 'Time', he had written, 'came into existence along with the Heaven, to the end that having been generated together they might also be dissolved together' (38B) and a little later he expanded on this:

> ... it is quite possible to perceive that the complete number of Time fulfils the Complete Year when all the eight circuits with their relative speeds finish together and come to a head, when measured by the revolution of the Same and Similarly-moving ... (39D)

Plato's emphasis here is on the completeness of creation, but for Heraclitus this circularity involved destruction and rebirth: the universe originated in fire and would end in fire. These two ideas were fused together by some Stoic thinkers of late antiquity and had a considerable influence in the ancient world. In his *De Natura Deorum*, written in about 45 BC, Cicero, in a passage on Stoic philosophy, writes that, 'the mathematicians have based what they call the Great Year, which is completed when the sun, moon and five planets, having all finished their courses, have returned to the same positions relative to one another. The length of the period is hotly debated but it must necessarily be a fixed and definite time' (II. xx. 51–2).[6] Then the entire cycle would repeat itself. G.J. Whitrow, in his treatment of this topic, quotes Nemesius, the fourth-century bishop of Emesa, who, in his treatise on human nature, first refers to Stoic beliefs and then sets out the recurrent cyclical nature of things with great clarity and circumstantiality:

> Socrates and Plato and each individual man will live again, with the same friends and fellow citizens. They will go through the same experiences and the same activities. Every city and village and field will be restored, just as it was. And this restoration of the universe takes place not once, but over and over again – indeed to all eternity without end. Those of the gods who are not subject to destruction, having observed

the course of one period, know from this everything which is going to happen in all subsequent periods. For there will never be any new thing other than that which has been before, but everything is repeated down to the minutest detail.[7]

It goes without saying that this was but one view – there were Greek and Roman thinkers who did not accept this essentially backward-looking recursive view of things. But it remained powerful and was enhanced by the emergence of the equally attractive and consolatory myth of the 'golden age', the age of Saturn, a time of pastoral ease from which the world had declined, a time when the earth looked after itself and there was no need for labour.

One of the earliest expositions of this myth appears in Hesiod's *Works and Days*, which is a practical moral treatise on how to live well in a world which has become increasingly wicked because it has declined by stages from its former perfection (106–201).[8] He distinguishes five ages – that of gold when men 'dwelt in ease and peace on their lands with many good things, rich in flocks and loved by the blessed gods', then an age of silver and one of bronze, followed by an age of heroes, and then his own age (in which he wishes he did not live), that of iron 'when men never rest from labour and sorrow by day or perishing by night': the only way to preserve oneself in decency is through honest, productive toil, he says, and much advice on agriculture and husbandry follows. There is no sense in this poem that the 'golden age' will return, but there were also those, like Hesiod, who accepted the idea of the decline but held to the cyclical nature of things and thought that the 'golden age' would return and repeat the idyllic conditions of the past. And these ideas appealed to the Romans too. Much later, in his celebrated 'messianic' *Eclogue IV*, addressed to Asinius Pollio during his consulship, Virgil elides the idea of the cyclical nature of time and the return of the 'golden age':

> Ultima Cumaei venit iam carminis aetas;
> Magnus ab integro saeclorum nascitur ordo:
> Iam redit et Virgo, redeunt Saturnia regna;
> Iam nova progenies caelo demittitur alto. (4–7)

> [Now comes the last age of the Cumean Sybil's prophecy; the great ordering of the centuries is born again from its beginning: now Virgin Justice comes back and the reign of Saturn; now a new race descends from the high heavens.]

The age of iron (*ferrea*) will pass and the 'golden race' (*gens aurea*) will rise up throughout the earth, though 'a few traces of ancient sorrow will remain' (*pauca tamen subeunt priscae vestigia fraudis*). But it is an age that will involve repetition: a second Tiphys will steer the Argo for Jason and his adventurers, and Achilles will again go to fight at Troy (34–6).

This dominant classical view of the shape of universal time was most significantly challenged by St Augustine of Hippo (AD 354–430), a convert to Christianity who, even after his conversion, continued to be influenced by neo-Platonic ideas. In *The City of God* (XI. 5) he wrote that 'those Platonist philosophers excel all others in reputation and authority, just because they are nearer to the truth than the rest, even though they are a long way from it'.[9] And, like Plato, he believed that the concepts of time and the universe depended in some way upon each other, and that time can have no existence unless something is taking place, but, like Plotinus, he subjected Aristotle's identification of time with motion to critical scrutiny: the idea that the turning of the heavenly bodies provided a standard by which time could be judged was not valid, he argued, because if they ceased to turn, time would not stop. He sought the standard in his own mind, his own perception of the passing of time. Though he could be sure only of the present he used memory as evidence of the existence of a past and expectation (and biblical prophecy), as evidence of the existence of a future because both were present in his mind: 'It might be correct to say there are three times, a present of past things, a present of present things and a present of future things ... if we may speak in these terms, I can see three times and I admit that they do exist' (*Confessions* XI. 20). He is careful also to distinguish firmly between eternity and time:

> If we are right in finding the distinction between eternity and time in the fact that without motion and change there is no time, while in eternity there is no change, who can fail to see that there would have been no time, if there had been no creation to bring in movement and change ...? (*City of God* XI. 6).

Basing his ideas on Genesis 1:1, 'In the beginning God made heaven and earth ...', he asserts that it follows from this that there could be nothing existing except the creator before 'the beginning' and that 'the world was not created in time but with time' – that is to say that time came into being only with the creation of the world. He supports this with the mention subsequently (in Genesis 1:3–2:3) of the six or seven days of creation, though he admits that there are difficulties in defining what kind of 'days' they were, especially as 'the first three days passed without the sun, which was made, we are told, on the fourth day' (*City of God* XI. 7), though the previous days have a 'morning and evening'.

However, these difficulties apart, the conviction that eternity and time were distinct and that universal time had a beginning, enabled St Augustine to refute the idea of circular time, recursiveness and the idea of the 'eternal return', in his terms 'the postulate of periodic cycles'. Those who hold this view, he wrote,

> ... asserted that by those cycles all things in the universe have continually been renewed and repeated, in the same form, and thus there will be hereafter an unceasing sequence of ages, passing away and coming again in revolution. These cycles may take place in one continuing world, or it may be that at certain intervals the world disappears and reappears, showing the same features, which appear as new, but which in fact have been in the past and will return in the future. (XII. 14).

His objection to this is in part moral in that this view allows no possibility or reward for improvement: 'they are utterly unable to rescue the immortal soul from this merry-go-round, even when it has attained wisdom ...'. But, if lasting change is allowed, 'we may escape from these circuitous courses ... by keeping to the straight path in the right direction under the guidance of sound teaching'. Universal time is rectilinear not circular and is sustained by the possibility of moral improvement: St Augustine has shifted the argument from the logical to the moral. He dismisses the idea of repetition that 'the same Plato, the same city, the same school, and the same disciples have appeared time after time and are to reappear time after time in innumerable centuries in the future'. Instead, he asserts, basing his argument on Romans 6:9, 'Christ died once for all our sins' and that 'in rising from the dead he is never to die again', and, turning to I Thessalonians 4:17, after the resurrection 'we shall be with the Lord forever'. Christ's death was a unique event and a revelatory demonstration that the future would not repeat the past and that there is eternity outside the sequence of universal time. It has to be stressed here that some of these arguments are based on the precept that 'the Bible cannot lie' and that St Augustine sometimes has a problem with texts, such as that from Ecclesiastes 1:9 that 'there is no new thing under the sun' (*nihil sub sole novum*), but argues that this refers simply to events in the natural world and does not impugn his view of universal time. On the other hand, he uses the text from Vulgate Psalm 11:9 '*in circuitu impii ambulant*' '[the ungodly will walk in a circle]' to be a condemnation of those believing in the cyclical nature of universal time and history.

There were, of course, Christian views of universal time that did not correspond to St Augustine's, but in general, circularity was replaced by linearity: universal time was framed by two events, a beginning and an end, the creation of the world and the promise in the future of the second coming, referred to in Romans 13:11–12, which St Paul thought was imminent, but which remained, in many ways logically, undefined and a feature of the indefinite future, though the subject of much speculation.

II

Although the Christian west established the idea of linear time as opposed to classical notions of cycles, it inherited the Roman calendar.[10] This had been established by Julius Caesar, on the advice of the Greek astronomer Sosigenes, on 1 January 45 BC, a modified version of which is still used practically all over the world. In an attempt to align the civil year with the solar year he established the true year as comprising 365¼ days: the ordinary civil year would have a duration of 365 days, but every fourth year would be a leap year of 366 days. Julius Caesar established months of alternating 31 and 30 days: January, March, May, July, September and November having 31 days and the others 30, except for February which had 29 days and 30 days each leap year. An elegant and logical system, but vanity interposed itself. In 7 BC the supporters of Augustus Caesar persuaded the Roman senate to rename the month which had been called 'Sextilis' after him (part of the argument was that the month had been particularly auspicious for him) and because it was held that it could not have fewer days than the previous month, which had been named July after his previously murdered great-uncle, a day was taken away from February and transferred to August. This would have meant that three months in succession would have 31 days, and so September and November were reduced by a day and October and December increased by a day. There were various later attempts to rename months after emperors, though none was generally successful. However, by the intrusion of Augustus into the calendar and the adjustments it entailed, Julius Caesar's simpler more logical system was disturbed and the necessity arose for mnemonics for the diversity to be remembered. A late medieval English verse from British Library MS Harley 2341 runs:

> Thirti dayes hath novembir,
> April, iune and septembir;
> Of xxviij ti is but oon,
> And all the remenaunt xxx ti and j.[11]

Later rhymes, such as the one I was taught as a child, tend to be longer and more specific about the anomalousness of February.[12]

Originally the Roman yearly calendar began on 1 March, which is still reflected in the names of the months September, October, November and December – whose names were based on numerals and were the seventh to the tenth in order. But in 153 BC the consuls, who were elected for a single year, began to take up office on 1 January, and the month named after Janus, the two-ways-facing god, the god of doorways, of exits and entrances, of endings and beginnings, came to be regarded as the beginning of the year. This aspect of the calendar proved to be problematic for the Christian west, since it was associated with pagan rituals, and they sought to establish their own chronological systems, which were more in line with the triumphalist advent and establishment of Christianity and their own sense of the linearity of time.

What Christian thinkers had in common was a wish to mark the beginning of the year with a date that was important in the Christian calendar, but the solutions they devised were various.[13] There was also the implication of the counting of the years. When in AD 596 Pope Gregory sent Augustine of Canterbury and his companions to England to evangelize the Britons, the monks were understandably reluctant to travel to somewhere so distant and barbarous, but Gregory insisted and sent them a letter of encouragement which he dated in the imperial form: '... the twenty third of July, the fourteenth year of the reign of the most pious Emperor Maurice Tiberius Augustus, and the thirteenth year of his consulship, the fourteenth indiction'. But Bede, who tells the story in his *Historia Ecclesiastica Gentis Anglorum* (I. 23),[14] has a different dating system from the one he quotes here – a system adopted from the work of the Scythian monk Dionysius Exiguus (*c.*500–60) whose work on the calculation of Easter in 525 had also included the suggestion of dating the Christian era from the birth of Christ, the *anno domini* (AD) system still in use. Bede referred to this system in his treatise on time, *De Temporum Ratione* (written in 725), and used it extensively in his later *Historia*, opening many chapters with an *anno domini* date and framing his closing summary (V. 24) in these terms; he also uses the BC dating in I. 2, '... sixty years before the birth of our lord'. But sporadically he refers to dates in terms of other systems – references to years after the foundation of Rome (I. 3; I. 11), the occasional regnal date (IV. 21) and sometimes an episcopal date (IV. 2), as well as the imperial dating of papal documents as seen above. He also adopted in *De Temporum Ratione* the date Dionysius had suggested for the beginning of the year – the 'incarnation' of Christ, Christmas Day, 25 December, but in his history he continued to use the indiction dates in September which were still used after Bede's time for the dating of charters. In this he was reluctant to change. 'Consequently', according to R.L. Poole, 'throughout his History, Bede made his Year of Grace begin in September'.¹⁵ But the Christmas Day date for the beginning of the year was adopted in Europe by the imperial chanceries and by the papacy, where it was used in formal documents until 1098 and longer in personal correspondence. It was used by French kings until 1111 'and generally in Western Europe, outside Spain, until the twelfth century'. Some Benedictine houses in England used it until the beginning of the fourteenth century.

This method of calculation was, however, challenged by other systems. It was eventually displaced in much of Europe by a system based on the feast of the Annunciation, 25 March, but this took two forms. The more logical of these, the *calculus Pisanus*, began the AD year-count in the year before Christ's birth. This system seems to have originated in southern France in the late ninth century, but was enthusiastically adopted in Pisa, where it persisted until 1750, and for a time in Lucca and Siena.¹⁶ Its use never extended over very much territory and it became a very inconvenient style to use, particularly because of Pisa's proximity to Florence, where the so-called *stylus Florentinus* held sway. This system began the year on 25 March, Lady Day, but counted the beginning of the Christian era from that date in the year following Christ's birth. This system was not developed in Florence any more than the *calculus Pisanus* was developed in Pisa, but seems to have originated again in France in the early eleventh century. But this style, despite its illogicality, had wide geographical use in Europe: it was adopted in England in the late twelfth century and remained the official mode of reckoning until 1751/2.¹⁷ This style can be seen in Chaucer: in *The Nun's Priest's Tale*, he dates Chauntecleer's misadventure with the fox as 3 May, a traditionally 'unlucky' date in Chaucer though rarely in anybody else:

> Whan that the month in which the world began,
> That highte March, whan God first maked man,
> Was compleet, and passed were also
> Syn March was gon, thritty dayes and two,
> Bifel that Chauntecleer ... (*CT*, VII. 3187–91)

The Lady Day start for the year also lies behind the naming of the ill-matched characters in *The Merchant's Tale*: January is meant to be an old man of sixty or so (*CT*, IV. 1252), while his unsuitable wife May is meant to be a teenager (1742–9).

Not so successful was the attempt to calculate from Easter – which had all the chronological disadvantages of being a moveable feast. There is evidence from Gervase of Canterbury, in about 1200, as he lists the various ways in which historians calculated the beginning of the year, that the reckoning from Easter was an idea he recognized: '*quidam vero a Passione*'. But this system appears to have flourished only in France: it became an established rule in the French chancery as early as 1215. It has been suggested that this extremely 'inconvenient' system had a political basis: Philip Augustus chose to adopt it because, according to R.L. Poole, 'he desired to mark his conquest of the English possessions in France by the use of a style different from those which had been current in them'. But its currency was limited: 'The court style seems never to have penetrated into Cahors, Rodez or Angoulême, and it is more than doubtful that it did into Poitou'. The Lady Day system was still current in the Auvergne in 1478.[18]

A lot of this diversity, however, was caused not so much by the logic of chronological investigation as by political considerations: the empire, the papacy, individual states and their rulers wished to impose their own configurations as to how time, in the Christian era, was to be calculated and expressed. And, because of the fractured state of Europe, with its plethora of diversely controlled (and often warring) territories, contiguous areas often had contrasting time-schemes. R.L. Poole's famous reconstruction of the predicament of the hypothetical traveller from Venice (which began its year on 1 March) to southern France in the mid-thirteenth century is still eminently apposite and worth repeating, as he demonstrates that, in terms of time-schemes, the traveller could arrive at his destination before he set out:

> If we suppose a traveller to set out from Venice on March 1, 1245, the first day of the Venetian year, he would find himself in 1244 when he reached Florence, and if after a short stay he went to Pisa, the year 1246 would have already begun there. Continuing his journey westward he would find himself again in 1245 when he entered Provence and on arriving in France before Easter (April 16) he would be once more in 1244.[19]

It would be reasonable to suppose that this traveller, considering the inadequacy of contemporary maps, might find himself puzzled as to where he was in terms of geographical space, but as this witty, but accurate and plausible vignette demonstrates, he might have also have had difficulties of locating himself, with any confidence, in time. However, if he had any memorial knowledge, or a reliable calendar or almanac, he would have been able to recognize the month or the day if not the year.

Both calendars and almanacs ran from January to December and 1 January remained, in the popular consciousness, as the first day of the New Year, even though other dates were used formally. The early Tudor poet John Skelton adopts this system at the closure of *The Garlande of Laurell*, published in 1523, perhaps because his dream of literary fame encompasses both the classical world and the world of contemporary writing.[20] The adoption of the 1 January beginning of the year, in this context, is very specific, as the two-faced god Janus, the Roman god of endings and beginnings, is described, using his astronomical tools ('tirikkis', 'volvell') as he constructs his almanac for the coming year. Disturbed from his dream by the congratulatory accolade for his entry into the rolls of Fame, Skelton awakens and looks to heaven:

> … Where I saw Janus, with his double chere,
> Makyng his almanak for the new yere;
> He turnyd his tirikkis, his volvell ran fast,
> Good luck this newe yere, the olde yere is past. (XXI, 1515–18)[21]

This could scarcely be clearer. But the beginning of the year was less simple and presented a special problem for Edmund Spenser in relation to his *Shepheardes Calender*, published in 1579. In a prefatory essay addressing 'the generall argument of the whole booke', attributed to E.K. (perhaps Edward Kirke, a Cambridge contemporary of Spenser's, or perhaps by Spenser himself with some contribution from his friend Gabriel Harvey), it is stated that 'it is wel known, and stoutely mainteyned with stronge reasons of the learned, that the yeare beginneth in March'. But there follows a circuitous argument, with much learned reference back to the Julian reform of the calendar in 45 BC, about alternative year-beginnings and a justification of the form of the poem (imitated from classical eclogues) which runs like an ordinary calendar from January to December: the author 'thinketh it fittest according to the simplicitie of common understanding to begin with Ianuarie', because shepherds would understand the structure of the year that way and not be cognizant of the subtleties of alternative calculations. Nevertheless, some trace of the system of beginning the year in March gets into the 'Argument' prefacing the February eclogue, which contains a lengthy discourse by Thenot on old age: 'The matter very well accordeth with the season of the moneth, the yeare now drouping, and as it were, drawing to his last age'.[22] It may be that Spenser refers to two systems because he was aware calendar reform was being discussed in learned papal circles at this time and in 1582 Pope Gregory XIII, following good mathematical advice, proposed a modification of the Julian calendar, adjusting the calculation of leap-years so as to bring the calendar more in line with the seasons, and proposing 1 January, the old Roman date, as the beginning of the year. This resulted in what is essentially the modern calendar, and was widely accepted in the states of Catholic Europe, but resisted, because of its associations with the papacy, by Protestant states such as England, where it only came into force in 1751/2.

The general acceptance and spread of *anno domini* dating, however configured, did not mean that other systems were discarded: they were sometimes used along with it, producing dates in which some elements were 'superfluous'. Michael Clanchy quotes a document drawn up by an imperial notary, Henry of Asti, which is dated: 'Anno a nativitate Christi millesimo ducentesimo sexagesimo octavo, indictione undecima, die Mercurii xviii intrante mense Januarii, pontificatus domini Clementis papae iiii anno tercio'. The date, Wednesday 18 January 1268 AD is precise and all that is necessary: the reference to the papal year, the third of Clement IV and the eleventh indiction, really add nothing. But whether because the writer is following some predetermined system of organization or whether because of opportune knowledge chronicles sometimes included dates by papal year, or regnal year, and some city chronicles refer to mayoral years if the chronicler chooses to be as comprehensive as he can. And, as Clanchy points out, sometimes along with a date, an event is recalled in order to enhance the memory of something: he quotes an agreement made 'in the year 1192 AD, namely the year in which Earl William de Ferrers took to wife Anneis, sister of Ranulf earl of Chester'.[23] Individuals sometimes also wrote the events of their own lives into dates, none more so than Ralph de Diceto, dean of St Paul's London, in his survey of the cathedral's charters:

> The 1181st year AD, the 21st year of Pope Alexander III, the 27th regnal year of King Henry II of the English, the 11th regnal year of King Henry the son of the king, the 18th year that time has passed since the translation of Bishop Gilbert Foliot from Hereford to London, when this inquest was made by Ralf de Diceto, dean of London, in the first year of his deanship.[24]

It is doubtful whether any document was ever more elaborately dated: there are six different systems involved here, which may be in a descending order of importance, but what is obvious also is that Ralph wants his own, newly acquired, position as dean to be recorded and remembered. Much later, and in a totally different context, John Skelton devised his own, very personal system of dating his poems. Its beginning date appears to be sometime in the late autumn of 1488 – which may have been chosen to celebrate his first laureateship (he referred to himself habitually as 'Skelton laureate') or, more likely, to mark his entry into the Tudor royal service, or conceivably both. Thus

'21' is written in a scroll at the end of his holograph copy of *A Lawde and Prayse Made for our Sovereigne Lord the Kyng*, a coronation poem written for Henry VIII in 1509. And the same system is used in relation to later texts.[25] It is not that Skelton wished to avoid conventional dating: conventional dates appear in several of his works and the poem in which he celebrates his career as a poet, *The Garlande of Laurel*, was printed, according to its colophon, by Richard Faukes in 'the yere of our lorde god M CCCCC xxiij the iij day of Octobre'. All the same, it is clear that Skelton wanted, in addition, a more personal way of registering his trajectory through time.

III

The acceptance of the concept of linear time, that the world had a beginning and an end, also had a profound effect on the way in which history was viewed in the Christian west, and the periodization of history, in strictly Christian terms, was a topic for exploration, though both of the major schemes used, in Beryl Smalley's terms, 'saddled medieval historians with a gloomy view of their times'.[26] The belief that the world would end proved particularly disturbing and generated a great deal of speculation, over many centuries, about the shape of Christian history and the coming of the 'last days'.

The 'four monarchies' or 'four kingdoms' scheme was generated by interpretations of two prophetic dreams in Daniel 2 and 7. In 2:32–3 Nebuchadnezzar sees an image whose 'head was of fine gold, his breast and his arms of silver, his belly and his thighs of brass, his legs of iron, his feet part of iron and part of clay'. This image, which is destroyed by a stone, figures the four kingdoms (2:37–41), the last of which is divided and partly strong and partly weak. In Daniel's dream he sees four beasts emerging from the sea (7:3–8), a lion with eagle's wings, a bear, a leopard and a large beast with iron teeth, and ten long horns and one shorter one, which 'shall devour the whole earth, and shall tread it down and break it in pieces' (23) – the ten horns being 'ten kings that shall arise, and another shall rise after them, and he shall be diverse from the first, and he shall subdue three kings' (24), but his dominion will eventually be destroyed by 'the Ancient of Days' (22). These mythographic texts prompted numerous illustrations, such as that finished in 1109 by a Spanish monk, now London, British Library MS Additional 11695, where the Ancient of Days sits in his mandorla throne above the four beasts: the middle horn on the fourth beast is, breaking the allegory, represented by a human head (see Plate 1).[27] This apocalyptic prophecy, not surprisingly, also gave plenty of scope for interpretation, but that offered by Jerome (*c.*347–420) in his

Commentary on Daniel was particularly influential: he understood the four kingdoms to be the Babylonian empire, the empire of the Medes and the Persians, the Greek empire presided over by Alexander, and lastly the Roman empire – which was still in being, though apparently destined for destruction, or at least for termination.[28]

The Old Testament book of Daniel was frequently interpreted along with the apocalyptic book of Revelations from the New Testament, and the beasts are recalled by John in 13:1:

> And I stood upon the sand of the sea, and saw a beast rise up out of the sea, having seven heads and ten horns and upon his horns were crowns, and upon his head the name blasphemy.

The next verse compares him to a leopard, a bear, a lion and a dragon, and in verses 18–21 the fall of Babylon is predicted. The beast, who is called a dragon, 'the old serpent', the Devil and Satan, is confronted, however, and overcome, bound with a chain and cast into a bottomless pit for a thousand years, though after that 'he must be loosed a short season' (20:1–3).[29] For those adhering to the four monarchies theory of world history, this gave fertile ground for speculation about the coming of Antichrist and the end of the world, especially as the year AD 1000 approached – none more so than Adso (c.910–92), abbot of Montier-en-Der, a hagiographer and a confidant of the West Frankish royal family. His *Libellus Anticristi* was written in about 954 and dedicated to Gerberga, wife of the future Louis IV.[30] Antichrist was usually identified with heretics, who divided the church, or the Jews and Adso chooses this second option and, relying on Genesis 49:17, avers that he will come from the tribe of Dan. By terror, gifts and miracles he will attempt to seduce mankind, and will produce troubled times and national and natural disasters such as have never before been seen (Daniel 12:1; Matthew 24:6–8, 24). 'This terrible and fearful tribulation will last three and a half years throughout the world', he writes, echoing the 'forty-two months' of Revelations 13:5, the specified duration of the power of the beast. Alluding to the four monarchies theory of linear history he mentions the passing of the Persian and Greek empires, but says that their Roman successors may not be destined for imminent destruction. Relying on II Thessalonians 2:1–3, he writes that the Day of Judgment will not occur unless there is a 'falling away of faith', and that 'as long as the kings of the Franks, who hold the empire by right, shall last, the dignity of the Roman Empire will not perish'. With a further gesture towards his masters he alters the pseudo-Methodius story of the 'last emperor',[31] which had predicted he would be '*rex Romanorum et Graecorum*' [a king of the Romans and Greeks], to a Frankish king (*rex Francorum*): one of the kings of the Franks will come in the last time and will be the last and the greatest of all rulers.

The constant rationalization of a postponement of the Day of Judgment is a feature of these prophecies of the duration of Christian lineal time: forty days will be allowed for penance for those who were led astray by Antichrist, but 'no man knows how great the space of time there may be after they have finished this penance until the Lord comes to judge'. Perhaps logically in the light of this and because the world did not end in AD 1000, Adso's *Letter* was edited, adapted, and revised extensively in the succeeding centuries.[32]

This scheme, however, was not as influential as Augustine's division of history into '*sex aetates*' [six ages], as expounded in *De Diversis Quaestionibus LXXXIII* and again, more elaborately, in *De Genesi contra Manichaeos*. Basing his division on the opening chapters of Genesis, and so on the Judaic hexameral tradition, he proposed that both the 'ages of the world' and the 'ages of man' corresponded to the six days of creation: there is an *infancia* [infancy] from Adam to Noah, a *pueritia* [childhood] from Noah to Abraham, an *adolescentia* [adolescence] from Abraham to King David, then a period to the Babylonian captivity corresponding to *juventus* [young manhood] and then a period to the coming of John the Baptist that he calls *gravitas* [middle age]. The sixth age, in which Augustine thought he was living, was the period that lasted from the coming of Christ until the end of time – the Christian era – which he equated with *senectus* [old age], but it is only the 'exterior' old man who decays, while the 'interior' is constantly renewed in the hope of the eternal rest of the Sabbath, when time is subsumed into eternity. He expounded it again, more simply, without the comparison with the ages of man, in the closing pages of *De Civitate Dei*: 'After the present age God will rest, as it were, on the seventh day, and he will cause us, who are the seventh day, to find our rest in him' (XXII. 30).[33] This scheme of the *sex aetates mundi* was adopted by Isidore of Seville in his *Etymologiae*, and from there it entered the encyclopaedic tradition and was frequently replicated.[34] In a Provençal verse encyclopaedia dating from the late thirteenth century, now London, British Library MS Yates Thompson 31, fol. 77r has a circular illustration of the six ages beginning with Adam and Eve and ending with Mary and the Christ child with a priest celebrating mass: an angel at the centre of the circle announces the coming of the seventh age.[35]

In another illustrated encyclopaedia, the *Liber Floridus*, Ghent University Library MS 02, compiled by Lambert of St Omer in the early twelfth century, the 'four monarchies' scheme and Augustine's six ages are run together: at the bottom of the picture Nebuchadnezzar dreams both of the metallic statue and the tree of his second dream (Daniel 4:1–25), which was to be cut down though its roots are to be allowed to remain. Daniel interpreted this dream to mean that a king would fall but would rise again when 'seven times' had passed over him. But in the illustration the 'seven times' are interpreted in Augustinian terms: the tree has seven branches with the '*aetates mundi*' noted beside them.³⁶

Augustine, like Adso, had been careful to make the point that the precise date of the end of linear time cannot be known. In *De Diversis Quaestionibus LXXXIII* he points out that *senectus* [old age] can last for a long time and that is why, he reasons, we cannot know how many generations will make up the last age of the human race before the ending of the world. But just as the date of AD 1000 focussed minds, so the indefiniteness of the date of the end of the world allowed a latitude of interpretation which was exploited, particularly by those with a political and moral agenda.

Wulfstan, bishop of Worcester, sought to improve the moral and political climate of England in a homily addressed to his countrymen 'quando Dani maxime persecuti sunt eos, quod fuit anno millesimo XIIII ab incarnacione Domini nostri Iesu Cristi' [when the Danish attacks were most severe on them, which was in the year 1014 from the incarnation of our Lord Jesus Christ]. The AD date of 1014 is clear, but the notion of the possible ending of the world, the coming of Antichrist and the signs of the 'last days' (Matthew 24:3–29), about which Wulfstan had written in other homilies,³⁷ hang over this text and are adverted to by its author:

> Leofan men, gecnawað þæt soð is: ðeos worold is on ofste, and hit nealæcð þam ende, and þy hit is on worolde aa swa leng swa wyrse, and swa hit sceal nyde for folces synnan ær Antecrystes tocyme yfelian swyþe, and huru hit wyrð þænne egeslic and grimlic wide on worolde. Understandað eac georne þæt deofol þas þeode nu fela geara dwelode to swyþe, and þæt lytle getreoþa wæran mid mannum, þeah hy wel spræcan, and unrihta to fela ricsode on lande, and næs a fela manna þe smeade ymbe þa bote swa georne swa man scolde …³⁸
>
> [Dear men, realize what the truth is: this world is in haste and is nearing the end, and for this reason the longer it is the worse it will become in the world, and so it will need to be much worse, because of people's sins, before the coming of Antichrist, and then, truly, it will become terrible and cruel widely in the world. Understand readily also that the devil has led this people astray too much for many years, and that there has been little truthfulness among men, though they have spoken well, and too many wrongs have dominated in this land, and there were not many people who sought a remedy as readily as they should …]

Wulfstan was an important political figure, a royal counsellor and a legislator as well as a homilist, and he saw himself, with some justification, as one of the leaders of his people who was capable of speaking to them collectively from a position of authority. Here he stresses to the English that their current misfortunes are the result of their sins and crimes: in the disturbed political situation, which he memorably describes, where the end of the world may be imminent, they needed to reform both morally and politically, to observe the laws and to show respect and consideration for each other. Whether this homily had any practical effect cannot be known, but it survives in five manuscript copies and evidently had a wider currency than most other surviving Anglo-Saxon texts.

This gloom about the present, however, ran deep in the imagination of other late Anglo-Saxon writers, not just in authoritarian figures with a moral and political agenda. Though the surviving text is damaged and incomplete, the poet of *The Ruin*, from the tenth-century Exeter Book, articulates the feeling that the world is running down as he contemplates a once beautiful but now ruined city: the line 'ofer harne stanas hate streamas' (43) [the hot water flowing over the grey stones] makes one think he may have had in mind the dilapidated Roman city of Bath, as does the later phrase 'þær þa baþu wæron' (46) [where the baths were]. But the poet's opening is important:

> Wrætlic is þes wealstan, wyrde gebræcon;
> burgstede burston, brosnaþ enta geweorc ... (1–2)[39]

> [Wonderful is this stone wall, destroyed by fate; the site of the city has crumbled, the work of giants is rotting away ...]

Whether this refers to Bath or not, it looks as though the remnants of Roman civilization in Britain left their mark and contributed to the sense that the present was inferior to the past. And this is also memorably expressed in a passage from *The Seafarer*, again from the Exeter Book, in which the poet contemplates his own personal situation in a declining world:

> Gedroren is þeos duguð eal, dreamas sind gewitene;
> wuniað þa wacran ond þas woruld healdaþ,
> brucað þurh bisgo. Blæd is gehnæged,
> eorþan indryhto ealdað and searað,
> swa nu monna gehwylc geond middangeard. (86–90)[40]

> [The whole company of warriors has fallen; their joys have slipped away; the weaker remain, and occupy this world, possess it with toil. Splendour

has been brought low; the nobility of the earth grows old and fades, just as now does each man throughout the middle earth.]

The decline of the world and the passing of its glories prompts contemplation of the poet's own aging in the lines that follow – the face that loses its colour, the greying hair (91–2), and from there to thoughts of the stability of eternity. Because 'seo molde onyrreð' (103) [this world will pass away] and men with it, he says, it is better to trust in God's 'ecan eadignesse' (120) [eternal blessedness], and it is with a consolatory faith in 'ece Dryhten' (124) [the eternal Lord] that he ends his profound meditation on the passing of things.

The fact that the world did not end in AD 1000, or anywhere near it, did not deter speculation and millenarian sentiments that surfaced from time to time, especially in situations of high political tension. Particularly influential in this regard were the writings of Joachim da Fiore (c.1135–1202).[41] Born near Cosenza in Calabria, he became initially, like his father, a notary and had a position, for a time, at the Sicilian court in Palermo. But he experienced a religious conversion, went on a pilgrimage to Jerusalem and on his return joined the impoverished Benedictine monastery at Corazzo in 1171 and soon became abbot of the house. In 1182 he was allowed by Pope Lucius III to give up the position and joined the Cistercians at Casamari, a much larger monastery just south of Rome, where he produced several of his most important works, including the *Expositio in Apocalypsim*, out of which came an influential and controversial periodization of history. Basing his analysis on the serial domination of the Trinity, he argued that there were three ages – that of the Father, corresponding to the time of the Old Testament, and characterized by obedience and the fear of God, that of the Son which dated from the coming of Christ, characterized by faith and filial submission, and a third age, that of the Holy Spirit, or the age of the 'everlasting gospel', which had not yet come about but which would be an age of love and freedom for the whole of humanity. His concept of the third age was based on Revelations 14:6:

> And I saw another angel fly in the midst of heaven, having the everlasting gospel to preach unto them that dwell on earth, and to every nation, and kindred, and tongue, and people.

Two other verses from Revelations, 11:3 and 12:6, which mention 'a thousand two hundred and threescore days' suggested that the beginning of the third age might be in 1260. Joachim also suggested a process through which the third age might be established. Between the time of his writing and the beginning of the third age a new order of monks would emerge who would preach the 'everlasting gospel' throughout the world, convert the Jews and lead all men from a love of the things of the world to a love of the things of the spirit. In Oxford, Corpus Christi College MS 255A, which is probably central Italian, this is shown diagrammatically on fol. 10r (see Plate 2). The three ages are represented as a tree with the Father, Christ and the Holy Spirit painted in roundels in ascending order up the trunk: the two peoples, the Jews and the gentiles, are represented as branches of the tree bearing leaves and fruits which signify virtues – these being most prolific in the third age.[42] In the three-and-a-half years (Revelations 13:5) before the coming of the third age a secular Antichrist figure would emerge who would chastise and destroy the corrupt church before his overthrow and the fulfilment of the age of the Spirit.[43] Joachim submitted all his writings to Pope Innocent III in 1200, but died before judgment was passed on them.

Though the sanctity of Joachim's life and the power of his preaching were much admired, and though he attracted disciples to him when he broke away from the Cistercians at Casamari and founded his own stricter order in Calabria at the abbey of Fiore in 1198, his writings did not immediately attract very much attention. But, to use Norman Cohn's word, they became 'explosive' when taken over, edited, and reinterpreted by the Spiritual Franciscans in the middle of the thirteenth century, who also forged prophecies which they fathered on Joachim: some of these, indeed, envisioned the Spiritual Franciscans as the new order which would replace the established church and lead mankind into the third age.[44] A number of ideas associated with Joachim were declared heretical: the Fourth Lateran Council of 1215, for example, condemned his ideas on the Trinity. But Dante places him in heaven, amongst the Franciscans: next to Hrabanus Maurus shines 'il calavrese abate Giovaccio / di spirito profetico dotato' (*Paradiso*, XII. 139–40) [the Abbot Joachim from Calabria, endowed with the spirit of prophecy]. What is perhaps most striking about Joachim's ideas and what has made them attractive over the centuries is that he envisions the perfectibility of the third age as being achievable not after the end of the world, but in the world and in time.

IV

As to the duration of man's life, the text from Psalm 90:10 is unequivocal: 'The days of our years are three-score years and ten, and if by reason of strength they be four-score years, yet is their strength labour and sorrow; for it is soon cut off and we fly away.' This was accepted as a good rough estimate: though some people did live beyond seventy in the Middle Ages and Renaissance the great majority never attained that age. But the idea was persistent and long-lasting. For example, in Charles Dickens's *Martin Chuzzlewit* (1842) there is a pretty exact reiteration of the sentiments of Psalm 90:10 in Mr Jonas's angry complaint to Miss Charity about his father's longevity:

> ... now he's gone so far without giving in, I don't see much to prevent his being ninety; no, nor even a hundred. Why, a man with any feeling ought to be ashamed of being eighty, let alone more. Where's his religion, I should like to know, when he goes flying in the face of the Bible like that? Three-score-and-ten's the mark; and no man with a conscience, and a proper sense of what's expected of him, has any business to live longer.[45]

And a little later, in 1896, A.E. Houseman contemplates how much time he needs to appreciate the Eastertide cherry blossom:

> Now, of my threescore years and ten,
> Twenty will not come again
> And take from seventy springs a score
> It only leaves me fifty more ...[46]

And in my own lifetime, as a child, I was taught the mnemonic jingle: 'The days of men / Are three-score years and ten'.

Perhaps the most notable use of this idea in the Middle Ages occurs in the opening of the *Divina Commedia*. Dante, with his customary attention to detail and his awareness of the implication of dates in the ecclesiastical calendar, situates the opening of the poem precisely:

> Temp' era dal principio del mattino,
>   e 'l sol montava'n su con quelle stelle
>   ch'eran con lui quando l'amor divino
> Mosse di prima quelle cose belle ... (*Inferno* I. 37–40)

> [The time was the beginning of morning, and the sun was climbing aloft with those stars that were with him when the divine love first moved those beautiful things ...]

Creation was supposed to have taken place in spring, when the sun was in Aries. It was the morning of Good Friday, 1300. But Dante also situates his poem precisely in terms of his own personal life:

> Nel mezzo del cammin di nostra vita
>   mi ritrovai per una selva oscura
>   che la diretta via era smarrita.
> Ah quanto a dir qual era è cosa dura
>   esta selva selvaggia e aspre e forte
>   che nel pensier rinova la paura. (*Inferno* I. 1–6)

[In the middle of this way of our life, I found myself again in a dark wood where the straight way was lost. Oh how difficult it is to speak of that wood, savage, harsh and obdurate, thinking about it again renews my fear.]

For a variety of reasons, political and personal, Dante describes himself as confused and fearful about his way forward, but he is also conscious that this is the year 1300 and that he is 35 years old, in the middle of his allotted 70 years, and this gives urgency to what he has to communicate. This consideration disappears somewhat as the poem develops, though Dante is always conscious of history and the trajectory of the lives of others.

Centuries later Henry King, who eventually became bishop of Chichester, uses the idea of 70 years for the span of human life in *The Exequy*, a poem on the death of his first wife Anne Berkeley in 1624.[47] He describes the poem as a 'complaint' (2) and meditates on her 'untimely fate': he notices without her 'how lazily time creeps' and experiences 'weary hours' (17–19). In the next section he develops the theme of 'time' and, in a passage full of wordplay and astronomical and temporal references, he adverts both to the expected 70 years lifespan and also to clock time:

> Nor wonder if my time go thus
> Backward and most preposterous;
> Thou hast benighted me, thy set
> This Eve of blackness did beget,
> Who was't my day (though overcast
> Before thou had'st thy Noon-tide past)
> And I remember must in tears,
> Thou scarce had'st seen so many years
> As Day tells hours. By thy cleer Sun
> My life and fortune first did run;
> But thou wilt never more appear
> Folded within my Hemisphear,
> Since both thy light and motion

> Like a fled star is fall'n and gon,
> And twixt me and my soules dear wish
> The earth now interposed is
> Which such a strange eclipse doth make
> As ne're was read in Almanake. (21–38)

Anne died in 1624 when she was 23 years old 'before thou had'st thy Noontide past', that is before she had reached 35 years, but not only this, before she had reached 'so many years / As day tells hours'. King here not only uses the idea of the 24-hour day, but also its division on the clock-face into twelve hours of day and twelve hours of night: she was 'my day' and like the 'sun', so that when she 'set' she 'benighted' him into an 'Eve of blackness'.

For these poets and for others the definition of the human lifespan as set out in Psalm 90:10 was clearly significant, but the tendency in the Middle Ages and the Renaissance to divide human life into smaller entities was pronounced. In *De Temporum Ratione*, after he has set out the theory of the *sex aetates mundi* in relation to the six days of Creation in much the same way as Augustine had, Bede makes the point that it is necessary to define the articulation of the human life span, the ages through which each individual passes, because Greek philosophers called man a *microcosmos*, that is a '*minor mundus*', a lesser world: the situation of the human individual reflects, on a lesser scale, the progression of the greater world through time. And Bede follows this with a six-age analysis, similar to that of Augustine considered above, except that he classifies the fifth age as *senectus* and the sixth as *aetas decrepita* [decrepitude].

The topic of the *aetates hominis*, the ages of man, was more often addressed by medieval authors than that of the 'ages of the world' – no doubt because it was closer to their individual experience – and it is impossible to treat it fully in a book of this sort, and, indeed, unnecessary because it has been so comprehensively studied by others. But something has to be said about it because it impinges on how time was regarded in the medieval and Renaissance world and how devices for measuring time, particularly clocks, came to be fashioned.

The six-age scheme alluded to above had a considerable vogue, largely because it was widely adopted by encyclopaedists, and was still being used in the fifteenth century when it appears in *A Stanzaic Life of Christ*, where it is introduced in the usual way by reference to the six ages of history. The anonymous author sets Christ's birth as taking place at the beginning of the sixth age of the world and then writes:

> And ri3t so as this world I-wys
> ffro bigynnyng to endyng
> In sex eldes diviset is,
> Mon is that has his fulle lyvyng.[48]

But apart from this scheme, the most important in the later Middle Ages were schemes based on three ages, four ages, and seven ages – though others were invoked sometimes in an impromptu fashion: towards the end of the period, for example, a twelve-age scheme became popular. What all these systems have in common is that they are usually, like the six-age scheme, predicated on a seemingly more comprehensive system of analysing the world.

Many three-age schemes, according to John Burrow, are based on biological conceptions, relating the human life-cycle to the natural world and so provide a scientific foundation for the widely held opinion that the sequence of aging itself follows, or ought to follow, a natural order.[49] It is easily observable that plants and animals, as well as human beings, grow, mature and decline, and these three stages provide the basis for the theory: it is frequently represented in art through triple portraits, as by Titian and Giorgione (Plate 3).[50] But this was interpreted not only in a physical way but in moral terms too. And here it had the powerful support of Aristotle who addressed the three-age system in *De Anima* III. 12 (in William of Moerbeke's Latin translation) and in his *Rhetoric* II. 12–14, where he first points out the faults of youth and old age before expressing a preference for the mean between them:

> As for men in their Prime, clearly we shall find that they have a character between that of the young and that of the old, free from the extremes of either. They have neither the excess of confidence which amounts to rashness, nor too much timidity, but the right amount of each …[51]

This was a position widely adopted by those who addressed the desirable qualities of rulers or those charged with governing, though not exclusively so: 'myddel age' was widely seen in the Middle Ages and the Renaissance as 'the perfect age of a man's life', and it was frequently illustrated in graphic form.[52] This age scheme was also interestingly adverted to by Langland in *Piers Plowman* where Ymaginatif explains his view of the Dreamer's position in relation to growing old:

> I have folwed thee, in feith, thise five and fourty wynter,
> And manye tymes have meved thee to mynne on thyn ende,

> And how fele fernyeres are faren, and so few to come
> And of thi wylde wantownesse tho thow yong were,
> To amende it in thi myddel age, lest myght the faille
> Of thyn olde elde, that yvele kan suffre
> Poverte or penaunce, or preyeres bidde:
> *Si non in prima vigilia, nec in secunda* … (B. XII. 3–9)⁵³

Here the invocation of the three-age scheme is clear enough, as is the sense that 'myddel age' is important, as is also the sense that the years are passing (*fernyeres*) and that the Dreamer needs to put his life in order while he has the power (*myght*) to do so. But its reference point is not biological or Aristotelian. As the Latin quotation, meaning 'It is not in the first watch, nor in the second …' (Luke 12:36–8), makes clear the framework of thought here is biblical – the three watches kept by the servants awaiting their lord's return from the wedding-feast, an alternative and emphatically religious validation of the scheme.⁵⁴

But 'myddel age' was not axiomatically regarded as the preferred area of life. There was a well-established tradition in the Middle Ages that associated old age with wisdom: 'men may the old atren [outrun] but not atrede [outwit]' was a widely popular proverb.⁵⁵ In relation to the three-age scheme this was often invoked, especially in works predicated on the famous texts from Ecclesiastes 1:2 and 12:8 that 'all is vanity'. This is plain from the fifteenth-century lyric which begins 'O vanyte off vanytyes & all is vanite':

> Lo! Here comys ȝouth with myrth & plays joly,
> With-outen thouȝt or care, fader & moderles,
> Bot mydell Age thinkis þat it was foly
> And ner peynes hym-selue with werdly besynes,
> But all his labour is to grete rysches.
> Than commys Age & seys þat he must dyȝe,
> Than he knaw ȝought & all was vanyte.⁵⁶

This is varied in a similar lyric, this time a *chanson d'aventure*, where the analogy with the three-age scheme is temporal and diurnal – the morning, noon and night of a single day:

> … one þe morov when hit is fayre & clere,
> After none hit wendys awaye,
> And commyth to the nyȝt as hit was ere:
> This word ys but a daye:

> Soo for ry3t all owre lewyng heyre;
> ffrow chyldwood vnto mannys degree,
> Owre enddyng drawyt nere and nere –
> This word ys but a wannyte.⁵⁷

The world [*word*] is a vanity for this poet. And similarly, in what is probably the most sustained and thorough examination of the three-age scheme, the alliterative *Parlement of the Thre Ages*, Elde argues down his younger disputants by demonstrating the superiority of his wisdom because of his age. He has experienced all that they have experienced because there is a sequential familial relationship (real or metaphorical) between the ages: 'for Elde es sire of Middill Elde and Middel Elde of 3outhe' (652).⁵⁸ But it is also significant that he ends his disquisition, which silences and therefore overcomes his younger opponents, with a quotation from Ecclesiastes: '*Vanitas vanitatum & omnia vanitas*' (639) [Vanity of vanities and all is vanity]. Like other schemes navigating the human trajectory through time this one tends to end in despair, because death destroys all that humans may take pride in – bravery, intelligence, love, riches:

> … doughtynes when dede comes ne dare noghte habyde,
> Ne dethe wondes for no witt to wende where hym lykes,
> And ther-to paramours and pride puttes he full lowe;
> Ne there es reches ne rent may rawnsone 3our lyues … (631–4)

In view of this, he argues, there is a necessity for penance (641–8). As is evident from these texts, the medieval church took over this scheme pretty effectively in relation to its established doctrines, though originally it was a scientific and moral scheme, and not in any way doctrinal.

More influential than the three-age scheme was that based on a four-fold division, which again claimed a scientific basis, this time on the basis of physiology, the elements, the humours and the seasons. Its origins may well have been Pythagorean. In his *Metamorphoses* XV. 199–200 Ovid puts a question into the mouth of Pythagoras:

> Quid? Non in species succedere quattor annum
> adspicis, aetatis peragentem imitatamina nostrae?
>
> [Or again, do you not perceive a year going through four seasons, imitating our own ages?]⁵⁹

And, as he develops this idea of constant change, he talks about the four elements, which give rise to bodies, being inconstant and that things change their appearance: 'nothing lasts long under the same form'. And he follows this with a wonderful exposition of geographical and ecological change. Furthermore, as this scheme was developed, by Ovid and by others, considerations other than nature and the seasons came to be invoked, all predicated on the number four, where the temporal is related to God and to a variety of features of the sublunary world.

This four-age scheme was widely adopted, but was defined and embedded in a logical and comprehensive form in England in two early eleventh-century texts probably written by Byrhtferth, a monk from Ramsey Abbey (Cambridgeshire), who addressed the subject in both Latin and Anglo-Saxon, in both words and diagrams.[60] One of these diagrams from Byrhtferth's *Manual* takes a basically circular form, but divided into quarters (see Figure 1). At the centre is God's name in Latin DEUS, and in the circle outside this is ADAM, the name of the first man, created and formed by God in his own image. Man faces inward towards God, but outside this he is related to the rest of creation. The four letters of Adam mark the four points of the compass, and in the next circle outwards come the four ages – *puericita* [boyhood], *adolescentia* [adolescence], *iuventus* [young manhood] and *senectus* [old age] with the four corresponding seasons of the year. Then come two rings naming the months of the year in Latin and in Anglo-Saxon, and in the outmost ring appear the twelve signs of the zodiac. Four lines radiating from the central circle of Adam, represent the solstices and equinoxes and divide the year into its four seasons, and each of these is associated with one of the four elements – air, fire, earth, water. None of these lines break the central circle of DEUS, because God is in eternity, outside the temporal. The manual, its diagrams and its bi-lingual explanations and discourses on the diagrams, are designed to provide instruction, 'so that the young priest who sees these things may be the wiser for it'. This may be a modest enough intention, but, in its reductive and simplistic way, this diagram locates man in relation to God and eternity, to the physical world (the elements), to space (the points of the compass) and especially to time (the solstices, equinoxes, seasons and months) and ordering of the heavens (the zodiac). The accompanying text expatiates on all this, and another text, the 'Ramsey *Computus*', adds other details – distributing the four qualities, hot, cold, dry and moist – and defining, in terms of years, the life expectancies of the four ages *puericitia vel infancia* ends at 14, *adolescencia* at 28, *iuventus* at 48, and *senectus* at 70 or 80.

But this four-age scheme, possibly because it could be interpreted in relation to so many different factors, was extremely malleable and could be framed to fit many contexts and agendas. Normally the framework was

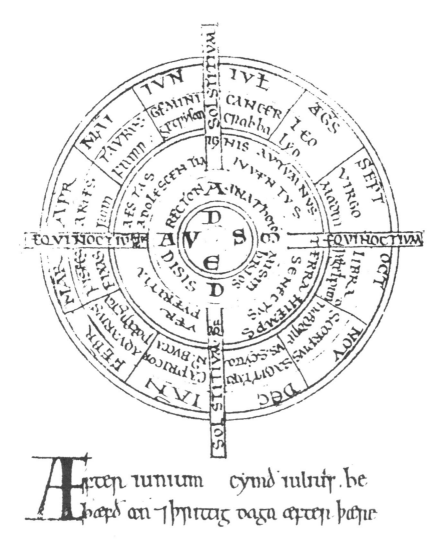

1 The four ages of man: Byrhtferth's *Manual*; Oxford, Bodleian Library MS Ashmole 328.

seasonal. In the February Eclogue of Spenser's *Shepheardes Calender* Cuddie draws a comparison between old age and winter: 'Age and Winter accord full nie / This chill, that cold, this crooked, that wrye' (27–8). This is more elaborately developed in the December Eclogue when Spenser has Colin Cloute review his life in terms of the four seasons, and now, in winter, describes the way age has affected his body:

> The carefull cold hath nypt my rugged rynde,
> And in my face deepe furrowes eld hath pight:
> My head besprent with hoary frost I fynd,
> And by myne eie the Crow his clawe dooth wright. (133–6)[61]

All the comparisons are from the natural world of the English countryside – Colin's skin is like the roughened bark (*rynde*) of a tree; the lines on his face are like the 'deepe furrowes' of winter plough-lands; the greying of his hair is compared to the effect of 'hoary frost'; and he uses the traditional metaphor of 'crow's feet' for the wrinkles round his eyes. The winter landscape has invaded and altered the aging shepherd's appearance. Like the good shepherd that he is, he thinks providentially and makes sure his 'little flocke' is protected 'in youre folds', and then prepares to face 'timely death', where the punning adjective summarizes the whole sequence of metaphors. Spenser, with great literary tact and decorum, aligns the four-age scheme with the pastoral mode of his poem.

But there were other possibilities, as can be seen from the widely-known thirteenth-century mnemonic verse:

> Consona sunt aer, sanguis, puericia verque.
> Conveniunt estas, ignis coleraque iuventus,
> Autumnus, terra, melancholia, senectus.
> Flema, latex et hyemps, senium sibi consociantur.
>
> [In harmony are air, blood, boyhood and spring. Summer, fire, choler and young manhood are congenial to each other, as are autumn, earth, melancholy and age. Phlegm, liquid and winter are associated with decrepitude.][62]

To the ages, the seasons and the elements, these verses add the four humours – blood, choler, melancholy and phlegm – all of which suggest a medical background: perhaps they come from Salerno, famous for its medical studies. But other contexts favoured other emphases, some of which could be personal, as individuals used the scheme to make sense of the trajectory of their own lives. John Lydgate, weak and ill (255–61), towards the end of his distinguished life, embarks on his *Testament*, 'to make rekenyng how I my tyme haue spent' (218), and invokes the traditional associations of spring to explain his unruly and erratic childhood, using not just the season but the appropriate humour, element, compass direction and, probably, wind if that is what 'meridien' indicates:

> Thus in vj thynges be order men may seen
> Notable accord and iust convenience,
> Blod, eyre, and ver, south, and medidien,
> And age of chyldhood by naturall assistence,
> Which, whill thei stonde in ther fressh premynence,
> Hete and moysture directeth ther passages,
> With grene fervence to force yong corages. (318–24)[63]

Not all of these items are used as he expatiates on his young years, but the general changeableness and instability of the season give him his theme: he was 'Stormysh as Marche, with chaunges ful sodeyne' (351) and 'voyd of resovn, youe to wilfulnesse' (614) in relation to practically every aspect of his life, he says, even after he entered the Benedictine monastery of Bury St Edmunds, preferring drink to learning:

> Holy histories did to me no chier –
> I savoured more in good wine that was clere. (729–30)

How far one can trust the accuracy of texts such as this is questionable: Lydgate does predictably reform and offers himself as an example of reformation (740–53). Furthermore, his use of the four-age system is interestingly selective: he does not use it further in this poem, though he clearly understood it. When he and Benedict Burgh came to write their *Secrees of Old Philisoffres*, a version of the influential *Secreta Secretorum*, the exemplary aspect of the whole four-age scheme is stressed: 'Thus four tymes makith us a merour cleer / Off mannys lyff and a ful pleyn ymage'. The traditional associations follow, but the end is unusual and personal: 'senectus' is associated with 'wynter last of alle / How dethys orlogge doth on us calle' (1457–63), where the summons of death is equated with the striking of the monastic clock.[64]

The seven-age scheme derives principally from the writings of the second-century astronomer Claudius Ptolemy who, in his *Tetrabiblos* (IV. 10) maintained that 'in the matter of the age-divisions of mankind ... comparison depends on the order of the seven planets', beginning with the nearest, the moon, and ending with Saturn, the most distant.[65] What is more, he argued, 'the accidental qualities of each of the ages are those which are naturally proper to the planet compared with it'. The first four years of infancy are governed by the moon, and are characterized by the 'body's growth', the 'moist nature' of its food, and changeability. The next ten years of childhood, dominated by Mercury, the god of learning, awaken 'the soul at this stage by instruction, tutelage and the first gymnastic exercises'. Then, until the age of 22, youth is influenced by Venus, who provokes 'an impulse towards the embrace of love' and unruly 'incontinence'. Between 22 and 41 comes young manhood governed by the sun, which implants 'desire for substance, glory and position and a change from playful ingenuous error to seriousness, decorum and ambition'. In the fifth age, which lasts from 41 to 56, dominated by Mars, men seek to accomplish something of note and so are ambitious, but these years are characterized by 'severity and misery' in day-to-day living and 'cares and troubles in the soul'. The sixth age, under the influence of Jupiter, brings a diminution of physical activity and a concentration on 'deliberation, admonition and consolation' and a concern with 'honour', but accompanied with 'modesty and dignity'. This lasts until the 68th year and for the rest of life, under Saturn, there is a physical decline and men become 'dispirited, weak, easily offended and hard to please' in keeping with the 'sluggishness' of the planet's movement round its orbit. However, a somewhat earlier scheme, set out by Philo Judaeus, who says he got it from Hippocrates, proposes a seven-age division, based on groups of seven years, but makes no mention of planetary influences.

As John Burrow has pointed out, neither of these schemes was very much used in England, particularly in the Middle Ages, but later Ptolemy's scheme was set out by Thomas Fortescue in 1571, when he reviews various 'ages of man' schemes and gives pride of place to that which proposed that 'the life of Man is divided into seven Ages, over every one of which ruleth and governeth one of the seven Planetes'. A similar exposition occurs in Sir Walter Raleigh's *History of the World* (1614) where there is an elegant and systematic series of comparisons between the stages of life and the planetary influences on them. But the scheme could be used selectively to apply to one or two ages, and could be interpreted in individualistic ways.[66] Among the many fourteenth-century wall-paintings in Langthorpe Tower, near Peterborough (Northamptonshire), is a partially ruined depiction of the seven ages, running round the top of an arch over a windowed recess (see Figure 2). *Infans* is in a cradle or cot of some sort; *puer* has what looks like a whipping-top; *adolescens* is very damaged and little detail can be discerned; but *juvenis* dominates the top of the arch with a hawk on his wrist; *senior* has a sword, *senex* a money-bag and *decrepitus* a stick or a crutch.[67] Even if the paintings had survived in a more complete state this is a pretty reductive interpretation of the scheme, but Mary Dove is surely right to point out that this gives the traditional pre-eminence to the fourth age, middle age, as 'the perfect age of man's life', as the confident figure of *juvenis* faces the beholder in an achieved stasis, while the others look sideways, in attitudes of becoming or decline.[68] But equally striking about the Langthorpe painter's interpretation of the seven-age scheme is that it appears, unless *senior*'s sword is a reference to Mars, to omit any sort of planetary influence.

2 The seven ages of man: Langthorpe Tower, Northamptonshire, photograph by Julie Potton.

Shakespeare's famous exposition of this scheme in *As You like It*, II. vii. 139–66, is also highly individualistic – though it incorporates, but not explicitly, the idea of planetary influences.[69] Shakespeare is candid about his way of using the scheme: he has a narrator, the 'melancholy Jaques', who is predisposed to see the worst in human life and who is prompted to expound the scheme by thinking about time because of a timekeeper – Touchstone's 'dial'. Jaques relates to Duke Senior and the outlaws how he met a 'fool' in the forest, who

> … drew a dial from his poke
> And looking on it with lack-lustre eye
> Says very wisely 'It is ten o'clock'.
> 'Thus we see' quoth he, 'how the world wags.
> 'Tis but an hour ago since it was nine,
> And after one more hour it will be eleven.
> And from hour to hour we ripe and ripe,
> And then from hour to hour we rot and rot;

> And thereby hangs a tale'. When I did hear
> The motley fool thus moral on the time
> My lungs began to crow like chanticleer,
> That fools should be so deep-contemplative,
> And I did laugh sans intermission
> An hour by his dial ... (II. vii. 20–33)

What initially amuses Jaques is not exactly clear: it could be the apparent incongruity of a fool in motley uttering moralistic statements, or the banality of the statements themselves, or the fact that they were made in relation to a shepherd's dial or a pocket watch in the countryside.[70] By comparing his laughter to 'chanticleer' he is associating himself with the bird which was reputed to be the natural timekeeper of the countryside, but it is interesting that he times his laughter in relation to Touchstone's timekeeper – 'an hour by his dial'. It is also interesting that this seemingly absurd event generates a serious meditation on the passing of time as the scene develops, coming out of the seasonal contrast of growth and decline, though measured in terms of the clock: 'from hour to hour we ripe and ripe, / And then from hour to hour we rot and rot'. Jaques begins to envy Touchstone's capacity for telling the truth and wishes he were also a fool: 'Invest me with my motley, Give me leave / To speak my mind' (58–9). At the end of this scene, Jaques, in his 'ages of man' speech, is himself thinking, like Touchstone, about growth and decay.

His exposition also has a framework which sees the 'world' as a 'stage' and those who people it as 'merely players' – but 'one man in his time plays many parts / His acts being seven ages'. This is avowedly a theatrical view, perhaps a theatre manager's or actor's view, because what Shakespeare does, with his wonderfully understated literary tact, is to incorporate the planetary comparisons, the wisdom of the *philosphi*, into the shifting parts available in an actor's career: he concentrates on changes of appearance, changes of voice and objects, perhaps theatrical props, which figurally serve as cues to or symbols of character. The 'infant' does not have much of a presence, and 'mewling and puking in the nurse's arms' indicates his helplessness: but in 'puking' the planetary association with moisture and the moon is suggested, and in 'mewling', which here means 'whimpering', gives him a voice, though admittedly a weak one. The unwilling and reluctant schoolboy, under the influence of Mercury, the god of education, 'creeping like snail', also has a voice – 'whining' – but he also has an object which associates him with his role, 'his satchel'. Equally with the third age, the 'lover' has a presumably written object, 'a woeful ballad / Made to his mistress eyebrow', but he also has a voice, replete with Venusian heat, 'sighing like furnace'. Jaques, perhaps predictably, leaves out the age associated with the sun and with achievement, success and triumph, but makes the next age that of Mars: appropriately aggressive, 'sudden and quick in quarrel' and ambitious in war seeking 'reputation … even in the cannon's mouth'. But even so, he has his appearance, 'bearded', and his voice 'full of strange oaths'. The next part, influenced by Jupiter, the law-giver among the Roman gods, is figured by the fat justice, with his own appearance showing his seriousness and conventional manner, 'eyes severe and beard of formal cut', and with his own voice and linguistic register: 'Full of wise saws and modern instances'. Here Shakespeare reminds the audience of the theatrical nature of this exposition: 'And so he plays his part'. And as he develops the sequence, he continues the theatrical implications:

> The sixth age shifts
> Into the lean and slipper'd pantaloon,
> With spectacles on nose, and pouch on side,
> His youthful hose well sav'd, a world too wide
> For his shrunk shank, and his big manly voice,
> Turning again towards childish treble, pipes
> And whistles in his sound.

This age, governed by Saturn, is one of decline, signalled physically in appearance by the shift from the 'round belly' of the justice on his bench into the old man at home, 'the lean and slipper'd pantaloon' with the 'shrunk shank', an allusion to 'Pantaleone', the standard old man of Italian *commedia dell' arte*, stressing again the actor's perspective in this seven-age scheme. Again there are the theatrical props, 'spectacles' suggesting a decline of the senses, and a 'pouch' suggesting the sin of avarice frequently associated with old age, as does the 'hose well sav'd' which is no use to him because it is now too big. But there is again attention to the actor's voice: the 'manly voice' is replaced by the 'childish treble'. This is the aging actor's last part, and this prepares the way for Shakespeare's exit from this wonderful but eccentric interlude interpreting the seven-age scheme, where the last age lapses into 'second childishness, and mere oblivion'. The decrepit old man is in some ways like the child of the first age, but is declining not growing, having lost some of his senses and all convincing appearance: 'sans teeth, sans eyes, sans taste, sans everything', and so worse than the child, but perhaps also, in this pitiless view of things, an actor past all use.

CHAPTER 2

Living in time: years, month, weeks and days

MOST MEDIEVAL PEOPLE OF Western Europe would have accepted, either explicitly or more likely tacitly, the Christian notion of linear time and would have known, from their own personal experience, that their own lives involved growth and decay, whether or not they were aware of or adhered to any of the various schemes relating to the ages of man. But as soon as they looked outside themselves they would have perceived a series of cycles in which time was experienced and understood, particularly in relation to the celestial and natural world – the solar and planetary cycles, the lunar cycle and, particularly, the turning of the seasons of the year, and the growth, decay and regeneration of plants and animals where there are everywhere repetitive patterns.

All this was regarded as part of the given order of things, as the author of *Sir Gawain and the Green Knight* makes plain as he contemplates Gawain's predicament as he has to wait out the year before he can fulfil his bargain with the Green Knight to accept a return blow for the one he gave in the 'Cristemas game' (283) at Camelot:

> Forthy this Yol overyede, and the yere after,
> And uch sesoun serlepes sued after other. (500–1)[1]

After Christmas comes the 'crabbede lentoun', as the seasons appear individually ('serlepes'), then the 'weder of the world' battles with 'wynter' so that spring comes, flowers grow, birds build nests and 'bremelyche syngen', because of their gladness at the 'softe somer' that follows ('sues thereafter'). All the emphasis is on a predetermined and orderly succession. Then, 'after the sesoun of somer' comes harvest which tells ('warnes') plants 'to waxe ful ripe' because of the approach of winter and what was growing has to decay: leaves fall, the grass loses its colour and 'then all rypes and rotes that ros upon firste' (516–28). By means of a sequence of adverbs connoting time, what the poet stresses in this passage describing the turning of the seasons is the inevitability of it, and so he can generalize having 'thus' proved a point:

> And thus yernes the yere in yisterdayes mony,
> And winter wyndes agayn as the world askes
>   No fage,
> And Meghelmasse mone
> Was comen with winter wage. (529–33)

Winter comes once more ('agayn'), as the world demands, in truth ('No fage'), with 'wyndes' and the Michaelmas moon, the September moon, brings a token ('wage') of winter, because it falls in the same month as the autumn equinox. But there may also be a pun on 'wage' here because Michaelmas (29 September) was one of the 'quarter days', when rents were due, servants hired and paid and bargains made.[2] In the next leash of lines the orderly turning of the year and the human obligations inherent in it receive further reinforcement. Gawain stays in Camelot for the All Hallows feast (1 November) and departs the next day: 1 November, in household calendars, was when increased winter allowances for lights (candles) and fuel for fires came in and winter clothing (livery) was handed out. So, in this deceptively simple passage, there is a rich concentration of time-schemes relating to the annual cycle. One is basically social, relating to the organization of noble households, but there is predominantly a natural cycle and, with the mention of Christmas, Lent, Michaelmas and All Hallows, an invocation of an ecclesiastical cycle also.

It seems clear from this piece of writing that these calendars were conventionally thought of together, as part of the given order of things, but for the purposes of what follows they have to be separated.

The seasonal cycle was most frequently articulated through the scheme of the 'labours of the months', which detailed when the work appropriate to the agricultural year should be performed – a tradition that has been extensively described and analysed elsewhere, but about which something has to be said here.[3] This tradition goes back at least to Virgil's *Georgics* and is predicated on philosophical and moral principles of prudential planning and good husbandry, and these are implicit in many medieval versions. Oxford, Bodleian Library MS Digby 88 is a mid-fifteenth-century collection, in English and Latin, of utilitarian material – relating to weather-lore, medicines, palmistry and so forth (see Figure 3). In it the following mnemonic verses on the 'labours of the months' appear, each appropriate to the designated month in a calendar, and the manuscript context suggests they are meant to be exemplary:

> Januar   By thys fyre I warme my handys;
> Febuar   And with my spade I delfe my landys.
> Marche   Here I sette my thynge to sprynge;

Aprile	And here I here the fowlis synge.
Maij	I am as light as byrde in bowe;
Junij	And I wede my corne well I-now.
Julij	With my sythe my mede I mawe;
Auguste	And here I shere my corne full lowe.
September	With my flayll I erne my brede;
October	And here I sawe my whete so rede.
November	At Martynsmasse I kylle my swine;
December	And at Cristesmasse I drynke rede wyne.[4]

The verses are accompanied by a set of rudimentary miniatures, drawn above each line, designed visually to reinforce the verbal precepts: a fire, a spade, a dibble, two birds, one on a branch, a hoe, a scythe, a sickle, a threshing flail, some seeds, a heavy axe and a goblet. Many of these occupations feature in other lists, and are often associated with the same months, but there is also variation, partly, no doubt, related to the different patterns of the agricultural year in different locations, but also partly determined by personal preference that privileged one of several seasonal occupations to another: this verse relates principally to arable farming and affords no mention of dairy farming, though most farmers kept cows for milk, though it may not have been their principal cash crop, as well as bullocks or horses for ploughing. This potential for variation is apparent in another copy of these verses that appears in London, British Library MS Additional 22720, again accompanied by a calendar and miniatures. But for March here the line reads, 'And with þis byll Y pare my vine', which refers to a different task, this time related to viticulture, though appropriate to the month of the year. And the lines for November and December read 'With þis ax Y kile my swyne' and 'O þese cuppes Y drynke boþe ale and wyn', which refers to the same occupations as in the other version of the poem, but removes the liturgical references and concentrates, in a way consistent with the features of the earlier lines of the poem, on the physical objects used.[5] Whatever the variation, however, both versions stay within the context of the annual calendar as it was appropriate to the rural labouring classes, and both take account of the weather: there are opportunities for outdoor enjoyment in April and May, but the indoor enjoyment in December is drinking red wine and in January one has simply to keep warm.

Some of these assumptions appear to be present in the description of the ideal husbandman, as set out in the opening of *How the Plowman Lerned his Pater Noster*, printed by Wynkyn de Worde in 1510, but undoubtedly older.[6] Though the title describes him as a ploughman, he is much more than this, clearly energetic and variously talented so that:

3 The labours of the months: Oxford, Bodleian Library MS Digby 88, photograph: © Bodleian Libraries, University of Oxford.

Januar At thys fyre I warme my handys.

February And w' my spade I delfe my landys.

Marche Here I sette my thynge to sprynge.

Aprell And here I her the fowlys synge.

May I am as lyght as byrde in bowe.

Juin And I wede my corne well I now.

July W' my sythe my mede I mawe.

August And her I shere my corne full lowe.

September W' my flayll I erne my brede.

October And her I sawe my whete so rede.

November At Martynes masse I kylle my swyne.

December And at Cristes masse I drynke redde wyne.

> ... he coude eke sowe and holde a plowe
> Bothe dyke hedge and mylke a cowe
> Threshe fane and gelde a swyn
> In euery season and in tyme
> To mowe and repe bothe grasse and corne
> A better labourer was neuer borne
> He coude go to plowe with oxe or hors
> With whiche it were he dyde no fors
> Of shepe the sole of for to shere
> His better was founde no-where ... (5–14)

Though the framework of his talents is defined by several of the 'labours of the months' (here work associated with July, August, September and October), there is much more to him: he can mend shoes, rear geese, graft trees, collect timber (for fires in winter, a labour of January), thatch and plaster his house. Some of these are not normally tasks involved in by personnel engaged in 'labours of the months' schemes. His operations also have a pastoral dimension – 'shepe ... for to shere'. His house was well-stocked with sides of bacon (presumably from his pigs killed in November), full of dairy and horticultural products such as 'egges butter and chese', 'good ale', 'martynmas befe', onions and garlic, 'chese and mylke of the cowe'. The poet concludes: 'by his laboure riche he was in dede' (15–31). But an important phrase in this description is 'In euery season and in tyme', which signifies that the ploughman became enriched by following the natural order of things as defined by the calendars. The ploughman is a traditional, hard-working, serious man, though eventually tricked out of much of his store of corn by an unscrupulous and opportunistic priest and various legal 'officials'. He has to learn his *pater noster*, but the priest will only teach him if he distributes his corn to the indigent poor 'for goddes sake' (125). Part of the rich satiric comedy of this consists in a listing of what each clause of the Latin paternoster costs the husbandman:

> Two peckes were gyuen to *qui es in celis*
> No wonder yf he halted for kybed were his helys
> Than came *sanctificetur* and *nomen tuum*
> Of whete amonge them they gate an hole tunne ... (117–20)

But the recipients of this generous charity waste it on drink, dicing and on singing 'a gest of robyn hode' as they go home from the tavern (128). When he is almost ruined by their demands and takes the matter to court, the priest who had promised him 'suretye' (164, 95) for his grain, reneges on his promise:

but he is 'praysed gretly' and the husbandman is pronounced a 'fole' (189–93). This poem manages at the same time to be an endorsement of the wisdom of the conventional 'labours of the months' calendar and also to register a social protest: like other, earlier poems, its protagonist is a resourceful, hardworking countryman who is here exploited by a priest and various officials. When he goes home to tell his wife 'how the parsone had hym betrayde', the ploughman says, 'preest shall I neuer truste agayne' (198–200). But the poet is more benign and inclusive, suggesting that the subterfuge of the priest and the officials may have led to some benefit for the poor. He ends by hoping that both of them (the husbandman and the priest) will go to heaven after their deaths (203–8).

The temporal sequence of the 'labours of the months' was ubiquitous and not only in writing: this scheme frequently appeared on clocks, along with representations of the sun and the moon and the signs of the zodiac and sometimes much else. Chaucer frequently used astrological dating in his poems (see, for example, *CT*, I. 7–8; IV, 1885–7, 2219–24; V, 48–51, 263–5) and in *The Franklin's Tale* the narrator's evocation of the 'colde frosty seson of Decembre' (*CT*, V. 1244) begins astrologically:

> Phebus wax old, and hewed lyk laton,
> That in his hoote declynacion
> Shoon as the burned gold with stremes brighte;
> But now in Capricorn adoun he lighte,
> Where as he shoon ful pale, I dar wel seyn,
> The bittre frostes, with the sleet and reyn,
> Destroyed hath the grene in every yerd.
> Janus sit by the fyr, with double berd,
> And drynketh of his bugle horn the wyn;
> Biforn hym stant brawen of the tusked swyn,
> And 'Nowel' crieth every lusty man. (1245–55)

Phoebus, the sun, has grown 'old' because it is nearing the end of the solar year and in the zodiacal sign of 'Capricorn', the sign of the winter solstice (13 December in the Julian calendar then in use). But the ending of the passage alludes to the traditional 'labours' of the winter months: the 'brawen of the tusked swyn' recalls the pigs killed in November; the 'wyn' is that traditionally drunk at Christmas ('Nowel'); and Janus, the two-faced god of endings and beginnings, who gave his name to January, is appropriately sitting 'by the fyr', his traditional posture in 'the labours of the months'. It may be that Chaucer is here using this material simply to signal the date, but it could be that he intends that there should be implications for the development of the story.

The characters involved in this part of the narrative are Aurelius, a love-sick squire, and a 'subtil clerk', an astrologer, who is being paid by Aurelius to devise a scheme whereby the dangerous rocks of the coast of Brittany may seem to disappear – so that Aurelius can acquire the love of Dorigen. The 'clerk' is working on his books, ultimately to some effect, such that 'thurgh his magik, for a wyke or tweye, / It semed that alle the rokkes were aweye' (1295–6), while Aurelius has been encouraging him with 'chiere and reverence, / And preyeth hym to doon his dilegence' (1257–8) as he 'awaiteth nyght and day on this myracle' (1299). They are not agricultural labourers by any stretch of the imagination, but the implication of these allusions to the 'labours of the months' is that they are, like agricultural labourers, confined at this time of the year to indoor activities.

In other poems on the months this set of assumptions was not always the case, and an alternative view of how the turning year might be occupied is set out by Folgore di San Gimignano, a pseudonym for Giacomo or Jacopo di Michele (c.1270–1332), in his *Sonetti dei Mesi*, which celebrates not a life devoted to productive labour but to a round of hedonistic pleasure indulged in by the Tuscan upper classes, to which he seems to have belonged.[7] It is true that in some of these sonnets there appear to be references to the traditional occupations of the months: the January poem refers to 'fuochi di salette accese ...' [fires of dried herbs burning ...] in splendidly furnished rooms, and in the December poem 'porci morti' [dead pigs] appear among the dishes enjoyed by the revellers, which perhaps allude to the November and December pig-killing and staying by the fire scenes of some calendars. It is true too that the spoils of hunting, 'cerbi, cavrouli e ... cinghiari' [stags, roebucks and ... wild boars] of the February poem are meant to be cooked in the smoky 'cuchina' [kitchen], as are 'pesce in tutta la riviera' [fish in all the river] caught in the March expedition, as are the birds taken through hawking in September and those acquired through shooting in October – so there is some utilitarian aspect to the activities of the 'brigata nobile e cortese' [noble and courteous group of friends]. But predominantly it is the sheer physical enjoyment of these activities that is celebrated and the wealthy, carefree lifestyle it represents. This is the turning of the year as it is experienced by the Tuscan 'signorelli e cavallereschi' [lords and gentlemen] of the early fourteenth century. Other outdoor activities, besides hunting, include jousting in May, dancing, and visiting the countryside in June, and the poems also celebrate indoor activities such as dicing and chess, in November and December. But predominantly and constantly the emphasis is on the opulence of this lifestyle – good horses, fine clothes, comfortable rooms decorated with fine tapestries and furnished with rich fabrics, large feasts with a variety of meats and poultry, followed by refreshing sweetmeats and, always, plentiful and varied types of wine. And then to warm bedchambers and soft beds.

This is a confident, secular rebuttal of the morally and economically aware prudential cast of mind that lay behind the more usual descriptions of the 'labours of the months'. It is also avowedly anti-clerical: the March sonnet ends with an expression of impatience with churches and monasteries and 'preti pazzi' [mad priests] who have 'assai bugie e poco vero' [plenty of lies but little truth]. It is also avowedly extravagant and not providential: the February sonnet includes a celebration of spending money and 'onta degli scarsi e degli avari' [shame on the skinflints and the misers]. It is through spending money, says the August sonnet, that one can acquire 'la miglior vivenda di Toscana' [the best way of living in Tuscany]. And the basic proposition throughout these poems is that, given wealth and freedom, one can enjoy the turning of the seasons in northern Italy, not only without working, but without even suffering the inconvenience of the changes in the weather. The July sonnet illustrates this:

> Di luglio in Siena, in su la saliciata,
> Con le piene ingiustare de' trebbiani;
> Nelle cantine li ghiacci vaiani …
>
> [In July in Siena, outside on the pavement, with full flasks of Trebbiano wine, and in the cellars with cool Fiano…]

The specificity of this is striking. Cooled by drinking Trebbiano, a wine made from the local grape, or chilled Fiano, which was perhaps imported from southern Italy, the company then goes on to consume jellies, then cold game-birds and meats flavoured with garlic sauce. One can enjoy a good time in these circumstances, says Folgore, and a good life, 'e non uscir di fuor per questo caldo' [and not go outside in this heat]. Similarly, to avoid the heat one can spend August 'in una valle d'alpe montanina' [in an alpine valley among the mountains]. Equally, in the cold of January one can venture out briefly to throw fine white snowballs ('gittando della neve bella e bianca'), but not for long and then one can retire to one's castle.

How influential Folgore's poetry was is hard to assess: it is specific to a certain area of north-western Italy, and it is difficult to know how widely it travelled and was read. How influential it was in foreshadowing the calendar painting of around 1400 is a question on which it is difficult to be precise. But what did happen, whether as a result of Folgore's assertiveness or not, was that accounts of the yearly cycle began to incorporate activities other than agricultural labour. It is true that the great majority of treatments of the 'labours of the months' stayed within the traditional ambit of agricultural tasks, though varied, where appropriate, with the pastoral – in Spenser's *Shepheardes Calender* the main characters are shepherds and goatherds – but particularly in later pictorial art there emerged a more socially inclusive sense of the meaning of the annual cycle, particularly if the patrons of this art were aristocratic and if they wanted their own lifestyles to be recorded. Amongst the many that could be given, I give two remarkable examples, one from a series of wall-paintings, the other from a lavishly illustrated manuscript book.

The *ciclo de' mesi* in the Torre dell'Aquila, Trento, was commissioned by the Prince-Bishop George of Liechtenstein in about 1400. The March fresco has been lost and a number of the other paintings have incurred damage over the years, but have been sensitively restored in places, so that the intended agenda of the sequence is still quite clear. It begins with a January fresco, overarched by the sun in Aquarius, which, unsurprisingly in the Alto-Adige at this time of year, depicts a snow scene (see Plate 4a).[8] In the foreground, outside a castle, elegantly and warmly dressed aristocrats, men and women, are snowballing, while in the middle-ground two peasants, up to their knees in snow, are embarking on a hunting expedition with dogs. In the background, two foxes lurk in a wood – a reminder, as elsewhere in this series, that animals and birds have a life on the edges of the world of men. The February scene also concentrates on aristocratic activity – here is jousting, which Folgore had described in relation to May. But as Master Wenceslas develops the sequence, the working year of agricultural labour and the life of the aristocracy are intercut in more interesting ways. The April fresco, with the sun in Aries, shows in the top left corner the houses of a village, clustered round a church, and in a field bordering the village a man on a horse harrowing already ploughed land and another peasant, on foot, sowing seed. Outside the village again, on the bottom left edge, a dog chases a hare through a small wood (see Plate 4b). In a fenced off enclosure, which appears to be a garden, two women tend the plants. Beyond the fence, on a track or road, two men load sacks from a mill onto an ox-cart. In the foreground, two other men plough a field with a heavy wheeled plough, pulled by two oxen and a horse. The activities of the farming year are under way and this fresco is almost entirely devoted to them. But, almost unobtrusively, through all this labour, walk two elegantly dressed aristocratic women, evidently not noticing their surroundings but talking to each other: one of the women passes through the pictorial border which separates this from the May fresco, which is entirely devoted to the aristocracy, to join others like herself assembled there enjoying themselves in a garden full of flowers, some eating at a table, others sitting on the grass or simply walking and talking, some of the conversations evidently of an amorous nature. And so it goes on. In July, for example, in the background scenes, some of the peasantry are scything and forking the hay-crop, the traditional 'labour', while others fish from a boat in a small lake. In the foreground of the picture is what is said to be the Castello Toblino, with stained glass windows, balconies with flowers and a stork's nest on the roof – again the natural invading the civilized world. Outside, across the drawbridge, the aristocrats, and their servants, are preoccupied with their falcons, in preparation for their late-summer hawking expeditions.

This same kind of separation of roles within a general inclusiveness can be seen in what is probably the most remarkable manifestation of calendar art, the *Très Riches Heures* commissioned by Jean, duc de Berry (1340–1416), third son of Jean II, king of France (1320–64), and executed by the Limbourg brothers and Jean Colombe, between 1409/12 and 1413/16.[9] The miniature for each month is crowned by a semicircular tympanum in which a man in a horse-drawn chariot carries the sun across the sky, beneath the appropriate zodiacal signs. Below this the 'labours of the months' are conceptually fairly traditional, but elaborately painted. January shows an indoor banqueting scene in an aristocratic setting presided over, presumably, by Jean de Berry and including other lords and prelates and their servants, sitting or standing around a long table, set before an elaborate fireplace, and covered with a damask cloth and crowded with elaborate tableware and a variety of dishes. On the wall behind the feasters is a tapestry depicting an appropriately martial scene: an army issues from a castle gateway to confront an attacking army, perhaps representing a scene from the Trojan War. February, by contrast, shows a snow-scene, set on a peasant farm. Inside a flimsy wooden building men and women can be seen warming themselves by a fire, while outside, in a fenced yard crowded with agricultural equipment, sheep huddle in a roofed enclosure and crows and magpies search for food on the ground. A muffled figure makes his way towards the farm-building, while outside the enclosure another figure cuts wood for fuel. A peasant, driving a laden donkey, makes his way towards a distant village in the hills – a cluster of dwellings around a church. The agricultural activities of spring dominate the March picture: in the distance, at the foot of the Château de Lusignan, one of Jean de Berry's favourite residences, a shepherd and his dog guard sheep; nearer, in an enclosure, three peasants prune vines; and to the right in a field a man with a sack is planting something. In the foreground, a ploughman guides his plough with one hand and goads his two oxen with the other. In fact, the compliments to the patron, as the sequence develops, seem largely to consist in depictions of the many castles belonging to the Duc de Berry, or places associated with him, which provide the backgrounds to practically all the miniatures and define their locale. Otherwise, the activities depicted are largely traditional and feature the peasantry – in June the mowing of the hay-crop, in July the cutting of the corn, in September the gathering of the grape harvest, in October harrowing and sowing winter corn, in November shaking down and gathering acorns for the pigs and in December the boar-hunt. The April miniature is set in an elegant parkland and features an aristocratic group of men and women celebrating a betrothal, perhaps that between Bonne de Berry, the duke's grand-daughter, and Charles of Orleans in April 1410, and May has an aristocratic company riding out into the countryside to gather greenery to celebrate the month. Only in the August miniature do aristocrats and the peasantry feature together: in the foreground an elegant company of men and women, with their falconer and dogs, ride out on a hawking expedition, while in the background labourers gather the grain harvest into carts (see Plate 5). But again, in its own way, this sequence seeks to convey something of the variety but inclusivity of the yearly activities of the different classes of people in contemporary agrarian society – how time was spent or, perhaps, how time should be spent – though almost everything which occurs appears to do so in the shadow of a castle, and the miniatures, advertently or not, appear also to articulate the power structures which underpinned that society.

II

Commentators have frequently seen these 'labours of the months' paintings as, in the words of Laurence R. Poos, 'tangible evidence of late medieval life and the attitudes or mental world of their patrons and artists'. A tendency towards 'idealization' is frequently noted: 'There is a consistent sense in these scenes of a placid, bucolic, unchanging world into which there seldom penetrates any of the hard work and harsh reality of this life'.[10] There is virtually no representation of life as it was lived in the increasingly important cities of Europe, or how time was spent there. It is also strikingly paradoxical, valuable though the evidence is, that these depictions of secular life, when they appear in 'books of hours' like Jean de Berry's, do so in contexts which are basically religious: these books, though the illustrations depict versions of 'the labours of the months' in terms of both the aristocracy and the peasantry, deal, as a whole, essentially with ecclesiastical time.

'Books of hours', or primers, as they came to be known, are prayer-books for the laity. Developed from the breviary, the prayer-book used by monastics for their varied daily round of services, 'books of hours' enabled laymen and laywomen to participate in formal worship but in a simplified manner. At the core of such books was a series of prayers called the Hours of the Virgin or the Little Office of the Blessed Virgin Mary. Each 'hour' consisted of psalms, hymns, liturgical songs derived from the Bible, readings and prayers, with various antiphons, versicles and responses and ideally was to be recited at various times of the day, following the monastic model of canonical hours: Matins and Lauds at daybreak, Prime at 6.00 a.m., Terce at 9.00 a.m., Sext at 12 noon, None at 3.00 p.m., Vespers at sunset and Compline later in the evening. Preceding the Little Office came a calendar of church feasts (usually arranged by month) and lessons from the four gospels. Following, usually, came the Hours of the Cross and the Hours of the Holy Spirit, two prayers to the Virgin – the 'Obsecro te' and the 'O Intemerata' – then the Seven Penitential Psalms and the litany of Saints, the Office of the Dead, and numerous petitionary prayers which could vary from book to book.[11]

'Books of hours' were immensely popular: more manuscripts have survived of this type of medieval book than of Bibles or psalters.[12] Though vernacular versions did emerge, especially after the advent of print, most were in Latin, though some of the closing petitionary prayers were sometimes in the vernacular. Despite a relatively settled set of contents, each manuscript 'book of hours' was unique, in one way or another. Most were relatively plain: illumination and decoration could be minimal and restricted to decorated or flourished capital letters at the beginning of sections, or individual psalms or prayers. Others could be extremely lavish, with elaborate borders of foliage, birds and animals enclosing the text, and miniatures, sometimes full-page, by recognized artists. Many of these were produced in Flanders and imported into England,[13] but some of the highest-quality 'books of hours' were produced in France – mainly in Paris and the big northern cities such as Rouen or Tours – and were sometimes the highly personalized result of commissions.[14] Among the well-to-do a 'book of hours' was sometimes a wedding gift to a bride, and a marriage appears to lie behind the 'book of hours' now Dublin, Royal Irish Academy MS 12 R 13. When Sir Thomas Hoo, the Chancellor of English-occupied Normandy, married Lady Eleanor Welles in 1444 he apparently commissioned this book in Rouen. It is an expensive book for Sarum use, consisting of 293 folios of fine parchment, and is highly personalized: on fol. 192r Sir Thomas is depicted with his armorials kneeling before the Trinity and on fol. 196v Lady Eleanor kneels before the Virgin and Child, bearing her husband's armorials impaled with her father's (see Plate 6). This book records a specific event in time. The texts are mostly in Latin, but with some French prayers and some not very accurately copied English introductions to prayers towards the end. It is written in an expert professional *textura* hand and is decorated with elaborate borders to the text and 28 high-quality miniatures.[15] It is a *de luxe* product, fitting for the people involved and the occasion, and the beauty of the book has no doubt contributed to its survival to the present day. But whether simple or elaborate, plain or decorated, 'books of hours' are important in the present context because they incorporate two important circular ecclesiastical time-frames, of which their owners cannot have been unaware – the daily round of prayers and the repetitive annual calendar of church feasts.

'Books of hours', partly no doubt because of their beauty, became themselves objects that acquired a social cachet. Eamon Duffy writes perceptively about their function as accessories in medieval art, about the 'images of Books of Hours on prayer-desks before devoutly kneeling donors, held in the hands of attendant saints, or being prayed from by the Virgin Mary herself as the Angel surprises her at her devotions at a hundred Annunciation scenes'.[16] Even when purchased ready-made, the wealthier owners would personalize them. Livia Visser Fuchs writes illuminatingly on the 'most intimate' of the books known to have been owned by Richard, third duke of York (1411–60) – Ushaw College MS 43. This was a small, fat pocket book of 152 folios, produced in Flanders in the 1450s: folios 24 to the end constitute a standard 'book of hours' but after the book had been imported, 'the first three gatherings were added and decorated in England … by an artist connected to the so-called Caesar Master, a foreigner working in England around this time' whose work appears in a number of contemporary manuscripts.[17] But besides being desirable objects to possess and show off, more importantly they were books in constant use: in a bequest to her daughter, Agnes Hull, the wife of a York merchant, mentions 'my primer which I use daily'.[18] They were often carefully bequeathed, staying in the same family for generations, but because they were sometimes personalized books, a change of ownership sometimes involved the erasure of one name and the substitution of another. One example must serve for many – in this case to the victor the spoils. After his death in battle at Bosworth in 1485, a highly personalized 'book of hours' that had belonged to Richard III passed, perhaps as a trophy and a gift from her son, to Margaret Beaufort, Henry VII's mother, who did not totally erase the former king's name, but added her own in a couplet on the back flyleaf:

> In the honour of God and sainte Edmonde
> Pray for Margaret Richmonde,

though this, in its turn, was scratched through by a subsequent owner.[19] 'Books of hours', as was the case in later centuries with family Bibles, were much written in, sometimes with material totally irrelevant to their primary function – notes about bed-linen and blankets, about rents due and rents paid, about debts due and paid. In some families the 'book of hours' was part of the fabric of everyday life, with all the implications of that in relation to conceptions of time. But sometimes, significantly, the entries relate to time, to dates and to memorialization. Most relate to family matters – births, deaths and marriages – but sometimes notable historical dates were added: Cambridge, Fitzwilliam Museum MS 54 has the dates of several of the battles of the Wars of the Roses written into its ecclesiastical calendar, with the names of the more important people killed.[20]

Occasionally, however, the material added is highly appropriate to the defining of the ecclesiastical calendar. Cambridge University Library MS Ff. 6. 8 is a fifteenth-century 'book of hours' written in Flanders for use in England. On one of the front fly-leaves is a simplistic mnemonic jingle on how to calculate Easter, which had been a massive problem for writers of *computus* texts, for centuries:

> In merche, after þe first C,
> Loke the prime wher-euer he be;
> The 3rd sonday, full I-wisse,
> Ester day trewly yt ys.
> & yf þe prime on þe sonday be,
> Rekyne þat sonday for one of the thre.[21]

This is written in a sixteenth-century hand and appears to be an attempt to replicate Bede's elegant and widely-accepted formula, from AD 725, for calculating this important date: 'the Sunday which follows the full moon, which falls on or after the [spring] equinox'. The MS Ff. 6. 8 formula is garbled and unhelpful, but at least the writer thinks he is contributing knowledge about the ecclesiastical calendar appropriate to the book in which he is writing.

The calendar of church feasts and saints-days was indispensable for any well-organized devotional life, religious or secular. Calendars were basically utilitarian, but could, for the wealthier, be elaborate and highly decorated, as is that produced in Bruges for Isabella of Castile (1451–1504) now surviving as BL MS Additional 18851, as can be seen from the January opening. At the top of the left-hand margin Aquarius appears. Below, running down the margin, is a countryside winter scene with bare trees beneath the falling snow and two muffled figures. In the bottom margin is an indoor scene in which a woman arranges jugs and plates on a table and a man warms his hands by the fire (see Plate 7). This is very traditional. Others could be highly personalized. The Benedictine monk John Lydgate wrote *A Kalendare* in rhyme-royal detailing the festivals of the church year, arranged month by month with the dates in the left hand margin. It is a simple, direct attempt to explain the significance of the saints and a prayer for intercession by them to make Lydgate and others spiritually better people. It is local and personal to some degree. In the following stanza, for late June, for example, he refers to several English saints:

> Prayeth for us, Marcellyan and Marke,
> Wyth Gervase and Prothase, martyrs ylkone,
> This world now, Seynt Edward, wenyth darke,
> For oure ynward syght ys almost agone,
> Lede us oure first martyr, Seynt Albone,
> Ethedrede of Ely, I pray now helpe me,
> Wyth Seynt Iohn Baptist, þe natiuite.[22] (169–75).

The poem may have been written for use in Lydgate's monastery of Bury St Edmunds, but six manuscript copies of it are extant, so it probably had some broader circulation. But ecclesiastical calendars were ubiquitous. They were the first item in 'books of hours' and no doubt these provided a constant reference point for negotiating one's way through the ecclesiastical year, and, for that matter, through the secular year also because the 'labours of the months', where they appeared in 'books of hours', are usually attached to the calendars.

But the decoration in illuminated 'books of hours' is also important; traditional biblical scenes, relating to church feasts, became attached to particular items in these books. Partly they function as book-marks, reminding those not particularly proficient in Latin where they were in the book and partly, no doubt, they were meant to prompt contemplation. But they also reinforce the chronology of the more important feasts in the ecclesiastical calendar. One example must serve for many. In Dublin, Royal Irish Academy MS 12 R 31, the Hoo Hours, already mentioned, the events relating to Easter are well represented: there are miniatures of the Man of Sorrows on fol. 202v, Bearing the Cross on fol. 212r, a Crucifixion on fol. 236v and a Pietà on fol. 226r. Earlier in the book, the Matins of the Little Office of the Blessed Virgin Mary begins conventionally on fol. 19r with an Annunciation miniature, set in a church with Mary reading the obligatory prayer-book, and recalls the feast day of 25 March. And a number of other miniatures advert to other Marian events and dates: Lauds has a miniature of the Visitation to St Elizabeth and

St Anne on fol. 28r, feast day 31 May; Sext has the Adoration of the Magi on fol. 57r, feast day 6 January; None has a complex miniature on fol. 61r of the Presentation of Christ in the Temple and the Purification of the Virgin, celebrated on Candlemas Day, 2 February. In addition, a number of saints, whose feast days are fixed, are also depicted: on fol. 75r at the opening of the Psalter of St Jerome there is a picture of the saint in his study, feast day 30 September, and elsewhere appear, on fol. 40r, a wonderfully accomplished St Christopher, feast day 25 July, and later, among others, on fol. 195r St Erasmus, feast day 2 June, and on fol. 199r St Leonard, feast day 6 November.

But all 'books of hours' were to some degree unique, and the choice of saints to be included may to some extent have rested with the patron, Lord Hoo, and if so it is no surprise that this highly-successful soldier should have included St George on fol. 41v, feast day 23 April, a legendary saint, here killing the dragon, but adopted as a patron saint, and much honoured by the English because of his supposed intervention on the English side in war, as a fifteenth-century carol, stressing his two functions, makes plain:

> He kepyd the mad from dragons dred
> And fraid al France and put to flight
> At Agyncourt, the crownecle ye red,
> The French hym se formest in fight. (311.1, 2)

According to R.L. Greene, 'The carol appears to have been suggested by a non-liturgical prayer, the Commemoration of St George, widely circulated in the Prymer or Hours of the Blessed Virgin Mary'.[23] The reference to 'the crownecle' is for the oft-repeated story of how St George was supposed to have appeared above the field at Agincourt in 1415. The ecclesiastical calendar is here invaded by political considerations.

III

But the ecclesiastical calendar was, in its turn, an influential feature of the organization of the great feudal households of the later Middle Ages and the early Renaissance: in the words of G.A. Woolgar, 'the household day was dominated by liturgical celebrations'.[24] The many surviving books of regulations for the good rule of noble and aristocratic households make this plain: in the household of Henry Percy, fifth earl of Northumberland, there was provision for five services during the day – Matins, Lady Mass, High Mass, Vespers and Compline – and rotas for 11 priests and choristers to celebrate these services.[25] This was, by any standards, a large household, but it is clear that some form of this organizational regimen was followed, to a degree, elsewhere. Ecclesiastical considerations dominated mealtimes also. This can best be seen, though it is validated by the household books, in imaginative literature. The settings in *Sir Gawain and the Green Knight* are various, but a significant part of the action takes place in two great households – Arthur's court at Camelot and Bertilak's castle at Hautdesert – and in both the considerations relating to prayer and diet are assiduously observed. After having resisted the first temptation of the Lady in his bedchamber, Sir Gawain

> ... ryches hym to ryse and rapes hym sone,
> Clepes to his chamberlayn, choses his wede,
> Bowez forth, quen he watz boun, blythely to masse
> And thenne he meued to his mete that menskly hym keped ... (1309–12)

Religious observance precedes meals, as it does with Bertilak, who has risen earlier to go hunting: he 'ete a sop hastyly, when he hade herde masse' (1135). The order is all-important. Bertilak's house, though it turns out to be enchanted through the power of Morgan le Fay, is disarmingly conventional in its organization, part of the seeming ordinariness that leads to Gawain's faulty behaviour.

The household accounts also make it clear what the regimen of diet consisted of. They set out amongst other things, according to the ecclesiastical calendar, a set of fast-days when a vegetarian or fish diet had to be observed: Wednesday, Friday and Saturday were regularly observed as fast-days. And to these, through the annual round, could be added fasts on the vigils of major feast days such as, over the Christmas period, from Christmas day to the feast of the Epiphany, or at Easter, Good Friday. Abstinence on the eves of major Marian feasts was also frequently observed – the Purification (2 February), the Annunciation (25 March), the Assumption (15 August) or the Nativity of Mary (8 September). Some households added further days – Corpus Christi, the Nativity of St John the Baptist (24 June) and All Saints (1 November). It is clear from the surviving account books of great households – the records and costs of provisions acquired on a daily basis – that these days of abstinence were widely adhered to, though there were those who chafed against them, and they are utterly rejected by the impecunious knight in the fourteenth-century debate poem *Wynnere and Wastoure*, who curses his more affluent opponent in the following terms:

> Now wolde God that it were als I wisse couthe,
> That thou Wynnere, thou wriche, and Wanhope thi brothir,
> And eke ymbryne dayes and euenes of sayntes,

> The Frydaye and his fere one the ferrere syde
> Were drownede in the depe see there neuer droghte come … (308–12)[26]

But Wastoure, as his name indicates, is seen as a figure of prodigality, who fritters away his inheritance, neglects his houses and lands, and instead provides himself with a 'rychely attyrede' retinue and spends his time with them at 'the tauerne byfore þe toune-hede' (270–7), drinking and womanizing – neither of which activities he can afford. But whether adhered to or resisted, the power and influence of the ecclesiastical calendar is demonstrable. It is interesting here that he alludes, aggressively, to the fact that the ends of the week – Saturday afternoon and Sunday – were regarded as being at once preparations and occasions for religious feast days. But there were many such feast days, and weekends did not assume the importance as they have come to acquire in modern times.

At some times in the annual round, however, festivity was conventional and, indeed, expected. This was mainly the case at Christmas, when household accounts itemize money spent on minstrels and music and where the evidence of imaginative literature bears this out. Staying with *Sir Gawain and the Green Knight*, at Arthur's Christmas feast at Camelot the 'rych brether' of the Round Table, after jousting, 'keyred to the court carols to make' and the festivities would be going on for 'ful fifteen dayes' (43–4), and, a year after this, at Bertilak's castle the retinue and their guests, on Christmas Day, 'wonderly thay woke, and the wyn drunken / Daunsed ful dreȝly wyth dere caroles' (1025–6) and on a later day there were 'mony athel songez / As condutes of Krystmasse and caroles newe …' (1654–5). Carols of this sort, celebrating Christmas, have survived in considerable numbers. One copied down by Richard Hill, a London grocer in the sixteenth century, is particularly revealing. 'Caroles' were originally ring-dances accompanied by a song, the refrain of which was sung by all the dancers or the dancers and the audience and the verses by what would now probably be called the lead-singer. In this one the refrain enjoins everybody, 'bothe more and lasse', to make 'mery' because it is Christmas, but, as it develops, begins to be coercive about merriment:

> Let no man cum in to this hall,
> Grome, page, nor yet marshall,
> But that sum sport he bring withall,
>   For now ys the tyme of Crystmas.[27]

'Yff that he say he can not syng' he should bring 'sum oder sport' to grace the festival, and if he cannot do anything he should be put in 'the stokkes'. This is humorous, but it does indicate that these celebrations were meant to have a large communal aspect and a broad participatory input from the household.

But Christmas was not only the time for music but for dramatic performances of various kinds – some less verbal than others. According to Bridget Ann Henisch, 'the disguising was weak on plot but very strong on costume'. She characterizes the typical performance thus: 'A group of people dressed as ingenuity and funds would permit, entered the hall at some suitable moment and performed a dance or sang a song before sweeping out in a stately exit'.[28] It was an expensive spectacle and the costumes were important: Edward III's Wardrobe Accounts for 1347 give details for the elaborate costumes for a performance of this sort at Guildford, for 14 angels, 14 men with bearded faces, 14 women and 14 people in other groups representing birds and beasts and suitably dressed.[29] In the following year there were comparable displays at Otford for Christmas and at Merton for Epiphany. Very similar were the 'mummings', which as their name indicates, were essentially silent performances. In origin a folk tradition, in which costumed groups, usually with blackened faces, might call on a household, offer to play dice, give presents and sometimes dance – all in silence except, sometimes, for a musical accompaniment. But this sort of performance was adopted by the higher ranks of society. In January 1377 an elaborate 'mumming' was performed, in both a public and private setting, by the substantial citizens of London, culminating in a visit to the young King Richard II at his palace in Kennington, where there was dicing (at which the king and his entourage were allowed to win) and dancing, after which the 'mummers' 'took their leave and departed to London'.[30] But this kind of performance clearly took hold on the imaginations of the London bourgeoisie. Between 1420 and 1430 John Lydgate, a poet with a courtly, social and ecclesiastical reputation, devised various 'mummings', which have been preserved with verses, spoken by a presenter, as a commentary on the silent performance. One was presented before the three-year old Henry VI and his mother at Eltham at Christmas 1424, and later two other Christmas 'mummings' for the king, one at Hertford and one at Windsor.[31] Another was devised for a feast organized by the Mercers' Company of London to entertain the Lord Mayor on 'þe twelffeþe night of Cristmasse' 1429, and another to honour the same person but for the Goldsmiths' Company in February 1429, 'upon Candlemasse at nyghte, after souper'.[32]

It is clear, too, that at celebratory feasts the food itself was sometimes presented in an elaborate way, like the boar's head, introduced at table at occasions such as Christmas, with a carol inviting the feasters present ('qui estis in convivio') to sing:

> The bores heed in hande bring I,
> With garlans gay and rosemary;
> I pray you all, synge merely,
> > Qui estis in convivio.[33]

Here the decoration appears to have been modest and includes an appropriate herb. But presentations could be more extravagant, to which Chaucer's Parson objects in his strictures against 'pride of the table': 'namely swich manere bake-metes and dissh-metes, brennynge of wilde fir and peynted and castellated with papir ...'. To him this was 'wast' (*CT*, X. 443–4). But elaborate presentations of food, known as 'sotelties', did become fashionable at feasts. Some were moralistic and educative. John Russell, at one time usher and marshal in the household of Humphrey, duke of Gloucester, in his *Boke of Nurture*, describes a four-course fish dinner given by the duke that was illustrative of a time-scheme, the 'four ages of man' with references to the four elements and the four seasons: it began with a 'galaunt yonge man', standing on a cloud (representing air), at the beginning of spring, and the other three ages with their associated elements and seasons followed, and verses explained the significance of the decorations.[34] But nobody did extravagance like Cardinal Thomas Wolsey in the next century. George Cavendish, his usher and biographer, describes a banquet for a party of French ambassadors given by Wolsey at Hampton Court in the autumn of 1527: accompanying the second course

> there were castles with images in the same, Paul's Church and steeple in proportion for the quantity as well counterfeited as the painter should have painted it upon a cloth or wall. There were beasts, birds, fowls of various kinds, and personages, most lively made and counterfeit in dishes, some fighting ... some vaulting and leaping, some dancing with ladies, some in complete harness jousting with spears, and many more devices than I am able with my wit to describe.

But he remembers a 'chessboard, subtly made of spiced plate, with men of the same ...' as a compliment to the French who 'be very expert in that play'. But, above all, this, like many of Wolsey's displays, was designed to impress: 'I suppose the Frenchmen never saw the like', writes Cavendish, with no apparent trace of irony.[35]

And then there were the plays. The outdoor civic drama of the later Middle Ages, the great mystery cycles, came under the general supervision of the municipal authorities, but were financed and staged by the trade guilds. Again, however, the liturgical calendar was important. These plays were traditionally associated with the feast of Corpus Christi: a Corpus Christi play at York is first heard of in 1376 and another is mentioned in 1377 at Beverley (though this play is no longer extant). The extant York cycle is designed to be played at Corpus Christi, but the Chester cycle, though it may have originally been meant for Corpus Christi, is, in its present form, intended for Whitsun. But plays were performed at other festivals too – particularly at Christmas and New Year, when the performances would have been indoors. It is clear that in some great households there were resident players. Henry VII maintained a troupe of four 'lusores regis, alias, in lingua Anglicana, "les playars of the Kings enterluds"' at a basic retaining fee of five marks a year each, together with liveries. For every performance given at court they received a gratuity and, when not required at court, were free to travel and perform in other households or guild-halls.[36] Henry Percy, fifth earl of Northumberland, had his own household entertainers who put on impressive performances, but he still budgeted for 20*d*. a play and 32*s*. in all for 'playes playd at Christynmas by stranegers'.[37] It is difficult to know what sort of performances these were. But in the moral interludes *Mankind*, written between 1465 and 1470 and played in the Cambridge area, the fashionably up-to-date vice figures at one point force their way through the audience into the playing space and offer a 'Crystmes songe':

> *Nowadays*: Mak rom, syrs, for we haue be longe!
> We wyl gyf yow a Crystmes songe.
> *Nought*: Now I prey al þe yomandry þat ys here
> To synge wyth ws a mery chere. (331–4)[38]

But the 'songe', which is grotesquely obscene, is not appropriate for a Christmas celebration or, indeed, for any religious festival, and the setting of the play is in one of the planting months, October or November, or March, since the protagonist Mankynde is 'a goode starke laburrer' (368), who attempts to till the soil and plant corn. Players of interludes obviously had a certain amount of latitude. But interludes were traditionally associated with calendar feasts. In *Sir Gawain and the Green Knight* Arthur seeks to explain away the Green Knight's dangerous challenge and reassure Guenevere and the rest of the court that such things were normal at Christmas:

> Dere dame, today dismay yow neuer:
> Wel bycommes such craft upon Cristmasse –
> Laykyng of enterludez, to laghe and to syng,
> Among these kynde carols of knyghtes and ladies. (470–3)

The Green Knight has misleadingly described his challenge as 'a Christmas game' (283) and Arthur responds in similarly misleading terms, though he knows 'at hert' (467) that it is a lot more serious than this.

There were dramatic performances, of one kind or another, throughout the Christmas season, including New Year. But New Year was, rather than Christmas Day, the day on which gifts were exchanged – 'hanselles', tokens of good luck for the coming year. In *Sir Gawain and the Green Knight*, 'while Newe Yere was so yep that it was newe comen' there are feasting and games at the Arthurian court at Camelot:

> And sythen riche forth runnen to reche hanselle,
> Yeyed yeres-yiftes on high, yelde hem by hande;
> Debated busyþly aboute tho giftes … (60–8).

There may have been some sort of game involved here because there is talk of winners and losers (69–70), but what the gifts consisted of does not appear. But the household accounts offer some information: in G.M. Woolgar's summary there is mention of monetary gifts to the household servants, brooches, rings with jewels, ornate rosary beads and knives for the boys – evidently a lot of small gifts, tokens of esteem. Rather different is the gift-giving relating to the earl of March, spending the Christmas season with Henry V at Eltham in 1414: he gave lots of gifts but also received two falcons 'and the falconers who brought the birds were rewarded handsomely'.[39] In line with this sort of gift comes John Lydgate's *Ballade of a New Year's Gift of an Eagle*, 'gyuen vn to þe kyng Henry ye vj and to his moder þe qwene Kateryne sittyng at þe mete vpon þe yeris day in þe Castell of Hertford'. This 'celestyal' bird is presented with good wishes, as the earlier refrains say, for his 'Honour and knyghthode, conquest and victorye', which is all pretty unrealistic for the boy king and was actually never achieved. Halfway through the poem, however, the refrain changes to more realistic wishes for his 'Helþe and welfare, ioye and prosparyte', again, as it turned out, not to be achieved.[40] Years later, in the Scottish court, William Dunbar presented no gift, except the poem, but similarly wished James IV prosperity and happiness in a New Year poem:

> My prince in God, gif the guid grace,
> Joy, glaidness, confort and solace,
> Play pleasance, myrth and mirie cheir,
>   In hansill of this guid New ȝeir. (18. 1–4)[41]

When this was written is not known, and doubtless, in these productions, it is the thought that counts, but James IV was not much more fortunate than the murdered Henry VI: he met an untimely death at Flodden on 9 September 1513. But this sort of gift-giving continued: on 1 January 1669 Samuel Pepys records the gift of 'a noble silver warming-pan' from a Captain Beckford.[42]

But small gifts were given at other times of the year also, usually in accordance with the liturgical calendar: gifts to the poor on Maundy Thursday, gifts to the cooks for their production of Easter feasts, and gifts at Lammas (1 August) to agricultural workers for their efforts in bringing in the harvest. And the calendar incorporated traditional days on which the normal hierarchical order was suspended temporarily. On 6 December, the feast of St Nicholas, patron saint of children, in some cathedrals a boy bishop was elected from among the choristers: he would be dressed as a bishop and his acolytes would be dressed as priests. There would be a procession through the streets where the boy bishop would bless the populace, and, with his acolytes, he would perform some of the functions of the cathedral clergy – but not the Mass. Some element of parody was evidently permitted. Their authority lasted until the feast of the Holy Innocents on 28 December. There were moves in some quarters to abolish this custom, but it lasted for a while and spread. The boy bishop could expect gifts. In 1383 Thomas Arundel, then bishop of Ely but later archbishop of Canterbury, gave 6s. 8d. to the boy bishop of Hatfield on the feast of St Nicholas and 40s. to the boy bishop in his own cathedral at Holy Innocents.[43] The feast of Epiphany on 6 January, 'Twelfth Night', closed the Christmas celebrations and was itself the occasion for celebration. Henry VII's household regulations, drawn up on 31 December 1494, have a section on 'the Voide on Twelfth Night and Wassail': the 'voide' was a drink taken before retiring, and the 'wassail' was the drink itself, usually spiced beer or mulled wine. The regulation stipulates: 'the chappell to stand on the one side of the hall, and when the steward cometh in at the hall doore with the wassell he must crie three tymes, Wassell, Wassell, Wassell; and then the chappell to answere with a goode songe'. There was also a relaxation of hierarchy on Shrove Tuesday. The same regulations say that 'there longeth non estate to be kepte, but onely a fellowshippe, the Kinge and Queene to be together, and all other estates'.[44] In 1482 there were unfortunate consequences deriving from this relaxation in the household of the Celys, wool merchants of the Staple. On 25 May, Richard Cely the younger writes to his elder brother George what is for the most part a routine letter on business matters, but in the middle of it confesses that he has something on his conscience and looks to his 'gostely brother' for help with a solution:

> Syr, hyt ys so that a chawns ys fawllyn that lyes apon myne oneste, byt I cannot kepe no cwnsell frome yow, for be polesy 3e and I may fynd

the meyn to sawhe awl thing clere at yowr comyng. Hyt ys so that Em ys wyth schyllde, and as Godde knowys byt that whons that hyt whas gettyn I desarwyd for myn. Hyt whos gettyn on Schrofe ȝeuyn, and sche has beyn seke heuyr syn ȝe departtyde of the axsys.⁴⁵

How matters developed is not clear or how the brothers devised the 'meyn' to rescue the situation, if they ever did: who 'Em' was never emerges and she does not figure further in the correspondence.

But 'Em's' predicament, occasioned by a relaxation of prudential behaviour associated with a festival, is reflected in a number of fifteenth-century carols, in which young girls are seduced (like 'Em') by male figures of somewhat higher status – usually priests or 'clerks'.⁴⁶ In one *carole* – a song with a refrain, to accompany a ring-dance – the narrator is one such girl and the occasion of her misfortune is the festivity associated with Midsummer Day. She begins: 'Ladd y the daunce a Myssomer day / y made smale trippys soth for to say ... ' (1–2).⁴⁷ She is joined in 'þe ryng' by 'Jak, oure haly-watur clerk' (6–7) – a rather lowly church official who carried the vessel holding the holy water. He promises her the traditional 'peyr of wyth glouus' (18), and when she comes to his chamber 'aftur euensong' to collect them he seduces her (21–24), with the consequence that in the final stanza she says 'my gurdul a-ros, my wombe wax out' (43). Each stanza ends with 'Thout y on no gyle' and in the refrain of the poem she expresses regret and blames dancing: 'Alas, alas þe wyle – / That euer y coude daunce'. R.L. Greene glosses the end of the poem by reference to a Latin sermon, which asserts: 'Juvencule, dum sunt virginnes et caste, cantant, sed cum venter ceperit inflari, mutant in lamentum' [Young girls, when they are virgins and chaste, sing, but when the stomach shall have suffered swelling, they change into weeping].⁴⁸ Despite the festive occasions celebrated in some of these poems and their associations with an enjoyable pastime, their message is often cautionary: it is perhaps ironic, in hindsight, that the sole surviving manuscript of this poem is that in Cambridge, Gonville and Caius MS 383, which Greene describes as 'a trilingual students's exercise and commonplace book', a book compiled by a 'clerk', 'very probably the work of an Oxford student', one of the class of people responsible for the unfortunate (but perhaps fictional) predicament of the girl.⁴⁹

IV

Something, finally, should be said about almanacs. Basing her judgement on the number of copies of this sort of book that have survived in English manuscripts and prints, Linne Mooney writes: 'it is clear that an almanack had become a necessary possession for hundreds, and by the end of the sixteenth century, thousands of Englishmen, not only for physicians, barbers and surgeons, but for merchants, churchmen, craftsmen and – yes – farmers'.[50] Almanacs developed from the Roman calendar of nones, ides and kalends, to which were added, in the early Christian period, the feast days of saints, calculations for the dates of leap-years and the dates of Easter in the coming years. Later, over the years, other material was added – lunar and solar conjunctions and oppositions, planetary conjunctions and oppositions, eclipses, the times of the rising and setting of the sun and of the moon, the sun's angle at its zenith and tables of shadow length to enable one to calculate the time. And, of course, much else. Some almanacs restricted themselves to scientific or quasi-scientific material, but some added prognostications for the coming year. Some, unsurprisingly, had to do with the weather, as the weather on a certain day might determine what it was to be on subsequent days. One such, long lasting and invoked in living memory, concerns the feast of St Swithun, of 15 July. A rhyme, stating a crude binary prognostication, runs as follows:

> St Swithun's day if thou dost rain
> For forty days it will remain.
> St Swithun's day if thou be fair
> For forty days 'twill rain nae mair.[51]

My grandmother and my mother, both country people from north Warwickshire who had access to a rhyme such as this, adhered to this prognostication well into the twentieth century, despite annual evidence to the contrary. But there were more comprehensive prognostications – such as those based on which day of the week Christmas Day or New Year's Day fell. One example must serve for many:

> If Cristemas day on A Satterday fall,
> That winter we mowen drede All.
> Yt shall be so full of tempeste
> Þat yt shall sley bothe man & beste;
> Ffruttes & cornes shall faile grete wone;
> And olde folke dye many oon.
> What woman that day of childe travaille,
> They shall bothe be in gret peraile.[52]

There were other prognostications for what one should do or not do on certain 'days of the moon', or on 'lucky' or 'unlucky' days. The texts on 'unlucky' days do not make for comfortable reading. One author, evidently relying on authorities ('masters'), states that on five days of the year it is especially necessary to avoid sickness:

> ... whoso in any of þer dayes
> In any sekenes down hym lyes –
> Masters says, þat war full wys,
> Of hys seknes shuld he neuer ryse.

Anyone born on these days, he continues, will have a short life; anyone going on a long journey will not return; anyone getting married will be unhappy and anyone taking up a difficult task will be unsuccessful.[53]

How seriously all this was taken is difficult to know, but even someone as sophisticated and practical as William Cecil, Lord Burghley, could advise his son in the 1580s – quoting authorities like the previous writer – to avoid beginning enterprises on certain days:

> Though I think no day amisse to undertake any good enterprise or businesse in hande, yet I have observed some, and no meane clerks, very cautionary to forbeare these three Mundayes in the yeare, which I leave to thine owne consideration, either to use or to refuse; viz. 1. The first Munday in April, which daie Caine was born, and his brother Abel slaine. 2. The secand Munday in August, which day Sodome and Gomorrah were destroyed. 3. The last Munday in December, which day Judas was born that betrayed our Saviour Christ.

Biblical associations account, as here, for many of these beliefs: 28 December, the day memorializing Herod's massacre of the Holy Innocents, was regarded as a particularly 'black letter day'.[54]

On the other hand, it is difficult to account for 3 May, which does not appear in any of the obvious lists as 'unlucky', but which was frequently regarded by Chaucer as such, particularly in relation to love: it is the date on which Pandarus suffers his 'tene for love' (*T & C*, II. 50–6) and the date on which Palemon breaks out of prison to fight his duel with Arcite for the love of Emelye (*CT*, I. 1462–9). Why this should be so is not clear: it may be that the date was inauspicious for love because the feast of the finding of the Cross by St Helena falls on this date and she also cast down the idol of Venus.[55] This date is also used by Sir John Clanvowe, Chaucer's friend and earliest imitator, as 'unlucky': in his *Boke of Cupide* this is the date on which the narrator dreams he hears the cuckoo sing before the nightingale, which was regarded as a 'tokenyng' inauspicious for lovers.[56] Perhaps there was some in-joke between them: there is at least one other instance in which they attach a special meaning to words and phrases.⁵⁷ And when Chaucer establishes the occasion, in the *Nun's Priest's Tale*, for Chauntecleer's terrifying encounter with the fox, it is 3 May (*CT*, VII. 3187–97) and, more than this, 'on a Friday fil al this meschaunce' (3341), a traditionally 'unlucky' day, on which, among other unfortunate events, Richard I met his death, which Chaucer mentions (3347–53) alluding to a lament for him by Geoffroi de Vinsauf. There is more than a little mockery here: death of a famous crusading king is recalled in relation to a mundane farmyard incident – in which the cock actually escapes.

But Friday was regarded in many cultures as an unlucky day. It is regarded as particularly ominous when it is the day on which any new enterprise is undertaken, especially if it involves a journey. Again, one example must serve for many. In one of the poems (dated *c.*1175) in the Old Irish Finn cycle, the 'hundred-slaying' warrior Cáel, 'son of the king of Leinster in the East', woos the beautiful Créide with a poem, which begins by explaining his dangerous mission:

> Turus acam Día hAíne
> (gé dech, isam fíraíge)
> co tech Créide (ní sním súail)
> re hucht in tsléibe an-airthúaid.
> A-ta I cinniud dam dul ann.
> co Créide i Cíchaib Anann,
> co rabar ann fo decraib,
> cethra lá ocus leithsechtmain. (1–2)

> [I travel in great anxiety on a Friday (though I do so, I am a true guest) to Créide's house which lies north-east of the mountain, facing it.
> It has been fated for me to go there, to Créide in the Paps mountains, to spend four days in trouble there and half a week.]⁵⁸

After this preamble, the poem develops into a *laudatio*, a praise poem of her beauty, her house and the circumstances of her life: 'Aíbinn in tech ina tá …' [Pleasant is the house in which she is …] (3) and details the fineness of her clothes, the smooth running of her household and the skill of her servants, the architectural features of the house, the rich furnishings, particularly the chairs and beds, the food and the drink, 'the cups and lovely goblets'. Twice more he refers to his journey – ominously keeping it within the consciousness of the hearer or reader – but hoping its outcome will be successful. Once he says 'if Créide wishes it (as I have said) my journey will have been a pleasant one' (5), and later he says that though he has brought no 'curly-haired cattle' as a present, only a poem, he hopes that 'she will be pleased with my journey' (23). His wooing is successful and they marry. But as the cycle develops the 'fated' nature of the journey interposes itself: Cáel and Créide go to assist Finn at the probably legendary battle of Ventry, fought against foreign invaders in a harbour in Kerry, on the final day of which Cáel is drowned. Créide fashions a moving lament for him, based on the 'nature mourns' trope, as she lies at his side before dying of grief for him: 'Why should I not die ... of grief for my husband, seeing that the restless wild creatures are dying for him ...?'[59] There is no ironic reversal associated with this instance: the misfortune associated with the initial 'fated' Friday journey simply works itself out in a relatively short time but in different circumstances.

There is irony though in the way that Shakespeare uses the concept of an 'unlucky' day in *Richard III*, V. vi, which is set on the morning of the Battle of Bosworth in which the king is to meet his death. The incident described is generated by the striking of a clock, and Richard seeks to read the future by consulting a 'calendar':

> (*Clock strikes*)
> *King Richard*: Tell the clock there. Give me a calendar.
> Who saw the sun today?
> (*A book is brought*)
> *Ratcliffe*: Not I, my lord.
> *King Richard*: Then he disdains to shine, for by the book
> He should have braved the east an hour ago.
> A black day it will be for somebody. (6–10)

Ostensibly, the king, as commander of his forces, is seeking quite reasonably to establish the weather conditions in which the forthcoming battle will take place, but the way in which Shakespeare constructs this staccato exchange has implications: the 'calendar' is actually an almanac, which has amongst its detail the time of sunrise, which is important not only militarily but symbolically too. The sunburst was a Plantagenet and therefore a Yorkist emblem as is established in the opening of the play, where the punningly referred to 'son of York' (Edward IV) has replaced the 'winter of our discontent' with 'glorious summer' and dispelled 'all the clouds that loured upon our house' (I. i. 1–4). But the sun is not shining at the time stipulated by the almanac for 22 August 1485 and Richard is initially disconcerted, but with some practical military realism says that the conditions are the same for the enemy: 'the self-same heaven / That frowns upon me looks sadly upon him' (16–17). But he also reacts with bravado and a pun: 'A black day it will be for somebody'. The important feasts in the ecclesiastical calendar and in almanacs were often designated by red script ('red letter days') while the less important were in black: in Richard's estimation this is going to be a 'black' day, unfortunate for somebody, him as it turns out.

This short but complex passage is set in clock-time: the striking mechanical clock, not seen but heard, has to be counted ('tell'). But this is not the only scene in which Shakespeare mixes clock-time with that of the almanacs. Before Duncan's murder, the sleepless and anxious Banquo and his son Fleance are in the courtyard of Macbeth's castle around or just after midnight, with all its menacing associations. It is a lightless night: they carry a torch, as do Macbeth and his servant when they appear:

> *Banquo*: How goes the night, boy?
> *Fleance*: The moon is down; I have not heard the clock.
> *Banquo*: And she goes down at twelve.
> *Fleance*: I take't, 'tis later, sir.
> *Banquo*: Here, take my sword – There's husbandry in heaven;
> Their candles are all out ... (*Macbeth*, II. i. 1–5)

Here 'candles' may allude to the stars, or to the graduated candles used to measure the hours of the night: 'husbandry' means 'economy', because candles were expensive and would be blown out when no longer necessary.[60] But 'she' is the moon (*Luna*) and the calculation of the setting of the moon is adverted to along with the midnight striking of the clock (here, not heard), when they are joined by Macbeth with ambition and murder in his thoughts. Both these passages only release their full meanings in terms of time schemes other than, or together with, that of the clock, here by reference to calendars and almanacs, a tradition of understanding time which has now largely disappeared in its fine detail – though solstices are sometimes still celebrated, especially at monuments such as Stonehenge or at passage-tombs such as that at Newgrange (Co. Meath), and the major feasts of the ecclesiastical calendar are observed – Christmas, Shrove Tuesday, Ash Wednesday and Lent, the ceremonies associated with Easter and Whitsun and, in some cultures, Halloween. Some peoples also celebrate national saints' days: the Irish greet St Patrick's Day (17 March) world-wide with processions. Friday the 13th is still widely regarded as an 'unlucky' day.

But even as Shakespeare wrote these lines this richly differentiated sense of time was being challenged and a greater sense of conformity was emerging, largely because of the increasing dominance of Protestant ideas. In England, the more Puritanical wing of Protestantism opposed and, where they could, eradicated, the sense of special days, particularly saints' days in the ecclesiastical calendar, which was a cherished part of the traditions of the Roman church, often in brutal terms with the destruction of religious images and the defacement of books. Instead they espoused and sought to establish a routine, for the week, based on the biblical authority of Exodus 20:9, of six days of work followed by a day of rest and worship on the Sabbath, which has come to be called the 'non-Conformist ethic' or the 'Protestant work ethic'. The mechanical clock, with its capacity for the regular division of time into definable segments and its regular public and private striking of the hours, became an important contributory factor in what became a revolution in the habits of daily life and work. But the earliest mechanical clocks were developed within the richer, more complex time-schemes that they eventually displaced, and their creators had to take account of this.

CHAPTER 3

Measuring time in the Middle Ages and Renaissance

IN HIS OVERVIEW OF *Feudal society*, Marc Bloch writes that people in the Middle Ages 'lived in a world in which the passage of time escaped their grasp, all the more because they were ill-equipped to measure it'.[1] As stated this is only partly true: linear time based on the AD system was generally accepted throughout the Christian west and numerous theories enabled people to make sense of history and the trajectories of their own lives. 'Books of hours', calendars and almanacs articulated the details of the ecclesiastical and the secular year, but matters were more difficult in relation to diurnal time. The Middle Ages had inherited the concept of the year, the lunar month, the seven-day week, the division of the day into two sequences of twelve hours for light and darkness and, in more intellectually abstruse analyses, the division of the hour into sixty minutes and the minute into sixty seconds. It was recognized that time is constantly moving and in a single direction, so that it is impossible to fix the instant, the 'now'.[2] Guillaume de Lorris in *Le Roman de la Rose* (lines 361–74) expressed this memorably in a much-imitated passage, translated as follows by Chaucer in his *Romaunt of the Rose*, lines 369–84:[3]

> The tyme, that passeth nyght and day,
> And resteles travayleth ay,
> And steleth from us so prively
> That to us semeth sykerly
> That it in oon poynt dwelleth ever –
> And certes, ne resteth never,
> But gooth so faste, and passeth ay,
> That ther nys man that thynke may
> What tyme that now present is
> (Asketh at these clerkes this)
> For er men thynke it, redily
> Thre tymes be passed by –
> The tyme, that may not sojourne,

> But goth and may never retourne,
> As watir that doun renneth ay,
> And never drope retourne may ...

Nevertheless, though the representation of 'present' time was recognized to be impossible, much ingenuity was devoted to calculating the rate at which time passed and much attention was paid to duration.

There was general agreement on how to measure years, months and weeks, but how to calculate the diurnal cycle was difficult – not least because the division of the day and night into twelve-hour periods involved accepting the concept of unequal hours, the length of an hour constantly changing as the hours of daylight and darkness varied throughout the year, being at their most differentiated at the solstices and being equal only at the equinoxes. In the Anglo-Saxon *Genesis B* Satan, confined to Hell, addresses his cohorts of fallen angels and wishes for a temporary release, even if it is short, so that he can create more damage on Earth and especially on Adam:

> Wa la, ahte ic minre handa
> And moste ane tid ute weorðan,
> Wesan ane winterstunde, þonne ic mid þys werode ... (368–70)[4]
>
> [Alas, if I could have control of my hands, and get out of here for a single hour, be outside one time in winter, then I with this troop ...]

He breaks off, speechless in frustration, recognizing that he is bound in iron fetters ('irenbenda'), but had it been possible for him to achieve any kind of, even limited, freedom, it would have been difficult for him to estimate how much time a winter-hour might have provided. There were time calculators that tried to adjust to the unequal hours of the natural world. Some astrolabes were marked with unequal hours as well as equal hours (as will be seen) and many sundials. Some clocks did this too. One such is the remarkable astronomical clock set into the wall of the town hall in Clusone (Lombardy) (see Figure 4). In its present form it was devised by Pietro Ferzango in 1583, but uses the medieval mechanism. The hand moves anti-clockwise, but the clock's dials show not only the hours, days and months, as usual plotted against the signs of the zodiac, and the movement of the sun and the moon, but also the 'unequal hours', the duration of day and night.[5] But the invention and development of the mechanical clock altered this.

As A.J. Turner puts it: 'instead of the machine being adapted in some way to indicate unequal hours following the norm prevailing in society, the machine itself forced a change in social life'.[6] From the latter part of the fourteenth

4 Town hall clock in Clusone, Lombardy, Zairon, CC BY-SA 4.0, via Wikimedia Commons.

century onwards: 'unequal hours' were beginning to be displaced by 'equal hours' as the norm. Later still, John Donne wrote about the winter solstice in his *Nocturnal upon S. Lucy's Day, being the shortest day*, which fell, in the Julian calendar still then in use, on 13 December. He begins:

> 'Tis the year's midnight, and it is the day's,
> Lucy's, who scarce seven hours herself unmasks … (1–2)[7]

Donne (as will be seen in a subsequent chapter) possessed a watch and wrote about clocks and watches, and here the short duration of the winter's day is appropriately calculated using the equal hours of the modern timekeepers.

But before the development of the mechanical clock, in order to measure the smaller units of time with any accuracy, tools and machines had to be devised and made. This involved the development of a different relationship with natural time: 'gradually time became manipulable. Time as a given element of the world gave way to a time which was created by the machines which measured it. In the process man became independent of nature'.[8] Some of the tools and machines developed, however, tried to work with the celestial and the natural world and to interpret observable phenomena so that they could be used to measure time.

II

The simplest and most prevalent of these instruments was the sundial, which basically measures diurnal time by plotting the apparent motion of the sun across the sky. Sundials normally consist of a flat plate, known as the *dial*, and a *gnomon* or *style*, set at an angle to the dial which in sunlight casts a shadow on it: the shadow aligns with time-lines precisely inscribed on the dial and so indicates the time of day.

Sundials are usually constructed in a single position and are accurate only when the latitude of their positioning is precisely related to the spacing and angle of the time-lines, though there are examples of portable sundials from the Middle Ages and later. This type of sundial was normally small and cylindrical in shape and could stand or be hung vertically from a ring with a gnomon set horizontally. The hours were marked on the surface of the cylinder and the position of the gnomon could be adjusted according to the time of the year.[9] The worldly monk Daun John in Chaucer's *Shipman's Tale* has an instrument of this sort, presumably since he is outside his cloister so that he can determine the proper time to say his prayers, though his single use of it relates to his wish for food – though Chaucer ironically relates it to one of the canonical hours ('prime'):

> Lat us dyne as soone as that we nay,
> For by my cylinder it is prime of day. (*CT*, VII. 205–6)

A number of these 'cylinders' have survived. On one of the shelves of the room in which Hans Holbein paints, in 1533, Jean de Dinteville, French ambassador to England, and Georges de Selve, bishop of Latour, there are, along with a celestial globe, two quadrants and a torquetum, no less than three instruments for measuring diurnal time: a cylinder or shepherd's dial, a small flat dial and a polyhedral dial.[10] Small cylindrical and polyhedral sundials were not expensive and were easily portable objects. The cylinder or shepherd's dial is apparently made of wood, and on its circumference are marked off, in two six-month cycles, the names of the months and the signs of the zodiac. The polyhedral dial has a compass set into it. But, these things were evidently not easy to use: 'In his letters from London to his brother Bishop François, Jean mentions a *compas*: "send me a drawing of the oval compass", he requests in his letter of 23 May, and writes that he is still puzzled by its details.'[11] Perhaps what he is referring to is a magnetic compass to help him align the dial correctly. These objects all suggest time passing and transience, but not as dramatically as the distorted skull at the bottom of the painting.

Fixed sundials, which were much more accurate and numerous, are very ancient tools for the calculation of diurnal time: perhaps the oldest, dated *c*.1500 BC, was found in Egypt in the Valley of the Kings. But they were used in classical Greece and Rome and had an extensive life in the Middle Ages and later. They were of various types, some of amazing complexity,[12] but the most common were the vertical, in which the gnomon or style is attached horizontally to a usually south-facing wall or other surface which is inscribed with time-lines onto which a shadow is cast; the horizontal, where the dial is inscribed usually on a metal plate on to which surface an angled gnomon casts a shadow; or the equatorial, where the dial is inscribed on a curved surface mounted on a plane set parallel with the equator of the earth. The horizontal type needs to be set in an open space and this type of sundial frequently served as a garden ornament and the equatorial type developed later into the more complex armillary sphere. The vertical type usually marks its time-lines on a semicircle, but the horizontal types usually use the whole circle. The number of time-lines varies considerably according to the intended function of the sundial: some simply divide the day into four 'tides', others are more complex, sometimes having as many as 24 lines radiating from the centre of the circle.

Early examples of vertical medieval sundials are usually found on the wall of churches, or, as at Monasterboice (Co. Louth), on a free-standing pillar in the churchyard,[13] and were almost certainly used principally for determining the times appropriate for Masses or, in examples from monastic houses, for the services associated with the canonical hours. But at times there is evidence that they were endowed with more specific significance. High on the south wall of St Mary the Virgin, North Stoke (Oxfordshire), an originally Saxon church rebuilt in 1223, is carved a sundial held in the hands of a figure whose head appears above it and who is thought to represent Christ, though this interpretation is disputed. It is almost certainly correct though: in a thirteenth-century Psalter map, in British Library MS Additional 28681 (fol. 9v), appears

5 Sundial, St Gregory's Minster, Kirkdale, Yorkshire.

a very similar depiction of Christ embracing the round earth, with angels around him and devils being trampled underfoot – an image of protection and custodianship,[14] which is replicated in this partial representation of Christ as the protector and custodian of time, particularly the time of the church. Meaning has to be elicited from this by minimalist iconographic gestures, but other sundials are sometimes accompanied by explanatory text.

The sundial on the south porch of St Gregory's Minster in Kirkdale (Yorks.) is semicircular and cut into eight divisions, very precisely executed according to David Scott and Mike Cowham, 'close to the ideal angles' (see Figure 5).[15] It is incised in a single block of stone and on either side are plaques explaining, in late Anglo-Saxon, the rebuilding of the church:

> Orm, son of Gamal, purchased St Gregory's Minster, when it was all broken down and completely fallen and he caused it to be made new from the ground up, for Christ and St Gregory, in the days of Edward the king and Earl Tostig.

The reference is to King Edward the Confessor and his brother-in-law Earl Tostig, brother of King Harold, killed at Hastings in 1066. Tostig held the earldom of Northumbria from 1055 to 1065, so the inscription must date from that decade. Orm clearly wishes to memorialize himself. On the sundial itself appears:

> ÞIS IS DÆGES SOLMERCA
> ÆT ILCVM TIDE
> AND HAWARD ME WROHTE AND BRAND PRS

> [This is the day's sun-marker at every tide and Haward made me and Brand priests]

There is the vanity of memorialization here too, it seems to me, but more than vanity: the time-measuring device establishes its own existence and the reasons for it, here by reference to a kind of regnal dating and a dating in terms of Tostig's elevation to and the holding of the earldom of Northumbria. But it also establishes that time can be harnessed to the service of the church, presumably for the benefit of the populace in that it can impose some sort of order on the regularity of worship.[16] Other motives are apparent elsewhere. Round the edge of a well-preserved circular sundial in St Batholemew's Aldbrough (East Yorkshire) is an Anglo-Saxon inscription to the effect that 'Ulf ordered this church to be built for himself and for the soul of Gunwara'.[17] This is thought to refer to Ulf Thoraldsen, a Viking prince who owned the land at Aldbrough in the early eleventh century, and here there appears to be a hope for spiritual benefits not only in time but in the afterlife. But, as is obvious from this, sundials came to acquire functions which were separate from the recording of time.

Mottoes on sundials are extant in many languages and scholars have assiduously compiled lists of them, but Latin is particularly favoured, presumably for its authority and succinctness.[18] Many topics are covered such as the idea that 'time flies': 'ruit hora', 'tempus breve est', 'tempus volet, hora fugit'. Some of these formulae are biblical in origin: 'Vidi nihil permanere sub sole' [I see nothing lasting under the sun] is from the meditation on 'vanity' in Ecclesiastes 2:11. But many are classical. The formula 'Tempus fugit velut umbra' [time flies like a shadow] appears to be based on Virgil's *Georgics* III. 284. 'Pulvis et umbra sumus' [we are as dust and shadow] is from Horace's *Odes* IV. vii. 16 and the injunction 'dona presentis cape laetus horae' [take the gifts of the hour gladly] is from *Odes* III. viii. 27. Many mottoes, in fact, recommend to their readers ways of using time, such as the quasi-proverbial 'Carpe diem' [seize the day] and 'festina lente' [hasten slowly], and there are injunctions against wasting time. The formula 'nobis pereunt et imputantur' [the hours are lost and will be charged to us], found in St Bunyan's Church, Cornwall, is from Martial's *Epigrams* V. xx. 13. That time should be used profitably was a powerful idea and seems to invade, by way of the metaphorical use of a sundial, the final stanza of Andrew Marvell's *The Garden*, which, in its opening, eschews 'the palm, the oke, or bays', symbols of military, civic and literary distinction, in favour of 'quietist' areas of contemplation in a garden whose 'flow'rs and all trees ... weave a garland of repose' where the 'mind' in 'happiness' can transcend this world and contemplate 'other worlds'.[19] Such a garden might have been described as including a sundial, but this garden in so constructed as to be its own sundial,[20] and this raises questions as to how time should be spent:

> How well the skilful gardener drew
> Of flow'rs and herbes this dial new;
> Where from above the milder sun
> Does through a fragrant zodiac run;
> And, as it works, th' industrious bee
> Computes its time as well as we.
> How could such sweet and wholesome hours
> Be reckon'd but with herbs and flow'rs! (65–72)

The vocabulary suggests the counting of the hours ('computes', 'reckon'd'): and words such as 'run', referring to the apparent motion of the sun, and 'works' and 'industrious', referring to the proverbial 'busyness' of the bee,[21] suggest that withdrawal and contemplation are not inert, but states that are themselves a kind of valid labour.

There were more impromptu ways of using sun and shadow to measure the time but, as Chaucer demonstrates when he has Harry Bailly attempt this, one needed to use a lot of resource:

> Oure Hooste saugh wel that the brighte sonne
> The ark of his artificial day hath ronne
> The ferthe part, and half an houre and moore,
> And though he were nat depe ystert in loore,
> He wiste it was the eightethe day
> Of Aprill, that is messager to May;
> And saugh wel that the shadwe of every tree
> Was as in lengthe the same quantitee
> That was the body erect that caused it.
> And therfore by the shadwe he took his wit
> That Phebus, which that shoon so clere and brighte,
> Degrees was fyve and fourty clombe on highte,
> And for that day, as in that latitude,
> It was ten of the clokke, he gan conclude … (*CT*, II, 1–14)

The seriousness of this passage is difficult to determine. It has been shown that Chaucer, in all likelihood, used the *Kalendrium* of Nicholas of Lynn for the calculations here, where it is in one place shown that the shadow of a man six feet tall would on 18 April at 10 a.m. measure exactly six feet – so on one level Harry Bailly's estimate is astonishingly accurate. What is interesting here is that though Harry Bailly measures his estimate in terms of the 'clokke' he evidently has no access to any timekeeping instrument, so he has to know the date (which was easy) and the latitude (which was difficult) and has to make estimates about the length of the artificial day (the time the sun is above the horizon), as well as having some fairly accurate sense of size and angle in relation to the shadow. On his date, according to Nicholas of Lynn, the length of the artificial day was 14 hours 26 minutes, the sun having risen at 4.47 a.m. – so at 10 a.m. the proportion of the artificial day that had passed was more like a third part rather than the 'ferthe part' he specifies. But this is the only inaccuracy, the only reason one might conclude that he was not very deeply learned in the knowledge of this subject (4). Otherwise his skill is wondrous to an incredible degree, particularly since Chaucer implies that the estimates were made without reference to any aids – instruments or books – of any description. It may have seemed to most readers or hearers of this tale that Harry Bailly had been invested, along with the other dimensions of his authority, with an unusual degree of giftedness in the instinctive calculation of time.

But he is infinitely practical. He follows this by warning the pilgrims not to waste time: 'the tyme wasteth nyght and day / And steleth from us …' (20–1) – stealing himself from Guillaume de Lorris. He alludes to classical authorities like Seneca and even becomes proverbial, modifying the saying 'time steals' and quoting 'los of catel may recovered be / But los of tyme shendeth us …' (27–8).[22] He warns the pilgrims that they should 'nat mowlen [grow mouldy] thus in ydelnesse' (31). He has to get the pilgrims, who are sometimes distracted by rivalries, arguments and quarrels, to Canterbury and to continue the storytelling contest: sometimes, to make matters worse, the stories themselves are interrupted and have to be abandoned. It is probably significant that the final story – told by the Parson – is preceded by another calculation of time, on this occasion by Chaucer himself, by means of studying the length of shadows with the sun low in the sky, giving 'foure of the clokke' in the afternoon (*CT*, X. 1–14). The day, like the pilgrimage, is moving towards its end.

III

A further dimension to these passages is the knowledge that could be expected of Chaucer's audience. The poet himself had written *A Treatise on the Astrolabe*, based in part on Johannes de Sacrobosco's famous work *De Sphaera*, which had addressed some of the questions involved here, particularly that of calculating latitude, but how general this knowledge was is hard to determine.

6 Astrolabe with Arabic markings: Jean Fusoris, *c.*1430, MAS | Museum aan de Stroom, CC0, via Wikimedia Commons.

Astrolabes came to Europe, by way of Spain, from the Muslim world, where they had been developed by Islamic mathematicians for, among other things, the astronomical determination of the direction of Mecca and the appropriate times for prayers. This was well recognized by European makers: Jean Fusoris, who designed astrolabes as well as mechanical clocks, produced an elegant astrolabe with Arabic markings in about 1430 (see Figure 6). But they could be of use in a number of other areas also, particularly astronomy and navigation – in order to measure the altitude above the horizon of celestial bodies, particularly the fixed stars and the planets and to determine latitudes on the basis of local time. A typical European astrolabe, such as the one on which Chaucer bases his treatise, consisted of a metal disk (usually brass), the *mater* [mother], the edge of which was marked in graduated degrees. Above this was a *tympan* [climate], made for a specific latitude, engraved with a stereographic projection of the great circles, denoting azimuths, describing the celestial sphere visible over the local horizon. This plate was fixed. Not so the *rete* [network] which came above the *mater* and the *tympan*: this was an openwork frame, bearing a projection of the ecliptic plane (the sun's apparent path amongst the stars in a given year) and an indication of the position of the brightest stars. On the more expensive astrolabes, the *rete* was often elaborately decorated. It was also, functionally, free to be rotated. So too was what came above it – the *label* [rule, pointer], again usually of brass. But there were many types of astrolabe and many designs.[23]

Chaucer's *Treatise on the Astrolabe* was written for 'lyte Lowys, my sone', in 'lyght', that is 'easy', English for the latitude of Oxford. He describes the instrument and how it is meant to be used, and propose, additionally, 'to teche the a certen nombre of conclusions', some of which have to do with time (Prologue, 1–14). One describes the calculation of 'houres inequales by day' (Part II, 10, 1–15), and this is followed by a section on 'houres equales' where the 'clokke' is referred to:

> The quantite of houres equals, that is to seyn the houres of the clokke, ben departid by 15 degrees alredy in the bordure of thin Astrelaby, as wel by nyght as by day, generaly for evere. What nedith more declaracioun?
>
> Wherefore whan the list to knowe hou many houres of the clokke be passed, or eny part of eny of these houres that ben passed, or ellis hou many houres or parties of houres ben to come fro such a tyme to such a tyme by day or by night, know the degre of thy sonne, and ley thy label on it. Turne thy ryet aboute joyntly with thy label, and with the point of it rekne in the bordure fro the sonne arise unto the same place there thou desirist, by day or nyght ... (Part II, 11, 1–16).

Earlier, like the good teacher and father that he was, he had provided a specific personal example: 'The yeer of oure lord 1391, the 12 day of march, I wolde knowe the tyde of the day. I tok the altitude of the sonne, and fond that it was 25 degrees and 30 minutes of height in the bordure, on the bak side. Tho turned I myn Astrelabye ...' and following the process described above he found 'that it was 9 of the clokke of the day'. An ancillary result of this calculation is that he 'fond there the 20 degre of Geminis ascendyng, which that I tok for myn ascendent' (Part II, 3, 15–35). The astrolabe enables him not only to locate himself precisely in time but astrologically also, which may have been important to him.

Both sundials and astrolabes could claim to be scientific instruments for the measurement of time in that they depended on the accurate interpretation of the positioning and movement of celestial bodies. But there were other devices, again of ancient origin, used in the medieval and Renaissance periods, which depended on more practical and recognizably less exact strategies.

IV

One was the flame-clock or candle clock. Theoretically, these could be made of anything that would smoulder or burn slowly: F.J. Britten cites an instance where a material resembling flax was used: 'knots were tied at particular distances, and the effluxion of time estimated as the divisions between the knots smouldered away'. But in its most simple and characteristic form, it consisted of a tall candle on the side of which were incised, at equal intervals, graduated marks indicating hours, so that as the candle burned down times could be read off.[24] How long timekeepers of this sort remained in use is difficult to establish, but Britten cites an example from 1560 and develops this: 'Lamp timekeepers of this kind were, I am told, to be met with in German and Dutch outlying dwellings till a comparatively recent date.'[25] So it could be some device such as this which Shakespeare has in mind when he has Romeo say to Juliet, as they must part after their night of love, 'Night's candles are burnt out, and jocund day / Stands tiptoe on the misty mountain tops ...' (*Romeo and Juliet*, III. v. 8–9).

Much earlier, in 878, according to his biographer Asser, Alfred the Great devised a more elaborate instrument such as this, 'a useful and shrewd invention',[26] in order to help him regulate his daily activities:

> ... [he] commanded his clerks to supply wax in sufficient quantity and to weigh it in the balance against pennies. When enough wax was measured out to equal the weight of seventy two pence, he caused the clerks to make six candles thereof, and to mark off twelve inches as the length of each candle. By this means, therefore, these six candles burned for twenty-four hours, night and day, without fail, before the sacred relics of God's elect, which always accompanied him wherever he went.

But in order to work well candle clocks need ideal conditions – a stable and quiet environment, with the minimum movement of air – which in Alfred's case, because he was regularly on the move, was not available:

> Sometimes, however, the candles did not continue burning the whole day and night, till the same time they were lighted the preceding evening, by reason of the violence of winds, which at times blow day and night without intermission, through the doors and windows of the churches, the sheathing and the wainscot, the numerous chinks in the walls, or the thin material of the tents …

But Alfred, determined and ingenious as ever, addressed the problem by 'a skilful and cunning invention':

> [he] ordered a lantern to be skilfully constructed of wood and ox-horn, since ox-horns, when sliced thin, are as transparent as a vessel of glass. Into this lantern … a candle was put at night which shone as brightly without as within and was not disturbed by the wind, since he also ordered a door of horn to be made for the opening of the lantern …

Asser's account of Alfred is, quite properly, laudatory and his account of the way Alfred sought to regulate his time-management is told to his credit. But it does, quite openly, also recognize the problems and limitations of the use of candle clocks.

V

Another instrument was the sandglass.[27] In this device time was measured by the passage of a fine material, usually sand, but it could be other material (such as finely crushed egg shells) from an upper bulb, usually of glass, through a narrow aperture to a lower bulb, as can be seen in the image of 'Tenperentia' [Temperance] painted by Ambrogio Lorenzetti in the Palazzo Pubblico, Siena (see Plate 8).[28] This device could be used, theoretically, in any context; it was not amenable to the difficulties encountered by the candle-clock in Asser's story. But it was particularly useful in maritime contexts, because weather and the movement of the ship did not affect its working. It was widely used into the nineteenth century, before reliable maritime chronometers – based on the brilliant work of John Harrison – were produced in large numbers. Earlier, the sandglass was an important instrument. Amongst his possessions at his death on 16 September 1380, Charles V of France possessed a maritime sand-clock which is precisely described in the administrators' exact and technical prose:

> Item ung grant oorloge de mer, de deux grans fiolles plains de sablon, en ung grant estuy de boys garny d'archal
>
> [Item a large sea-clock, of two large sand-filled phials, in a large wooden box, bound with brass][29]

This had been given to him by his aunt Yolande of Aragon at some time before 1335, and was obviously to be used for practical navigational reasons. But these instruments could be decorative, widely used in social contexts, and sometimes became the subject of *coterie* writing – witty and metaphorical – as in Ben Jonson's *The Hour-Glass*,[30] where the inert matter in the glass is transposed into the ashes of a disappointed lover:

> Do but consider this small dust
> Here running in the glass,
> By atoms moved:
> Could you believe that this
> The body ever was
> Of one that loved?
> And in his mistress' flame, playing like a fly,
> Turned to cinders by her eye?
> Yes; and in death, as life unblessed,
> To have't expressed,
> Even ashes of lovers find no rest.

This is based on Girolamo Amaltei's *Horologium Pulverum*, and this poem, and Jonson's, were later used by Robert Herrick in his *The Hour-Glass*:

> That hour-glass, which there ye see
> With water filled (sirs, credit me),
> The humour was (as I have read)
> But lovers' tears encrystalled;
> Which, as they drop by drop do pass
> From th' upper to the under glass,
> Do in a trickling manner tell
> (By many a watery syllable)
> That lovers' tears in lifetime shed
> Do restless run when they are dead.[31]

This is affectionate and witty: Herrick admired Jonson. The phrase 'as I have read' signals the reference and deference to the earlier poems, and there is a pun on 'humour', which also means 'liquid' or 'moisture'. Sandglasses were not particularly accurate: as every sailor knew, if jolted or knocked the sand ran a little faster and their four-hour 'watch' might be over more quickly. But their derivatives became much-loved, unofficial timekeepers and are present in domestic contexts today as decorative hourglasses or humble egg-timers.

VI

But probably the most important timekeeping instrument before the development of the mechanical clock was the *clepsydra* or water-clock. This device was again of ancient origin – being found in Babylonian, Greek and Roman cultures, as well as in China.[32] There were two basic forms, but both depended on the regular flow of water into or out of a cylinder, the walls of which bore incisions, graduated in terms of the hours. A float, which either rose or fell, measured the level of the water so that the time could be read off. Most were fairly simple, but some, especially those from the Islamic world, could be very elaborate. The water-clock in Dar-al-Magana, Fez (Morocco), which overlooks a street, has twelve windows, below each of which, on a platform, is a brass bowl (see Figure 7). Water was drained from a reservoir behind the clock at an even pace, and a weight-driven mechanism caused the doors to be opened in turn, out of which fell a brass ball into one of the bowls. One could then count the hours by counting the balls.[33] It is interesting that this clock was completed on 6 May 1357, by which date many of the European water-clocks were being replaced by the mechanical clock. *Clepsydrae* were expensive to make and needed to be constantly refilled and managed. They were also regarded as not particularly accurate: Seneca, in Rome, famously complained that it was not possible to tell the exact time 'since it is easier for philosophers to agree than clocks'.[34]

Nevertheless, *clepsydrae* or water-clocks were very popular for a long time in monasteries and other religious houses, especially if accompanied by a striking mechanism and an alarm system.[35] In the Cistercian Rule of the early twelfth century, item CXIV specified that the sacristan was to set the clock each night so that it would sound on weekdays in winter before lauds unless it was daylight. He was to use it as an alarm to get him up so that he could light the lamps and candles. And other monastic rules contained similar instructions.[36] Before the fourteenth century, monastic life was largely regulated by means of water-clocks. A clock of this sort, according to Jocelin of Brakelond, proved useful for more than timekeeping at the Benedictine monastery of Bury St Edmunds on the morning of 22 June 1198 when a fire started on a platform which held two candles close to the shrine of the saint:

7 Clepsydra or water-clock: Dar-al-Magana, Fez (Morocco), photograph by Mike Prince, Bangalore, India, CC BY 2.0, via Wikimedia Commons.

Eadem enim hora cecidit horologium ante horas matutinas, surgensque magister vestiarii, hec percipiens et intuens, cuccurit quamtocius et, percussa tabuls tamquam pro mortuo, sublimi voce clamuit dicens feretrum esse combustum. Nos autem omnes accurrentes flammam invenimus incredibiliter sevientem, et totum feretrum amplectentem, et non longe a trabibus ecclesie ascendentem. Iuvenes ergo nostri propter aquam currentes, quidam ad puteum, quidam ad horologium, quidam cucullis suis impetum ignis cum magna dificultate extinxerunt, et sanctuaria quedam prius diripuerunt.

[Around the same time the clock struck for Matins, and the vestry master, on getting up, saw the fire, and ran as fast as he could, and beat upon the board as if someone was dead, and shouted in a loud voice that the shrine was on fire. We all rushed up, and met the incredibly fierce flames that were engulfing the whole shrine and almost reaching up to the beams of the church. Our young monks ran for water, some to the rain-water tank, some to the clock, and some, with great difficulty, when they had snatched up the reliquaries, put out the flames with their hoods.][37]

This must have been an elaborate clock with a very large water-tank. Of course, water-clocks were also used outside religious houses. A guild of makers of water-clocks existed in Cologne as early as 1183, and by 1220 there were enough of them working in one place to cause a street – Urlogingasse – to be named after them.[38]

Time, before the development of the mechanical clock, was very much dominated by the church. There is evidence that the organization of daily life, particularly in towns, centred on the sound of bells in churches and monasteries, which were regulated by their clocks.[39] Dante, in *Paradiso* XV, into the mouth of his great-great-grandfather Cacciaguida puts an idealizing description of Florence in the twelfth century, within its 'old walls', regulated, as it still was in his own day, by the sound of the bell of the Badia, the church of the Benedictine Abbey founded in 978, as it rang for *terce* and *none*:

> Fiorenza dentro dalla cerchia antica,
> ond'ella toglie ancora e terza e nona.
> si stava in pace, sobria e pudica. (97–9)

> [Florence, inside her old walls, from which she still takes *terce* and *none*, was in peace, sober and chaste.][40]

And this continued throughout the Middle Ages. François Villon describes how, on a cold December night in 1456, he came to end his poem *Le Lais*, because he heard the bell of the Sorbonne sounding nine:

> Finablement, en escripvant,
> Ce soir, seulet, estant en bonne,
> Dictant ce laiz et descripvant,
> J'ouis la cloche de Serbonne,
> Qui tousjours a neuf heures sonne
> Le salut que l'ange predit;
> Si suspendis et y mis bonne
> Pour prier comme le cuer dit. (273–80)

> [Finally, as I was writing this evening, in a good mood, describing this legacy and writing it down, I heard the bell of the Sorbonne, which always strikes the Angelus at nine, so I set myself to pray as the heart tells me to.][41]

Records show that the bell he refers to was made by a certain 'Galterus' and was called 'Marie' because it struck the Angelus. In calm weather it could be heard all over Paris. It sounded the curfew inside the precincts of the University

1 Four Monarchies: BL MS Additional 11695, the Silos Apocalypse © The British Library Board.

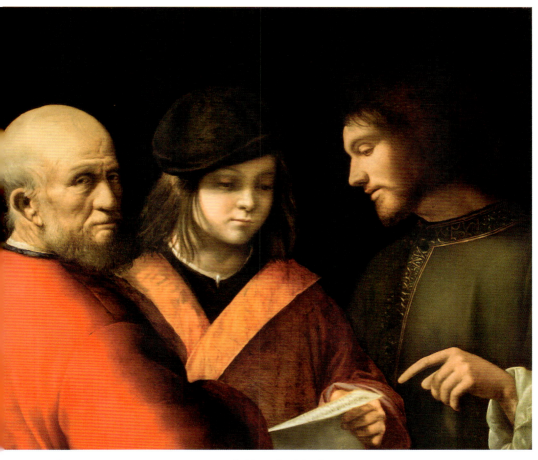

3 Giorgione, *The Three Ages of Man*, Gallerie degli Uffizi, Firenze.

2 Joachim da Fiore: Oxford Corpus Christi College MS 225a, fol. 10r. By permission of the President and Fellows of Corpus Christi College, Oxford.

4a January: Trento, Torre d'Aquila, photo by Andrea Carloni, Rimini.

4b April: Trento, Torre d'Aquila, photo by Andrea Carloni, Rimini.

5 August from *Les Très Riches Heures du Duc de Berri*, Limbourg brothers, public domain, via Wikimedia Commons.

6 Lady Eleanor Welles kneeling before the Virgin and Child: Dublin, Royal Irish Academy MS 12 R 31, fol. 196v. By permission of the Royal Irish Academy © RIA.

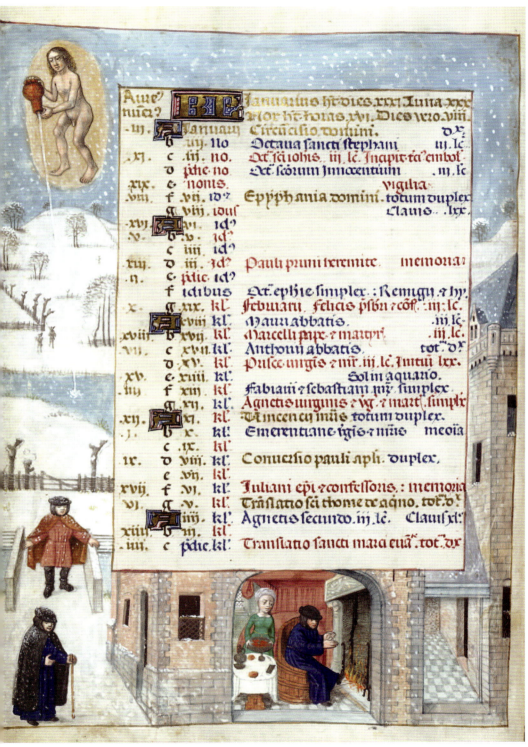

7 January: BL MS Additional 18851, fol. 1v © The British Library Board.

8 Hourglass: Ambrogio Lorenzetti, 'Fresco of good government', Palazzo Pubblico, Siena (*detail*), public domain, via Wikimedia Commons.

pitiatu. Iterū iussit sieri celaturam
tecto quod est sup illam i loco quo
sti Amphibali collocat. Et puidit
baculū pastoralem pulcrū ualde. n
nomen eius.

Ricardus
...inus octa
...huina scientia
...struxit horolog
...aedinius omni
...horologia ante
...tas tribulation
...pro ecclie sue u

9 Richard of Wallingford and his clock. BL Cotton Nero D. VII, fol. 20. © The British Library Board. Miniature shows Richard of Wallingford, abbot of St Albans. He is pointing to a clock, referring to his gift to the abbey, and his face is disfigured by leprosy.

10a The Wells Cathedral clock: Jack Blandiver, photograph by Fr Lawrence Lew OP.

10b The Wells Cathedral clock: the black and white knights, photograph by Fr Lawrence Lew OP.

11 The Prague town-square clock, Uoaei1, CC BY-SA 4.0, via Wikimedia Commons.

12 Heinrich Suso's *Horloge de Sapience*: a detail from Bruxelles Bibliothèque Royale MS IV. 111 © KBR, Bruxelles.

13 Abraham Mignon, *Stilleven met Bloemen en een Horloge, Still life with flowers and a watch*, c.1660, oil on canvas, h 75cm × w 60cm × d 8cm, by kind permission Rijksmuseum Amsterdam.

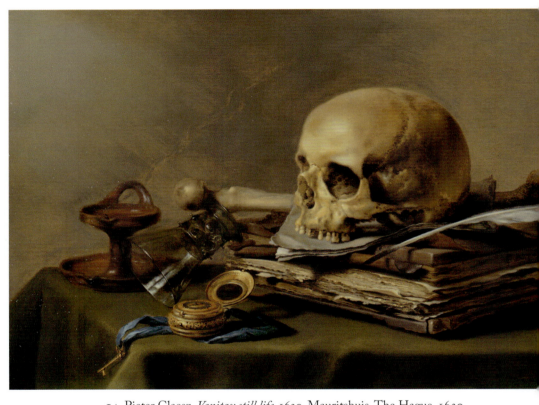

14 Pieter Claesz, *Vanitas: still life 1630*, Mauritshuis, The Hague, 1630.

15 *Nicholas Kratzer*, after Hans Holbein the Younger, oil on panel, late sixteenth century, based on a work of 1528, NPG 5245 © National Portrait Gallery, London.

16 Charter of the Worshipful Clockmakers of London MS 6430. The Clockmakers' Charter, granted by King Charles I on 22 August 1631 (vellum).

of Paris, and at this point Villon gives up writing and prays. He dozes, and 'dame Memoire' fills his mind with thoughts of scholastic philosophy so that, on awakening, he finds he can write no more of his poem: the ink was frozen; the candle had gone out. And since there is no other light by which to continue writing he makes himself as warm as he can and sleeps through the chilly night. Effectively, his working day, because he was a scholar, had been defined by the time of the church – though it is clear he did not wish to stop work quite when he did.

Just how instinctive it was to measure diurnal time by the services of the church is apparent from the following extract from a letter dated 13 May 1482 from Richard Cely, in London, to his elder brother George, who was in Calais. The details of dealing in wool and woolfells in the Cotswolds are suddenly interrupted by a passage on a prospective marriage, which is also construed as a matter of some financial moment. William Midwinter, a wool merchant, tries to interest Richard in marrying a rich heiress, Elizabeth, the daughter of Thomas Limrick or Lymeryke of Cirencester, MP for Gloucestershire and a JP who was coming to Northleach to preside at a sitting of a court:

> Syr, I whryte to yow a process: I pray God sende therof a good heynd. The same day that I come to Norlache, on a Sonday befor mattens from Burforde, Wylliam Mydwynter wylcwmyd me, and in howr comynycacyon he asked me hefe I wher in any whay of maryayge. I towlde hyme nay, and he informeyd me that ther whos a yeunge genttyllwhoman hos father ys name ys Lemryke, and her mother ys deyd, and sche schawll dyspend be her moter xl li. a yer, as thay say in that conttre, and her father ys the gretteste rewlar and rycheste mane in that conttre, and ther hawhe bene grete gentyllmen to se hyr and wholde hawhe hyr, etc. And hewyr matens wher done, Wylliam Mydwynter had meved thys mater to the gretteste mane abot the gentyllman Lemeryke, and he yeyd and informyd the forsayd of aull the matter, and the yewng gentyllwomane bothe ...[42]

Whether any of the people involved in this story actually attended matins at St Peter and St Paul, Northleach, the big perpendicular church which graces the town, is uncertain, but the time frame of the story is dominated by the church service: it is its consistent temporal reference point. The Celys and their correspondents were perfectly capable of measuring time by the clock: William Maryon writes to the Cely brothers at Calais on 8 November 1478 that 'the same day that Y departed fro Calles Y londed in the Dovnys at iij a clokt at afternoon, and Y cam to London the Freyday at non after.'[43] But in Northleach they seem to have relied entirely on the church bells. And in the hours of darkness the sound of bells was even more important. What wakes Chaucer from his dream in *The Book of the Duchess* is the striking of the Richmond castle clock:

> Ryght as me mette, as I yow telle,
> That in the castell ther was a belle,
> As hyt had smyten houres twelve,
> And fond me lyinge in my bed (*BD*, 1321–5)

And in the fiction of his *Miller's Tale*, the night of illicit love enjoyed by Alison, an Oxford carpenter's wife, and Nicholas, their student lodger, is brought to an end by the sound of bells signalling the beginning of the first service of the monastic day:

> ... Ther was the revel and the melodye;
> And thus lith Alison and Nicholas,
> In busynese of myrthe and of solas,
> Til that the belle of laudes gan to rynge,
> And freres in the chauncel gonne synge. (*CT*, I. 3652–7)

Here, with quiet irony, Chaucer terminates their metaphorical secular 'melodye' with the ecclesiastical plainchant of the friars. He has here taken a French fabliau, and recreated it in England as a rich social urban comedy, grounded in contemporary space and time.[44]

But it was not only monastic houses that treasured their bells: there is evidence in late medieval wills that parishioners were interested in keeping the bells of their local churches in good order. The will, dated 1463, of John Baret of Bury St Edmunds is typical:

> I will yeve and beqwethe yearly to the Sexteyn of Seynt Marie chirche viij s. to kepe the clokke, take hede to the chymes, wynde vp the peys and the plummys as ofte as need is, so the seid chymes fayle not to goo thorough the defawte of the seid sexteyn who so be for the tyme ...[45]

In the countryside, away from urban centres, there was no alternative to listening to the bells. John of Garland, at the beginning of the thirteenth century, offers the following bizarre but significant etymology: 'Campane dicuntur a rusticis qui habitant in campo, qui nesciant judicare horas nisi per campanas' [Bells are named because of rustics who live in the country, who may not know how to calculate the time except by bells].[46]

CHAPTER 4

The development of the mechanical clock

IN CHAPTER XX of the first part of his *Repressor of Overmuch Blaming of the Clergy*, written in 1449, Reginald Pecock, bishop of Chichester, sought to demonstrate that the Bible was not an infallible guide to everything – a position assumed by some of the more extreme followers of the heretic John Wyclif whom he was seeking to refute. Many things, Pecock says, are not mentioned in the scriptures, yet it is, nevertheless, legitimate to use them in the service of God, and among the examples he cites is the interesting one of the mechanical clock:

> … for though in eeldist daies, and though in Scripture mensioun is maad of orologis, schewing the houris of the dai bi schadew maad bi the sunne in a cercle, certis neuere save in late daies was eny clok telling the houris of the dai and nyght bi peise and bi stroke …[1]

With his customary exactness Pecock tells the reader how clocks work, by means of a weight (*peise*) and a striking mechanism, that they coexisted with and partly replaced sundials which showed the hours by means a gnomon which produced a shadow on a graduated circle, and what the advantages of the clock were: sundials showed only the hours of the day, clocks indicated the hours of the day and night. Even the choice of verbs denotes a distinction. A sundial works by showing the hours, that is, one needs to be able to see it to use it, a clock by counting (telling) the hours by striking. One can, therefore, calculate the time if one hears the clock – a reference to the fact that most early clocks did not have dials, only bells: the English word 'clokke' is related etymologically to Latin 'clocca', French 'cloche', German 'glocke' meaning 'bell'. As A.G. Rigg puts it: 'Middle English uses suggest that a clock was primarily something one heard rather than saw'.[2] One of the world's oldest working clocks – that in Salisbury Cathedral, dated before 1386 – has no dial but an elaborate striking train (see Figure 8).[3] Most notable of all, though, is Pecock's recognition that, though the calculation of time is an ancient practice, the use of mechanical clocks is recent: it is a product invented 'in late daies'. Quite what Pecock means by 'in late daies' is not exactly clear, though it is apparent that he knows that the development of the mechanical timekeeper is

8 The mechanism of the Salisbury Cathedral clock, photograph by Immanuel Giel, 21 August 2007, public domain, via Wikimedia Commons.

something relatively new and that clocks were still recognized as unusual things, though familiar enough to serve as an example.

As G.J. Whitrow authoritatively says; 'the actual origin of the mechanical clock remains a mystery, although it probably occurred towards the end of the thirteenth century'.[4] And there are differences of opinion among historians of horology over whether the escapement mechanism which was critical to the

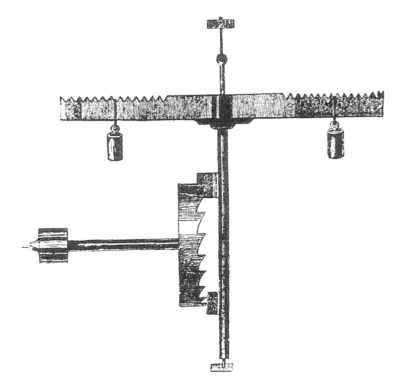

9 The verge and foliot escapement mechanism.

development of mechanical clocks was imitated from Chinese technology or whether it was developed in Europe.[5] Carlo Cipolla suggests that mechanisms developed to ring bells with greater efficiency, which may have used toothed wheels and oscillating levers, may have 'helped to prepare for the development of mechanical clocks'. But this is difficult to establish with examples, and he is on firmer ground when he points out the likely contribution of 'astronomers, astrologers, and those interested in making globes and spheres and in supplying them with movements that would imitate the movements of the stars and the planets'.[6] At any event, it is plain that as early as the second half of the thirteenth century engineers were looking at the problem. This is clear from the lecture notes of Robertus Anglicus, in his commentary on Sacrobosco's *De Sphaera* dating from 1271:

> Nor is it possible for any clock to follow the judgment of astronomy with complete accuracy. Yet clockmakers are trying to make a wheel which will make one complete revolution for every one of the

equinoctial circle, but they cannot quite perfect their work. But if they could it would be a really accurate clock and worth more than the astrolabe or other astronomical instruments for reckoning the hours, if one knew how to do this according to the method aforesaid.[7]

And he goes on to describe a mechanism powered by a falling weight which would turn a dial through one complete revolution between sunrise and sunset.[8] Not long after this the first mechanical clocks begin to appear. They were weight-driven and worked with a fairly rudimentary verge and foliot escapement mechanism (see Figure 9).[9] The foliot was a horizontal bar with a weight at each end: at its mid-point it was attached to a vertical rod ('verge') on which were two flanges, set at an angle, which engaged with a toothed wheel, given motive power by a falling weight. This pushed the verge first one way then the other which made the foliot oscillate causing the toothed wheel to disengage ('escape') from the flanges one tooth at a time so that the clock moved on. Later, particularly in Italy, a balance wheel was substituted for the foliot, as a device for regulating the speed of the clock.[10]

Most early clocks were public ones: they were built for churches, monasteries and towns. A clock made of iron was set up in 1309 in the church of St Eustorgio in Milan. Before 1324 the cathedral at Beauvais probably had a clock with a bell for sounding the hours. According to one Italian source the church of St Gothard in Milan in 1335 had 'a wonderful clock, with a very large clapper which strikes a bell twenty four times according to the twenty four hours of the day and night, and thus at the first hour of the night gives one sound, at the second two ... and so distinguishes one hour from another which is the greatest use to men of every degree.' From this time onwards mechanical clocks spread rapidly: the monastery of Cluny had one by 1340, and Chartres Cathedral two by 1359. In 1353 in Genoa a public clock was installed which struck the hours, another in Bologna in 1356, and another in Ferrara in 1362. King Charles V of France had one installed on one of the towers of his royal palace in 1362 and two others in the Chateau de Vincennes and the Hotel Saint-Paul.[11] It is assumed by many scholars that most early clocks were Italian, French or German and some clockmakers came to England to pursue their trade from these countries. A record survives of a grant of protection and safe-conduct by Edward III in 1368 to three Dutchmen '... *orlogiers* coming into the realm to practice their art'.[12] Edward III saw the importance of clocks and ordered them to be installed at various royal residences – Westminster, King's Langley and, on the Isle of Sheppey, at Queensborough.[13] But C.F.C. Beeson has another version of events: 'It has long been supposed that the mechanical clock was born in Italy or central

Europe and that the knowledge gradually spread westwards. Yet the following cases show that England was from the outset not less well informed than other countries' and he goes on to argue, with instances, that there is an English 'claim for a superiority in the making of the first mechanical clock'. His instances or 'cases', from records of English churches, begin with an annal of Dunstable Priory of the Austin Canons (Bedfordshire) dated 1283 related to an 'horologium quod est supra pulpitum collacatum' [a clock which is placed above the pulpit]. 'This', he says, 'is the earliest English record of what is considered by the author an escapement controlled clock, and equally is the earliest European record'.[14] He follows this by a detailed cataloguing of evidence of the existence or installation of clocks in Exeter Cathedral (Devon) in 1284, in Old St Paul's London in 1286, probably in Merton College Oxford in 1288, in Norwich Cathedral Priory (Norfolk) in 1290, and so on down into the middle of the fifteenth century. It is not always clear from the records what the exact configuration of these clocks was, but they do overwhelmingly demonstrate how rapid and extensive the idea of the mechanical clock became in ecclesiastical contexts.

The earliest clockmakers were non-specialist metalworkers, often blacksmiths, locksmiths or gun-makers.[15] And blacksmiths continued to be associated with the making of clocks, particularly large public clocks: a will dated 1578 says:

> … whereas Thomas Hall blacksmythe hath the greateste parte of a clocke of myne I will that the parishonerys of Coppinghall shall have both yt and certen timber of myne to make the frame with all upon condicioun yt be sett upp and maynteyned to go to Coppinghall steple …[16]

The objects they produced were often heavy and crude. But, quickly, highly skilled clockmakers emerged – Richard of Wallingford in England, Jean Fusoris in France, and Giovanni de' Dondi in Italy – the last of whom produced the celebrated *astrarium*, a wonder of its age, between 1348 and 1364: according to Philippe de Mézières, 'solemn astronomers came from far regions to see [it] in great reverence …'.[17] And, as the technology developed, clocks got smaller. One of the earliest mentions of what appears to be this sort of chamber clock comes in Jean de Meung's part of *Le Roman de la Rose*, lines 20815–18, where Pygmalion, having successfully completed his ivory statue, celebrates by singing love-songs, playing on his stringed instruments and getting his clocks to chime:

> Et refet sonner les orloges
> Par les sales et par les loges
> A roes trop sotivement
> De perdurable movement.[18]
>
> [He made his clocks sound out, through his rooms and through his chambers, with wheels arranged skilfully, with never ceasing motion]

But he cannot bring her to life: this is a 'deaf image'. In 1377, according to an inventory made at his death, Charles V of France had an *'orloge portative'* in his oratory. In 1430 Philip le Bel possessed what appears to have been a spring-powered chamber clock, and in 1459 Charles VII of France purchased a *'demi orloge dore de fin or sans contrepoix'* [a small clock gilded with fine gold without counterweights].[19] On the front flyleaf of Cambridge University Library MS Dd. 5. 76, written in a small sixteenth-century hand, along with several other more traditional riddles, appears a modern *double entendre* riddle:

> Two stones yt hath or els yt is wrong
> With a bald hed & a tag somwhat long
> & in the night when women lie awake
> Wit ther conscience they doe yt take.[20]

The respectable interpretation in the right-hand margin is 'a clocke', a lantern clock: evidently weight driven with a striking train – hence the 'two stones'. The 'bald hed' is the bell which characteristically was positioned on top of the clock. Lantern clocks became popular in England in the sixteenth century,[21] and it was at this time also that what may be described as the earliest watches developed, and it became possible, for the better-off, to possess a personal timekeeper and there were simply more of them around. For a domestic clock to be adverted to in this context argues that they were becoming familiar objects, though deliberately de-familiarized in the riddle.

II

Many of the earliest clocks were simply utilitarian timekeepers. But others were more elaborate and along with the calculation of diurnal time had more complex but related agendas. The large mechanical clock constructed at Norwich Cathedral between 1321 and 1325 appears to have been set up with monastic rituals in mind: besides an astronomical dial with models of the sun and moon, it had automata in the form of a procession of monks.[22] A similar clock was constructed, at about the same time, by Richard of Wallingford at

THE DEVELOPMENT OF THE MECHANICAL CLOCK 105

10 Giovanni de' Dondi's Astrarium, Museo della Scienza e della Tecnologia 'Leonardo da Vinci', CC BY-SA 4.0, via Wikimedia Commons.

St Albans (see Plate 9). He was the son of a blacksmith, orphaned at the age of ten, but adopted by William of Kirkeby, the Benedictine prior of Wallingford, who provided for his education at Oxford. He became a considerable scientist and many of his observations are preserved in London, British Library MS Cotton Julius C. vii. He became abbot of St Albans in 1328 and spent many years designing and constructing the clock. He also spent a great deal of money on it, so much so that he quarrelled with his brethren and was criticized by Edward III who visited the abbey and noticed the sumptuousness of the work on the clock and contrasted it with the ruinous state of some of the abbey buildings. It was unfinished at his death in 1336. But when John Leland visited the abbey in 1534 and saw what it had become he pronounced it without equal in Europe: 'One may look at the course of the sun or the moon or the fixed stars, or again one may regard the rise and fall of the tide measured at London Bridge, and a moving image of changing human fortune'. This description, and Richard of Wallingford's notes in Oxford, Bodleian Library MS Ashmole 1796, enabled John North to reconstruct its main features and describe it 'as much a celestial theatre as a timepiece'. One particularly original feature of it was that it evidently had an escapement system that was superior to the verge escapement then in use. The tidal dial is a partly utilitarian feature which appears on later clocks also, but in part it is a demonstration of the logic of the universe.[23] Much the same was Giovanni de' Dondi's clock (see Figure 10). It impressed Philippe de Mézières when he went to look at it in part because it was so skilfully made that 'all goes by one weight', but also because it exposed and demonstrated the workings of the universe: it '... shows all the movements of the signs and the planets with their circles and epicycles, and differences, and each planet is shown separately with its own movement in such a way that at any time of the day or night one can see in which sign and to which degree the planets and the great stars appear in the sky ...'.[24] It also had a twenty-four hour dial, a dial for the times of the rising and setting of the sun, a dial for the nodes or intersections of the orbit of the moon, and separate dials for the fixed and movable feasts of the church year – this last item locking it firmly into an ecclesiastical agenda.[25] The magnificent clock, designed by Nicholas Kratzer for Henry VIII and installed on the gatehouse of Hampton Court Palace in 1540, had, like Richard of Wallingford's clock, a tidal dial – useful if one travelled to and from London by barge on the Thames (see Figure 11). But the clock had much else besides. It registered the time of the day and night, the position of the sun in the zodiac, the phase and age of the moon: again, though it had a practical use, it also provided a description of the universe.[26]

Medieval clocks became complex before they became accurate. Early on it became customary, especially on the bigger clocks, to have figures – 'jacquemarts' or 'jacks' – which struck the bells, and these were sometimes affectionately given names: 'Jack Blandiver' struck the bell on the clock at Wells Cathedral (see Plate 10a), and 'Jack the Smiter' performed a similar office at Southwold. Two figures with long hammers strike the quarters on the Matthew

11 The Hampton Court clock, photograph by Mike Cattell, CC BY 2.0, via Wikimedia Commons.

the Miller clock on the tower of the church on St Mary Steps, Exeter.[27] Hammers were normally used, but the jacks, dating from about 1480, on the York Minster clock are soldiers dressed in plate armour and they strike the quarters on tubular gongs using their halberds. These figures provided entertainment. The use of automata in early mechanical clocks was, in fact, fairly common. They are little regarded by historians of horology, but better than anything else they articulated the meaning that time had for the constructors and the commissioners of medieval clocks. Some are fairly straightforward. The jacks fitted to the clock on the belfry in Ghent features Adam, who strikes the hours, and Eve, who strikes the half-hours. But since it also includes a snake, it is probably meant to be a warning against temptation.[28]

12 The Strasbourg Cathedral clock, photograph by David Iliff, CC BY-SA 3.0, via Wikimedia Commons.

However, some are not always easy to interpret. In addition to two bands marking the hours and the minutes of the day and night, each with an indicator with a gilt star, and a device for showing the phases of the moon, all of which, according to a barely legible inscription, shows the wonders of the universe, the Wells clock, made in about 1392, has four equestrian knights, two white two black, equipped for a tournament, who joust against each other, figuring, presumably, the alternation of light and darkness, day and night (see Plate 10b).[29] The show in about 1340 at Cluny was, according to Viollet le Duc, much more complicated. In addition to indications of the movement of the sun and the phases of the moon, and a cock which crowed twice at every hour, marionettes enacted various scenes – the Annunciation, where an angel greeted Mary, the Holy Ghost descended on her head, and God the Father gave his benediction; death; the mystery of the Resurrection. When the carillon chimed all the figures retreated back into the clock. Something of the same sort appeared on the first Strasbourg clock, begun in 1352 and completed two years later (see Figure 12). An astrolabe was in the middle, whose pointers showed the movements of the sun, moon, and hours. There was a calendar and an indication of the movable feasts. Then, in an upper compartment, the Magi bowed before the Virgin Mary. The whole thing was topped by a crowing cock, which also moved its beak and flapped its wings. Whether this last feature was there as a reminder of the most celebrated of timekeepers from the natural kingdom, or whether as an antitype of sloth, or a type of Christ, is difficult to tell.[30] However, this clock has been modified over the years, and it is difficult to be certain about how much of what remains is medieval.[31] Not quite as elaborate is the astronomical clock in the Cathedral of St Etienne in Bourges, designed by Jean Fusoris and installed in 1424, when the court was at Bourges, at the instance of Charles VII, to celebrate the baptism of his son, the future Louis XI (see Figure 13). It is housed in a tall wooden case and has two dials, one above the other. In the upper dial two hands indicate the time. In the lower dial there is a zodiac against which the movement of the sun and moon are plotted. It chimes 'Salve Regina' on the hour. It was repaired and restored in 1782, 1822, 1841 and several times later. It was completely restored and reinstalled in 1994 with a replica mechanism. The original clockwork has been preserved and is on show in the cathedral.[32]

In some later clocks this essentially religious agenda was modified to incorporate more secular subjects. The astronomical clock in the town square in Prague, perhaps dating from as early as 1410, has a lower roundel that shows the signs of the zodiac and the labours of the months, while above the marionette performance begins with a skeleton who shakes an hourglass and

13 The Bourges Cathedral clock, Zairon, CC BY-SA 4.0, via Wikimedia Commons.

rings a bell (see Plate 11). Various other figures appear, including a miser who rattles his purse and a vain man who looks at himself in a mirror. The agenda seems to be cautionary: death and time preside over the sinful world of men. Others were apparently advisory: according to Bartolomeo Manfredi in 1473 the cosmological indications of a clock in Mantua showed '… the proper time for phlebotomy, for surgery, for making dresses, for tilling the soil, for undertaking journeys, and for other things very useful in this world'.³³ Early clocks were not simply timekeepers: they claimed to be able to suggest how people might organize their lives in the religious, social and moral spheres.

III

Early clocks were neither accurate nor reliable. They had to be reset frequently by reference to sundials; and they needed constant repairing. They were frequently the subject of ironic comment. Chaucer's Nun's Priest says of Chauntecleer

> Wel sikerer was his crowyng in his logge
> Than is a clokke or an abbay orlogge.
> By nature he knew ech ascensioun
> Of the equynoxial in thilke toun;
> For whan degrees fiftene weren ascended,
> Thanne crew he that it myghte nat been amended. (*CT*, VII, 2853–5)

Here Chaucer is comically preferring the reliability of the natural timekeeper to that of man-made machine. The cock has internalized the science: he knows 'by nature' what would normally have to be calculated using an astrolabe. Chaucer is intervening in a light-hearted way in what was a serious debate on this issue.³⁴ There was a rhyme current in Paris in the latter part of the fourteenth century which referred to the inaccuracy of the clock installed by Charles V, again ironic because it registers the failure of the king to rationalize time in the capital, which had been his object:

> … l'horloge du palais
> Elle va comme il lui plait.³⁵
>
> […the clock of the palace goes as it pleases]

In 1387, King John of Aragon decided he would employ two men to strike the bells of the clock in Perpignan because the striking mechanism could not be made to work perfectly – an ironic reversal because the 'jacquemarts' became human again.³⁶ But it was not simply elaborate public clocks which went awry. On about 20 February 1470, John Paston II wrote to John Paston III about two clocks, both in the hands of someone who mended clocks:

> I praye yow speke wyth Harcort off the Abbeye fore a lytell clokke whyche I sent hym by James Gressham to amend, and þat ye woll get it off hym, and it be redy, and sende it me; and asfore mony for hys labore, he hathe another clokk of myn whyche Syr Thomas Lyndez, God haue hys sowll, gaue me. He maye kepe that tyll I paye hym ...

In a reply, dated 1 March 1470, John Paston III makes it clear that there will be some delay: 'as for your clok at Harcortys, it wyll be nye Estern er it be redy, for ther is stolyn owt of hys chambyr som of the ger þat belongyd therto, and þat must haue leyser to be mad ayen'.[37] It must have been a chiming chamber clock, or a domestic clock of some sort in the Stonor household, to which Thomas Betson refers in an affectionate love-letter to the much younger Katheryne Ryche (whom he subsequently married in 1479) – a clock which, though not broken, was perpetually, it seems, fast, so as to cause some social embarrassment:

> I praye you, gentill Cossen, comaunde me to the Cloke, and pray hym to amend his unthryffte maners, ffor he strykes ever in undew tyme, and he will be ever affore, and that is a shrewde condiscion. Tell hym with owte he amend his condiscion that he will cause strangers to avoide and come no more there. I trust to you that he shall amend agaynest myn commynge the which shalbe shortely ...

He writes this from Calais, a staple town, where he was in the wool trade in partnership with Sir William Stonor, and dates and closes his letter with the interruption of another clock, which was presumably a bit more accurate than that at Stonor: '... the ffyrst day off June, whanne every man was gone to his Dener, and the Cloke smote noynne, and all oure howshold cryed after me and bade me come down, come down to dener at ones ...'.[38]

A century later, Thomas Nashe jibed at religious differences in England by comparing preachers to clocks: 'the preachers of England begin to strike and agree like the clocks of England, that never meete jumpe on a point together'.[39] Of course, clocks improved in accuracy as the technology developed, but even in the seventeenth century to agree 'like the clocks of London' was an ironic proverbial saying indicating difference rather than consonance. At his death, Giovanni de' Dondi's wonderful *astrarium* and clock fell into disrepair, despite the elaborate written account of how he made it, because nobody knew how to maintain it. It was eventually put into the library of the Visconti castle at Pavia and fell to pieces through neglect: when the Emperor Charles V saw it in 1529–30 it was not working.[40] Good clocks at this date were rare, good clockmakers even rarer, and reliability was almost impossible to attain.

Yet despite all this, despite the experience-based recognition that they were not infallible, mechanical clocks became associated with precision, reliability and perpetual motion – partly no doubt because they brought a new orderliness into timekeeping through using equinoctial hours, partly because they did not need so much attention as *clepsydrae*, which needed frequent resetting, and partly because, if you could hear clocks, they were a constant reminder, day and night, of the passing of the hours. The mechanical clock, with its division of time into regular pulses so that every moment was the same as the last and the next, became a model, an image of the logical arrangement of things, of unerroneous constancy, of temperance. It gave writers an instrument which served as a religious, social and moral measure. Clocks could tell mankind how to organize its life in this world and prepare itself for the next. Inevitably, it came to be perceived as a threat too, an image of the remorselessness of passing time.

Whether the diurnal mechanical timekeeper developed more or less as a by-product of the need to provide a mechanical image of the universe, or whether it developed in response to mundane necessities is an issue on which there is some debate.[41] There are arguments – incomplete because of the paucity of the evidence – which can be adduced to support either position. But what is not in doubt is the fact that the comparison between the workings of the universe and the workings of the clock emerged at an early stage. The earlier view that the comparison emerged co-terminously with the mechanistic philosophy of the seventeenth century is not sustainable.

IV

Who first compared the cosmos to a clock is in doubt. It could be argued that any clock which attempted to account for the turning of the heavens, the movements of the stars and the planets, the sun and moon, the circuit of the seasons, the logical alternation of day and night, the division of the day into ever smaller but equal parts, could be said to be a universal model. Furthermore, David S. Landes has argued that the automata on public clocks served to support this idea. He points out that 'the sums paid to painters and woodcarvers bear witness to the growing importance of the clock as a spectacle as well as a time signal'. He further argues that the automata 'offered lessons in theology and astronomy to the upward gazing multitude that gathered to watch and wonder' – though it is hard to establish this since few testimonies or comments have come down, though the automata on the Strasbourg clock certainly impressed Robert Boyle in the seventeenth century, enough to prompt a comparison with the workings of the universe. But Landes is surely right when he concludes: 'the clock as pageant was a miniaturization of heaven and earth.'[42]

There is early evidence that medieval thinkers entertained the possibility that the clock mirrored the universe. The German mystic Heinrich Suso (died 1366), in his *Horologium Sapientiae*, described a vision, to be dated 1334, in which he had been privileged to see Christ in the form of an elaborate contemporary clock chiming the hours: God's eternal time, he thought, provided a model for the soul which needed to operate in consonance with it. This was a very well-known text, which exists in many copies in several languages, often elaborately illustrated. In the fifteenth-century French version in Bruxelles, Bibliothèque Royale MS IV. 111 the relevant passage has *Sapientia*, acting as Temperance, show Suso

> ... ung horloge ou orloge de tresbelle et de tresnoble forme, dont les roes estoient excellentes et les cloches doulcement sonnans, et par la diverse et subtille facon de lui, tout cuer humain semerveilloit et esjoissoit en regardant ycelui ...[43]

> [... a timepiece or a clock of very beautiful and very noble form, of which the wheels are excellent and the bells chime sweetly, and by the various and subtle fashion of it, each human heart marvelled at it and rejoiced in looking at it ...]

This appears on fol. 14r. Opposite to it on 13v is an elaborate illustration showing Suso and *Sapientia*, including no less than eight timekeepers of which three are clocks (see Plate 12). The Middle English translation of this, which may date from the late fourteenth century or the early fifteenth century, the *Orlogium Sapientiae or The Seven Poyntes of Trewe Wisdom*, though organized differently, makes the same point in its opening. The translator explains that it is called the 'Orloge of Wisdame' because the 'matere' of Suso's book was shown to him 'in a visione undere þe figure and liknesse of a wondere fayre Orloge, sette & arayede with passynge fayre Roses, and with Cymbales swete sownynge, þat ȝevene wondere liking & heuenlye sowne, stirynge and excitynge vpwarde to hevene þe hertes of alle þat it hyrre.'[44] And in 1377, Nicole Oresme, in his *Livre du Ciel et du Monde*, compared the universe to a clock (*horloge*) which worked whatever the season, by day and night, was never fast or slow, and never stopped.

> Et selon verite, nulle intelligence n'est simplement immobile et ne convient pas que chascune soit par tout le ciel que elle meut ne en

chascune partie de tel ciel, pose que les cielz soient muez par intelligences, car par aventure, quant Dieu les crea. Il mist en eulz qualitez et vertus motivez aussi comme Il mist pesanteur es choses terrestres, et mist en eulz resistences d'autre nature et d'autre matiere que quelcunque chose sensible ou qualite qui soit ici bas. E sont les vertus contre ces resistences telement moderees, attempres et accordees que les mouvemens sont faiz sanz violence; et excepte la violence, c'est aucunement semblable quant un honme a fait un horloge et il le lesse aler et estre meu par soy. Ainsi lessa Dieu les cielz estre meuz continuelment selon les proporcions que les vertus motivez ont aus resistences et selon l'ordenance etablie.[45]

[Actually, no intelligence is absolutely immobile, and, if we assume the heavens to be moved by intelligences, it is unnecessary that each one should be everywhere within or in every part of the particular heaven it moves; for when God created the heavens, He put into them motive qualities and powers just as he put weight and resistance against those motive powers in earthly things. These powers and resistances are different in nature and in substance from any sensible thing or quality here below. The powers against these resistances are moderated in such a way, so tempered, and so harmonized that the movements are made without violence; thus, violence excepted, the situation is much like that of a man making a clock and letting it run and continue its own motion by itself. In this manner did God allow the heavens to be moved continually according to the proportions of the motive powers to the resistances and according to the established order.]

This is a remarkable passage, not least since, when the language of philosophical discourse becomes punctuated by the image of the clock and its maker, Oresme knows precisely what he is talking about. Orderly movement, depending on power and resistance, is at the heart of the mechanics that account for clockwork. So God became a sort of divine clockmaker: having constructed the 'horloge' of the universe and set it in motion he could leave it to move by itself.

Whether Dante knew about mechanical clocks is much argued about, but the likelihood is that he did. *Paradiso X*, which deals perhaps significantly with the circle of the sun, begins with a cosmological description of the universe and ends with a monastic clock signalling the time for matins by means of a striking mechanism:

> Indi, come orologio che ne chiami
> > ne l'ora che la sposa di Dio surge
> > a mattinar lo sposo perche l'ami,
> Che l'una parte e l'altra tira e urge,
> > tin tin sonando con si dolce nota
> > che 'l ben disposto spirto d'amor turge;
> Cosi vid' io la gloriosa rota
> > muoversi e rendere voce a voce in tempra
> > ed in dolezza ch'esser non po nota
> Se non cola dove gioir s'insempra. (139–48)

[Then, like the clock which calls us at the hour when the Bride of God rises to sing matins to the Bridegroom that he may love her, when one part draws or drives another, sounding the chime with notes so sweet that the well-ordered spirit swells with love, so I saw the glorious wheel move and render voice to voice in harmony and sweetness that cannot be known but where joy becomes everlasting.]

The word Dante uses here, 'orologio', could indicate a *clepsydra* or a mechanical clock, and 'rota' does not help because wheels were part of the mechanism of both types of timekeeper. But whatever he was thinking of it was clearly fairly intricate: there appear to have been several parts to the drive mechanism. But a later passage is clearer. The circling of the Fellowship of the Lamb in *Paradiso* XXIV is also compared to a clock and here the description is more precise. Perhaps Dante, who was interested in the significance of number, used the comparison in this context because the number of the canto corresponds to the number of hours in a day and to the number of numerals on some clocks:

> ...e quelle anime liete
> > si fero spere sopra fissi poli,
> > fiammando forte, a guisa di comete.
> E come cerchi in tempra d'orioli
> > si giran si, che 'l primo a chi pon mente
> > quieto pare, e l'ultimo che voli;
> Cosi quelle carole, differente-
> > mente danzando, della sua ricchezza
> > mi facieno stimar, veloci e lente. (10–18)

[... and those happy spirits formed themselves in circles on fixed poles, flaming brightly like comets. And as wheels in the structure of a clock revolve so that, to one watching them closely, the first seems to rest and the last to fly, so these choirs, dancing severally fast and slow, made me gauge their bliss.]

On this particular passage David S. Landes writes: '... it takes excessive ingenuity to see here anything but the wheel train with reduction gearing characteristic of the mechanical escapement clock'.[46] The orderliness of this heavenly dance is like the orderliness of a mechanical clock, and, because of the language of astronomy (*spere, fissi poli, comete*), it is further suggested that the universe moves in a similarly logical way – so Dante may here have been thinking of a clock which was also an *astrarium*. Two other points are important in relation to these passages. One is that in hell there is no time: clocks appear only in heaven, where they are seen as images of orderliness and constancy.[47] The second has to do with the phrase 'in tempra', meaning something like 'in measure' or 'in harmony', which here has important etymological overtones and other semantic nuances, some of them musical: orderly movement and orderly sound are features of both passages, and both are associated, like Nicole Oresme's word 'attempres', with the clock.

And much the same can be said of a passage from Christine de Pisan's *Epistre d'Othea*:

> ... raison peut estre figuree a l'orgue qui a plusieurs roes et mesures et toutfois ne vault rien l'orloge si se n'est pas atrempe, semblablement non fait notre corps humain se attremperance ne l'ordonne ...[48]
>
> [...reason may be figured in the organ which has several wheels and gauges, and, moreover, the clock is worth nothing if it is not regulated, and in the same way nor is our human body if temperance does not order it ...]

Here again, temperance appears in association with music and the clock: the mechanical clock was making its presence felt in all sorts of contexts. Philippe de Mézières went even further. In a passage from the third part of his *Songe du Vieil Pèlerin* he writes, describing 'la belle orloge du monde' [the beautiful clock of the world] by means of which God governs the world:

> ... Dieu gouverne cestui monde en peys et en nombre et en measure par troys moyens singuliers, c'est assavoir par nature misericorde et par justice, qui adroisse et attempres l'orloge; c'est assavoir que, faisent son adroit cours, l'orloge ne soit pas destourbee. Et pour ce fut elle, c'est assavoir justice, au grant et pesant plomb de l'orloge compare ...
>
> [... God governs the world in weight in number and in measure through three separate means, that is to be understood by nature, mercy and

> justice, which direct and moderate the clock; that is to say that, following its correct course, the clock will not be disturbed. And for this reason, it is she, that is to say justice, that is compared to the great and heavy lead weight of the clock ...]

This passage takes its origin from the apocryphal *Liber Sapientiae* 11:21 where God's power, his justice and his mercy are being addressed: 'omnia in mensura, et numero, et pondere disposuisti' [you have arranged all things by measure, number and weight], and de Mézières applies these three things, by analogy, to a clock which, powered by a weight, measures time and expresses itself by numbering – either by countable striking, or by the figures on a dial, or both. He then compares this triad to nature, mercy and justice, by means of which God governs the world. It is driven by his power (*justice*), but this is moderated (*attempres*) so that the world and all things in it are stable, and not disturbed (*destourbee*). As in a clock, the power of governance has to be ordered by restraint. My sense of this passage is that it is deliberately stated in generalized and universal terms, but it could clearly have political and social implications – a point made more trenchantly by others.[49]

Early clocks often consisted simply of a frame, holding the clockwork, without a case, so that the workings of the machine could be seen. And there is evidence that watching the intricacies of clockwork proved fascinating: when he looked at Giovanni de' Dondi's astrarium Philippe de Mézières, as has been seen, was impressed by its complexity, but marvelled that 'all goes with one weight'.[50] Pondering the workings of clocks in his *Treatise of Melancholie* (1591), Timothy Bright is equally impressed by the paradoxical complexity and unity of the machines and sees a similarity with the workings of the universe:

> We see it evident in automaticall instrumentes, as clockes, watches, and larums, howe one right and straight motion, through the aptnesse of the firste wheele, not only causeth circular motion in the same, but in diverse others also: and not only so, but distinct in pace, and time of motion: some wheeles passing swifter than other some, by diverse rases; now to these devises, some other instrument added, as hammer, and bell, not only another right motion springeth thereof, as the stroke of the hammer, but sound also repeated, and delivered it at certaine times by equal pauses; and that either larume or houres according as the partes of the clocke are framed. To these if yet moreover a directorie hand be added; this first, and simple, and right motion by weight or straine, shall seeme not only to be author of deliberate sound, & to counterfet voyce,

but also to point with the finger as much as it hath declared by sound. Besides these we see yet a third motion with reciprocation in the balance of the clocke. So many actions diverse in kinde rise from one simple first motion, by reason of variety of ioynts in one engine. If to these you adde what wit can devise, you may finde all the motion of heaven with the planets counterfetted, in a small modill, with distinction of time & season, as in the course of the heavenly bodies.[51]

Bright has clearly looked closely at the gearing of mechanical timekeepers and appreciates what can be driven by a weight or a spring (*straine*) – a complex striking mechanism to register the hours or to act as an alarm, a hand on a dial, and an *astrarium* if desired, which might model 'the course of the heavenly bodies'. Implicit in this is the idea that the mechanical clock is like the universe. But though he makes that point in this passage here it is not his main point: a little later he returns to the issue of unity and diversity and argues that the soul may seem to be three different souls, but is really one in which '… the same facultie varieth not by nature but by use only'.

So when Johannes Kepler asserted that 'the universe is not similar to a divine living being, but is similar to a clock' and when Robert Boyle described the universe as 'a great piece of clockwork' neither was using a particularly new analogy. They had, however, more reason to use it than earlier writers, because by the seventeenth century the best clocks had improved somewhat in both accuracy and reliability – though they were far from perfect.[52]

CHAPTER 5

The use of time: some social and moral implications of the mechanical clock

THE DEVELOPMENT OF THE MECHANICAL method of calculating time also provided an incentive and an opportunity for seeking to establish greater social and political orderliness, and the clock became an image of this orderliness: after all, it was widely believed that ordered society should be a reflection of the order found in the universe, especially in terms of hierarchy. In 1370 Charles V of France tried to organize time to his own standard: he decreed that all the clocks in Paris should be regulated by the one he was installing in the palace. The churches were to ring their bells when his clock struck the hour. The control of time by the church passed into secular hands. As Jacques le Goff puts it: 'the new time became the time of the state'.[1] However, to establish a standard time for a whole state, in the late Middle Ages and the early Renaissance, was beyond both the technology available and the social organization, and the most interesting practical attempts to regulate society by regulating time concern nothing larger than cities and towns and concern nothing more complex than the hours of the trading and working day. Perhaps the earliest example of this comes from Salisbury in 1306 where it is stipulated that 'before the clock of the Cathedral has struck one no person was to purchase or cause to be purchased flesh, fish or other victuals'.[2]

Traditionally, the working day had been co-terminus with the hours of daylight, largely because of the unavailability, on a large scale, of reliable, efficient and inexpensive sources of artificial light. It was a tradition formulated in relation to the rhythms of the natural world: it meant that the working day was longer in the summer than in the winter, which suited a largely agricultural economy, though the tradition held in urban contexts too. It had all the moral weight of the church on its side. In the thirteenth century, in his *Summa de Vitiis et Virtutibus*, Gulielmus Peraldus proposes the sun as the ideal agricultural worker:

> Posuit Dominus praeceptum soli ut de singulis diebus ab oriente veniat ad occidentem & singulis noctibus revertatur in orientem, & numquam

praeteriit sol illud praeceptum. Non pigritatur nec de die, nec de nocte, nec aestate, nec hyeme, implere illud praeceptum. Quantumcunque laboret in uno die nihilominus tamen summo mane surgit in sequenti die, & tandem non expectat talem remunerationem laboris sui, nec talem poenam negligentiae suae qualem homo. Ad huc videtur habuisse respectum. Augustinus cum dicit: Indecens est Christiano si radius solis eu inveniat in lecto. Posset enim dicere sol si potestatem loquendi haberet: amplius laboravi heri quam tu, et tamen cum surrexerim tu adhuc dormis.[3]

[The Lord gave a rule to the sun that every day it should come from the east to the west, and that every night it should go back to the east, and never did the sun neglect that rule. It is not lazy neither by day nor by night, neither in the summer nor in the winter, in fulfilling that rule. However much it may labour in one day, nevertheless, it also gets up very early on the next day, and, in the same way, it does not expect a reward for its labour, nor punishment for negligence, as a man does. For this one should have respect. Augustine says: It is unfitting for a Christian if the orb of the sun should find him in bed. The sun, indeed, might say, if it had the power of speech, I worked longer than you yesterday, and now when I am up you are still asleep.]

Peraldus's main aim in this passage is to expose the vice of sloth and to promote its countervailing virtue, *labor* or 'busyness'. But though the focus is primarily moral, there is no mistaking the social assumptions about the working day that lie behind it: the labourer is to get up with the sun and to work all day. These assumptions derive from a system of feudalism in which an unfree peasantry was expected to work the manorial demesne as an obligation. But even after the collapse of feudalism and the emergence of contract labour based on agreed wage rates and fixed hours of working, these ideas about the duration of the working day proved tenacious. In a Parisian labour dispute of 1395 the provost remarked, summarizing the proceedings, that a number of workers in different trades, 'weavers of linen or cotton, fullers, washers, masons, carpenters', were trying to start and stop work at precise hours during the day but still wanted to be paid as if they were working 'the whole day long' and reminded them that the working day was 'des heure de soleil levant jusqu'a heure de soleil couchant, et prenant leurs repas a heures raisonnables' [from the hour of sunrise to the hour of sunset, with meals to be taken at reasonable times].[4]

    These ideas proved to be long lasting. Two centuries later, John Donne, in 'The Sunne Rising', like Peraldus, meditates on the vice of sloth – staying in bed, in Donne's case, compounded with the vice of lechery, because he is with his lover, after the sun has begun to shine through their windows.[5] Unapologetically and comically, he tells the 'busy old fool, unruly sun' to leave the lovers alone, because the divisions of time are not relevant to them: love 'no season knows nor clime, / Nor hours, days, months, which are the rags of time'. He advises the sun to concentrate instead on his duties of getting people to start their working days: 'go chide / late school-boys and sour prentices, / Go tell court huntsmen that the King will ride …' (1–10).[6] Similarly, Shakespeare, a little earlier, adverts to much the same ideas, but without the comedy or the assertion that the time of lovers is different, when he has Henry V, unable to sleep and anxiously wandering through his army on the night before Agincourt, seeking to ascertain their mood, expresses envy for the simple lifestyle of the 'wretched slave' who:

> Never sees horrid night, the child of hell,
> But like a lackey from the rise to set
> Sweats in the eye of Phoebus, and all night
> Sleeps in Elysium; next day, after dawn
> Doth rise and help Hyperion to his horse,
> And follows so the ever-running year
> With profitable labour to his grave … (*Henry V*, IV. i. 268–74)

This is an eloquent and moving restatement of the traditional norm – working hours are from the 'rise to set' and are here associated with two classical sun-gods – though by this date the working day was becoming increasingly to be calculated not by the sun but by the clock.

Initially, the time of the church was the standard, but modified often by considerations of light and darkness. W. Rothwell has pointed out that according to a statute of 1324 the tanners of Paris worked from sunrise to sunset in the summer, but in winter they should begin when it was possible to recognize someone in the street. Silk makers of Paris stopped work in summer when the bell of Sainte-Marie-des-Champs sounded for alms. When the bell on Notre Dame sounded for noon on Saturday, the carpenters stopped work.[7] Towards the end of the fourteenth century, a not entirely dissimilar situation appears to have existed in York. As Chris Humphreys has demonstrated, in detail, that ordinances regarding the workers refurbishing York Minster stipulated that the works of masons, and others engaged in the project, were committed by the ordinances of the project that, from Michaelmas to the first Sunday in Lent, they should work 'as early as they might see skilfully by daylight for to work'. At noon or just before, they could eat, but the meal should be at 'high noon smitten by the clock when holy day falls at noon'. At other times of the year, other arrangements could be made, but 'at no time of the year … should they be away from their work … more than the space of an hour.' Here clearly daytime working hours, defined by the light, were modified by those of the clock – probably a mechanical clock with a striking train: in 1360 the minster invested in a new clock and a 'new bell' to replace the broken one.

It is clear, though, that there were other clocks and bells in the city, but that the minster clock was the main reference point for the definition of the working day. The ordinances of the Girdlers' Guild stipulated that members should not work on a Saturday after twelve was struck by the clock at York Minster 'on pain of a fine of a pound of wax'. In time, however, other clocks – civic clocks – came to be used. There were bells on Ouse Bridge probably as early as 1380 and a clock system came into being. From 1428 comes an order that the butchers, who were not opening their shops on Sundays, were to open them until 'eight of the bell of the clock of the commonalty on Ouse Bridge'. They could close them during vespers at their local parish churches, but had to open again after vespers. In these York city records, which are very rich and well preserved, a complex sense of urban time exists: the duration of the working day is in some cases defined by the hours of daylight, but is substantially modified by church bells and by clocks, both religious and public.

Labour disputes over the duration and the calculation of the duration of the working day are a particular feature of the fourteenth century and appear, to a large extent, to have been generated by the availability of mechanical public clocks or work-bells. This meant that the site of conflict was cities and towns, particularly those connected with the cloth trades. It was not always the case that the employers demanded a longer working day. In fact, the earliest evidence available comes from a request in 1315 by the fullers' apprentices of Arras for a lengthening of the working day and a corresponding increase in wages – an early case of a demand for overtime. But shortly after this work-bells begin to proliferate, almost always at the instigation of the employers. A work-bell was installed in Ghent in 1324 for the fullers, authorized by the abbot of St Pierre. On 24 April 1335 Philip VI (le Bel) granted a request from the mayor and aldermen of Amiens that they could

> … faire une ordenance quand les ouvriers de ladicte ville et banlieue d'icelle iroient chascun jour ouvrable a leurs ouvrages au matin, quand ils deveroient aler mengier et quand ils deveroient repairier a leurs ouvrages apres mengier et aussi au soir quand ils deveroient laissier

oeuvre pour la journee; et que par la dite ordenance que il feroient, il peussent sonner une cloche que il on fait pendre au Beffroi de ladicte ville, laquelle se differe des autre cloches ...⁸

[... issue an ordinance about when the workers of the said town and its suburbs should go each working day to their work in the morning, when they should go to eat and when they should return to work after eating, and also in the evening when they should leave work for the day; and by this ordinance that they made they might sound a bell which might be hung in the Belfry of the said town, which differs from the other bells ...]

Similar arrangements were authorized in other places. At Aix-sur-Lys on 15 August 1335 Jean de Picquigny, governor of Artois, gave permission for a belfry to be constructed with a work-bell because of the 'cloth trade and other trades' who needed their workers to arrive and leave work at predetermined times.⁹

It is apparent that in some places the public clock was a valued part of the city, at once decorative and useful. An inscription on a striking clock on the bridge at Caen in 1314 refers to the bell:

Puisque la ville me loge
Sur le pont pour servir l'orloge,
Je ferai les heures ouir
Pour le commun peuple rejouir¹⁰

[Because the town has set me on the bridge to serve the clock, I make the hours heard to please the common people]

Galvano Flamma, chronicler of Milan, proudly described a newly-restored city clock in 1333 as 'the greatest necessity for every rank of men'.¹¹ From the next century, Carlo Cipolla quotes from a petition in 1481 to the town council of Lyon arguing that the town needed 'a great clock whose strokes could be heard by all citizens in all parts of the town. If such a clock were to be made, more merchants would come to the fairs, the citizens would be very consoled, cheerful and happy and would have a more orderly life, and the town would gain in decoration'. He makes the point that civic pride as well as utilitarianism contributed to the spread of town clocks. There was also a certain amount of emulousness involved: he points out that in the 1420 the town council of Romans had installed a beautiful and expensive clock, and that in 1557 the citizens of not-too-distant Montélimar decided they wanted one 'a la forme d'icelluy de Romans' [in the manner of that of Romans].¹² And it was no doubt his appreciation that a clock represented an aspect of a town's civic pride in

14 Jacquemarts on the Cathedral of Notre Dame, Dijon. François de Dijon, CC BY-SA, via Wikimedia Commons.

itself which caused Philip the Bold, duke of Burgundy, after his defeat of the burghers of Flanders at the battle of Roosebeke in 1382, to have the clothiers' belfry clock in Courtrai dismantled as a punishment and to have it taken back to Dijon with him.[13] He presented the clock to the people of Dijon and had it set up on the tower of the church of Notre Dame (see Figure 14). In a turret that covered it were a bell and, on either side of it, figures of a man and a woman who struck the hours.[14] He compounded the humiliation of the rebellious town by removing one of the things in which it took pride: to him the clock may have appeared almost to be a totemic object, as well as a socially useful one.

But work-clocks, no doubt partly because they were new and partly because they could be used coercively by employers, became contentious objects. It is clear that there were those among the workforce who resisted the new discipline of the clock. In Ghent, between 1358 and 1362, fines had to be instituted for those who did not obey the summons of the work-clock. In Commines, in 1361, weavers who did not appear on time were fined 'five Parisian *solz*'. Fines were also threatened if unauthorized persons interfered with the work-bells. But there is evidence of resistance, which sometimes succeeded. On 6 December 1349 the aldermen of Ghent issued permission for the weavers to return to the city within a week and conceded that they could stop work at hours they determined. And at Thérouanne, on 16 March 1367, the dean and chapter had to promise the 'workers, fullers and other mechanics' that they would 'silence forever the workers' bell' so that no trouble would be caused.[15] However, despite resistance and conflict, labour time in cities and towns, particularly in those dependent on the cloth trades, became dominated by work-bells and work-clocks. Not only was the organization of the natural working day displaced, but the organization of the working day governed by the time of the church came to be increasingly silenced, or at least compromised: in York, between 1352 and 1370, when the minster was being constructed and reconstructed, a work-bell was set up, relieving the bells of the church of that function.[16] No doubt the two sets of bells – one traditionally religious, one newly practical and secular – found a way of coexisting amicably and differentiating their functions. But it is clear where the future lay.

II

The possibility of the exact measurement and quantification of time which the mechanical clock promised appears to have increased the sense of its value.

> Tempus donum dei est
> Inde vendi non potest.
>
> [Time is the gift of God, so it cannot be sold]

So ran an anti-usury jingle. But as early as the first half of the fourteenth century Domenico Calva of Pisa, in his *Disciplina degli Spirituali*, compared wasted time to the unused talent of the biblical parable, so, in a sense, even for somebody in orders, time was money.[17] And for those engaged in commerce or trade this sense quickly became highly developed. In the London Merchant Tailors' Records for the years 1488–93 comes a complaint from a master against one of his apprentices because he has fallen in love. Indentures between masters and apprentices frequently stipulate that the apprentice shall not commit fornication. This complaint, however, is not brought on those grounds, but on the grounds that the apprentice wastes time he ought to be spending on his work because he '... used the company of a woman which was to his (the master's) grete losse and hynderyng for as moch as he was so affectionate and resorted daily unto hyr ...'.[18] How time was spent was always something of importance. Sloth was one of the capital sins: as Chaucer's Parson put it, 'Certes, the hevene is yeven to hem that wol labouren, and nat to ydel folk' (CT, X. 716–17). But in the late Middle Ages and the Renaissance, with the increased possibility that time could be calculated more precisely, the sense of how important it was to use time profitably was increased: '& therfore take good keep into tyme', advises the author of *The Cloud of Unknowing*, 'how that thou dispendest it. For nothing is more precious than tyme. In oo litel tyme, as litil as it is, may heven be wonne & loste'. And, he continues, God will want to know what a person did with his time 'in the dome & at the gevyng of acompte of dispendyng of tyme ...'.[19] He is, of course, primarily interested in persuading his reader that time profitably spent in contemplation can lead to the salvation of one's soul. But the vocabulary of commerce, which runs through the whole passage, suggests that the spiritual was being invaded by the secular sense.

The reorganization of the working day had profound and far-reaching social consequences, and not everybody was happy about the compromising of the norm that the day was for work and the night for rest and recreation. Of course, there had always been those who, in order to make a living, had had to work at night as well as during the day. In about 1168, more than a century before the appearance of the first mechanical clocks, Chrétien de Troyes, in *Yvain*, had set in a castle, which the hero visits, a scene in which ill-dressed and undernourished silk-workers are being exploited by (literally) diabolical employers. One of the women explains that they are allowed to keep only fourpence out of every twenty shillings they earn:

> ... nos somes ci an poverte,
> s'est riches de nostre desserte
> cil por cui nos traveillons.
> Des nuiz grant partie veillons
> Et toz les jorz por gaignier.[20]

[... we are here in poverty while the man we work for is rich because of our earnings. We stay up a large part of the nights and all day to make money ...]

Whether Chrétien is here protesting about the exploitation of the female workforce in the newly developing silk industries of Champagne, or about the silk-making workshops to be found in some seigneurial households is much debated. But what is interesting for the present argument is the feeling that the necessity to work at night is of itself indicative of the poor conditions in which the women found themselves.

On the other hand, long after the advent of the mechanical clock had made it possible to negotiate hours of work that did not simply correspond to the hours of daylight or to what were called 'working days', those who chose to work at night, or on the Sabbath, or on 'holy days' came under some social and moral stigma. Most of the criticism attaches to moneylenders and merchants, who are memorably linked, under the metaphor of the clock, by Roger Fenton in *A Treatise of Usurie* (1611): 'Usury is so twisted into every trade and commerce, one moving the other, by this engine, like the wheeles in a clocke, that it seemeth the very frame and course of traffick must needes be altered before this can be reformed.'[21]

Strictures against taking interest for money loaned were many: throughout the Middle Ages and into the Renaissance canon law always condemned it, and civil law sometimes did and sometimes allowed it under certain strict conditions. It was morally disapproved of for a variety of reasons: it contravened the biblical text which said 'lend, hoping for nothing again' (Luke 6:35); it was held to be unnatural for money to beget money; it exploited those in need; and the like.[22] However, bankers and moneylenders were too useful, politically and socially, to be dispensed with totally. Most kings, and a great many noblemen and heads of religious houses borrowed money at one time or another for a variety of reasons. Nor could international trade have operated efficiently without a highly developed banking system which turned on credit and interest. Thomas Aquinas, in his *Summa Theologica*, is humane and understanding on this matter:

> The civil law leaves certain sins unpunished to accommodate imperfect men who would be severely disadvantaged if all sins were strictly prohibited by suitable sanctions. Human law, therefore, allows the taking of interest, not because it deems this to be just, but because to do otherwise would hinder the utilities of a great many people. (IIa, IIae, q. 78)

But, useful or not, lenders of money, usually called 'usurers' pejoratively, were especially vulnerable in relation to time, which is a critical issue in relation to the charging of interest. The banker or moneylender or usurer was regarded as a thief of time. Jacques le Goff quotes the *Tabula Exemplorum*: 'Usurers are thieves, for they sell time that does not belong to them and sell someone else's property, against the owner's wishes, and that is theft'. It was especially serious theft, too, for time, by common consent, belonged to God. Thomas Chobham is typical, when he says: 'Thus the usurer sells his debtor nothing that belongs to him, but only time that belongs to God *(tempus quod dei est)*. Since he sells a thing belonging to someone else, he should make no profit from it'. Time may have become equated with money in some commercial and mercantile circles, but money had to be earned through labour: the stipulation in Genesis 3:19 – 'In the sweat of thy face shalt thou eat bread' – valorized work as a way of atoning for the fall. But moneylenders did not work in any obvious way, hence Chobham's accusation: 'The usurer wants to make a profit without doing any work, even while he is sleeping, which goes against the precepts of the Lord who said "By the sweat of your face shall you get bread to eat"'. John Bromyard in his *Summa Praedicantium* compares, to their detriment, usurers to robbers:

> The usurer is worse than the robber, because the robber usually steals at night. The usurer, however, robs by day and night, having no regard for time or solemnity, for the profit which accrues to him through a loan never sleeps, but always grows.[23]

Francis Bacon, in his essay *Of Usury*, makes most of these points, but adds, among the 'witty invectives' made against usury, 'that the usurer is the greatest Sabbath-breaker, because his plough goeth every Sunday'.[24] As an abuser of time – making a profit while he slept and on the Sabbath – the usurer came at the top of the list: his only means of attaining salvation was to make restitution of what he had unlawfully obtained, and that was not easy. Chobham, as le Goff makes clear, is very explicit on this point: 'Since the canonical rule states that "the sin is never pardoned unless a stolen object has been returned", it is clear that the usurer cannot be considered penitent unless he returns everything that he extorted through usury'. In practical terms, time was the moneylender's friend: it enabled him to conduct a necessary trade and make a living from it. In spiritual terms it placed him in a situation that was at best difficult, at worst impossible.

Nor did merchants fare a lot better in the public imagination. It was often argued, in justification of merchants, that their activities were necessary for the public good of the towns in which they did business, that the profits that they made could be justified because they paid for the labour they expended in buying goods and in transporting them, that their profits compensated for the risks (the 'ventures') they took. But merchants were economic individualists in a society which set much store by the common good and the care for one's neighbours. And the sometimes large profits that they made rendered them suspect: there was a feeling that they helped themselves to too much when the social theory said that they should have laboured simply to sustain themselves and keep up their social positions. And because they bought cheap and sold dear there were suspicions that merchants were devious, unscrupulous and tricky.

> Money to incresse, marchandys never to cease
> Wyth many a sotell wyle;
> Men say the wolde for sylver and golde
> Ther owne faders begyle.[25]

So ran one stanza of a fifteenth-century poem complaining about the materialism of contemporary culture. But it was their perceived obsessiveness, their reluctance to 'cease' to work to make a profit, that condemned them as abusers of time. According to a fifteenth-century sermon in London, British Library MS Additional 2398 the merchant's obsessive lust for gain, causing him to work 'by nighte', when he should be taking 'slepe' and 'reste', as well as by day is likely to destroy him:

> [it] ne suffreth him nought to have slepe, ne reste, by nighte ne by day; bot maketh him travayle in water and in londe, in chele and in hete, in feyntyse and in werynesse. Ryght as a spythur destroyeth here-self in makynge a webbe for to take a flye, ryght so the coveytous man destroyeth his owene body for to gete thys worldes goed.[26]

To work hard was a virtue. To work too hard, especially if this involved working at unconventional times, left one open to criticism, especially if the obsessiveness caused one to neglect the spiritual side of one's obligations. On 21 February 1401 Francesco Datini, a merchant from Prato, wrote to Cristofano di Bartolo, one of his partners in Spain, trying to persuade him to spend less time making money and come back to Italy:

> You take no account of time and do not remember that you must die ... You count on your fingers and say, 'In so much time I shall have made so much, and shall have so much time left, and when I am rich indeed, I shall go back to Florence and take a wife' ... You do not remember

our five men, who died in the same year: Falduccio and Manno, Niccolo di Piero, Andrea di Bonanno, Bartolomeo Cambioni, and a hundred others ... I do otherwise: I give more thought to how things will go after my death, than to those of this world.[27]

In old age, or in bequests after their deaths, merchants often made money available to acquire spiritual benefits for themselves: a good many of the late medieval parish churches of England, especially in Yorkshire, East Anglia, the Cotswolds and the south-west, were splendidly refurbished in the late Middle Ages by the profits from the wool trade.

III

The general issue of what constituted the proper time for work, therefore, was an important one, and legislation begins to be put in place to regulate night-work. Not all trades needed regulation: for an individual silk-worker or spinster to work at night would have offended nobody. But the metalworking trades were noisy and, because they used forges, potentially dangerous, and metalworkers, particularly blacksmiths, sometimes had good reason to work at night: equipment, particularly farm equipment, might have to be repaired overnight so that it could be used next day. It is a blacksmith who is making or repairing farm equipment in Oxford to whom Absolon goes towards the end of Chaucer's *Miller's Tale* as he plots his revenge on Nicholas and Alison:

> A softe paas he wente over the strete
> Until an smyth men cleped daun Gerveys,
> That in his forge smythed plough harneys;
> He sharpeth shaar and kultour bisily. (*CT*, I, 3760–3)

It has already been established that 'derk was the nyght as pich, or as the cole' (3731) and Gerveys himself draws attention to the fact that it is very early when he asks Absolon: 'Why rise ye so rathe?' He is at work well before sunrise, and this seems to be taken for granted: he is mending or improving ploughs so that they can be used the next day.[28] Some guilds tried to outlaw night-work, but found it difficult. In the early years of the reign of Edward I, for example, the spurriers of London insisted that their members take an oath not to work except between sunrise and sunset, and had recourse to the consistory court in the case of one offending journeyman and won the case, with the result that 'the said Richard, after three times being warned by the official, had been expelled from the church and excommunicated, until he would swear to keep the ordinance'.[29]

There were various complaints about night-work. In the articles of the spurriers of 1345 it was argued that work done at night was often inferior in craftsmanship, 'because no man can work so neatly by night as by day', and that it often led to the use of inferior materials. Usually, though, complaints centred on the danger created by metalworkers' forges and by the noise they made as they worked, as the spurriers' articles again make plain: 'many ... are wandering about all day, without working at their trade; and then, when they have become drunk and frantic, they take to their work to the annoyance of the sick and of all their neighbourhood ... and then they blow up their fires so vigorously that their forges begin at once to blaze, to the great peril of themselves and of all the neighbourhood around ...'.[30] In 1394 the 'reputable men' among the London blacksmiths proposed a set of articles 'for the common profit and advantage' of the city to restrict night-work. These articles were proposed, they say, because a number of their trade were coming under pressure to 'quit their houses' because of 'the great nuisance, noise and alarm experienced in divers ways by the neighbours around their dwellings'. The proposal, when it comes, is very precise:

> ... it is ordained that no-one of the said trade shall work by night, but only from the beginning of daylight to 9 of the clock at night throughout all of the year, except between the feast of All Hallows and the feast of Candlemas, between which feasts they shall work from 6 of the clock in the morning until 8 of the clock at night ...

There are several interesting things about this. One is that it both prohibits night-work and allows it: to define a working day which can extend for 14 hours between 1 November (All Hallows) and 2 February (Candlemas) is to allow for many hours to be worked in darkness. A second is that part of the old definition of the working day survives in the mention of 'the beginning of daylight', but it has largely been superseded by time calculated in terms of the clock. A third is that not very much is said in this document about enforcement of the ordinance, and in this it is characteristic of other documents from other places dealing with other trades. Because this document comes from the 'reputable men' of the trade in London, one can assume that there were others who would not have felt themselves bound by these rules.

And complaints about night-work continued, though there were restrictions in force in many cities and towns. From possibly the first quarter of the fifteenth century comes an alliterative poem, usually entitled *Blacksmiths* (though it has no title in the manuscript), which complains about the noise and inconvenience of night-work. It begins:

Swarte smekyd smethes smateryd wyth smoke,
Dryve me to deth wyth den of here dyntes!
Swech noys on nyghtes ne herd men never:
What knavene cry, & clateryng of knockes!
The cammede kongons cryen after 'Col! Col!'
& blowen here bellewys that al here brayn brestes.
'Huf, puf!' seyth that on; 'Haf, paf!' that other.
Thei spytten & spraulyn & spellyn many spelles;
Thei grauen and gnacchen, thei gronys togydere,
And holdyn hem hote wyth here hard hamers.
Of a bole hyde ben here barm-fellys;
Here schankes ben schakled for the fere-flunderys;
Hevy hamerys thei han that hard ben handled;
Stark strokys thei stryken on a stelyd stokke.
'Lus, bus! Las das!' rowtyn be rowe –
Sweche dolful a dreme the devyl it todryve ... (1–16)[31]

[Black, smoked smiths, begrimed with smoke, drive me to death with the din of their blows. Men never heard such a noise at night. What a noise from the lads, what a clatter from their blows! These pug-nosed rascals shout out for 'Coal, Coal', and blow their bellows until their brain bursts. 'Huff, puff' says one; 'Haff, paff' says another. They spit and they sprawl about and tell many stories. They grate and gnash their teeth and complain together. They keep themselves hot with their hard hammering. Their leather aprons are made of bull's hide; their legs are wrapped up against fiery sparks. They have heavy hammers which are vigorously handled. They strike heavy blows on a steel anvil. 'Luss, buss, Lass, dass' they snort in turn. May the devil get rid of such a miserable tune ...][32]

The setting here looks urban and the workshop seems quite large, since a number of people are present in it, and the poet may intend the smiths to be makers of horse-armour or harness: he calls them 'clothemeres' (21). But to contextualize the poem further is difficult. The dialect of the poem as we have it has been identified as north-west Norfolk, and certain features of the vocabulary are East Anglian. The sole surviving manuscript of the poem, London, British Library MS Arundel 292, once belonged to Norwich Cathedral Priory, and it may be that the poem was copied there.[33] It may have been composed there, too, and the author may have been a cleric: the slightly envious disapproval of the gross physicality of the smiths is characteristic of the non-manual worker. But whoever he is, the complaint is made in the usual terms: the flames, and particularly the noises, offend him as does the crucial fact that the work takes place 'on nyghtes'. Later in the poem the speaker complains that, because of those who burn water (*brenwateres*), nobody can 'on night han his rest'. What he sees in the night-working smithy is a vision of hell. Working at night is not just antisocial but diabolical too: 'the devel it to dryve'. This poem has all the appearance of having been written from experience, but whether regulations, governed by the mechanical timekeeper, were in force which would have permitted night-work, when and where this was written, is not possible to determine. Perhaps it really does not matter. This is a restatement of the old certainties that the day is meant for work and the night for rest.

From much later comes a highly imaginative, and famous, confrontation which turns on the issue of when it is appropriate to work, a confrontation which specifically invokes the mechanical clock and is largely defined by it. In *1 Henry IV* when Prince Hal and Falstaff first appear on stage together they talk about time, and its licit and illicit uses:

> *Falstaff*: Now, Hal, what time of day is it, lad?
>
> *Prince*: Thou art so fat-witted with drinking of old sack, and unbuttoning thee after supper, and sleeping on benches after noon, that thou hast forgotten to demand that truly which thou would'st truly know. What a devil hast thou to do with the time of day? Unless hours were cups of sack, and minutes capons, and clocks the tongues of bawds, and dials the signs of leaping houses, and the blessed sun himself a fair hot wench in flame-coloured taffeta. I see no reason why thou should'st be so superfluous to demand the time of day. (I. ii. 1–12)

Hal responds to Falstaff's question about 'the time of day' by anatomizing his daytime activities in terms of a mechanical timekeeper, which had both a bell (*clock*) and a 'dial': 'sleeping upon benches after noon' drinking 'sack', eating 'capons', talking to 'bawds' and going to brothels (*leaping houses*). Falstaff does no work during the day, merely indulges himself when he is awake – gluttony, lechery and sloth were the traditional 'sins of the flesh'. The clock was also obviously assumed to have a hand that marked the hours of daylight, often on a separate dial, which had on it 'the blessed sun himself', and it is this feature which determines Falstaff's reply and defines the shape of the scene as it develops. Falstaff admits, tacitly, that his lifestyle does not involve spending the daylight hours working, but says that he works at night, and alludes to the fact that many contemporary clocks had a dial for the hours of night, which were indicated by a hand with a moon on it:

> *Falstaff*: Indeed, you come near me now, Hal, for we that take purses go by the moon and the seven stars, and not 'by Phoebus, he, that wand'ring knight so fair'. (13–15)

Where the iambic pentameter about Phoebus, which Falstaff quotes, comes from is not known (he may have invented it), but it is clear that he is rejecting the daytime world of work for the night-time world of crime. And he follows this by seeking, only half humorously, to persuade Hal, when he is king, to give sanction to such activities as he indulges in by inventing parodic titles of actual royal offices – 'squires of the night's body', 'Diana's foresters', 'gentlemen of the shade'. But Hal reminds him that crime leads not to titles, but to prison or the gallows. Falstaff defends 'purse-taking' as his vocation ''Tis no sin for a man to labour in his vocation' (105).

But Hal is not to be deflected, and in the famous closing soliloquy to this scene (192–214) he commits himself to work and to daytime values associated with the sun, and determines that he will begin 'redeeming time', which he knows he has hitherto wasted. He will put up with the 'unyoked' [not working] 'idleness' of his companions, but for 'a while' only. If 'playing holidays' become everyday things, he argues, they become 'tedious'. He vows instead to 'imitate the sun'. In this context such a statement has multiple resonances. One, by way of a pun, is that he will become the dutiful and responsible 'son' that his father wishes him to be. Another is that he will live up to his family traditions, since the 'sunburst', or the sun emerging from clouds, was a Plantagenet badge, though technically he is a Lancastrian, but related to the Plantagenet line. But in view of the way the clock has shaped this scene and in view of the vocabulary of the final soliloquy, the commitment to work of a licit and useful kind is important in his scale of priorities: he intends to reform and conform, to commit himself to order and regularity, to become a useful member of the community, to live his life in relation to the instrument that had come to govern social life. Falstaff has chosen a different way, and as the play develops there are reminders of this choice. In the play-acting scene in Eastcheap, Falstaff, in the role of Hal's father, marvels 'where thou spendest thy time' and accuses Hal of truancy using this imagery: 'Shall the blessed sun of heaven prove a micher, and eat blackberries?' (II. iv. 411–12). In Falstaff's painful interview with the Lord Chief Justice, the latter alludes both to Falstaff's part in the Gads Hill robbery and his (supposed) good performance at the battle of Shrewsbury – where he claims to have fought with Hotspur, 'a long hour by

Shrewsbury clock' – in the following terms: 'Your day's service at Shrewsbury hath a little gilded over your night's exploit at Gads Hill' (*2 Henry IV*, I. ii. 149).

In fact, throughout *2 Henry IV*, whenever Hal is with his old companions, he is haunted by the feeling that he is not spending his time profitably. In the course of a desultory conversation with Poins emerging from a discussion of a letter from Falstaff, he pulls himself up short with: 'Well, thus we play the fools with time and the spirits of the wise sit in the clouds and mock us' (II. ii. 133–4). And again, a little later in Eastcheap, he confesses to Poins that he feels 'much to blame / So idly to profane the precious time' (II. iv. 565–6) when there is national business he should be attending to at court.

IV

A short poem entitled *On Tyme* appears in a small collection of Skelton's poems published in about 1545 by Kynge and Marche, and was republished in a number of later collections. It also exists in several forms – with added stanzas.[34] Although some have doubted that it is by Skelton it is followed in the Trinity College Dublin MS 661 version by 'Quod Skelton', one of the ways he signed his poems.[35] Whichever view is true, it is, however, interesting in that it provides a conspectus of late medieval and early modern views on the subject, none of them particularly original. In the Trinity College Dublin MS 661 version, which I use, the opening stanza makes the point that time is 'trancytory', 'irrecoverable', and 'mutable' and ends with the proverb 'Byde for tyme who wyll, for tyme wyll no man byde' – a testimony to the power and unreliability of time, and how it is beyond the control of men. As the poem develops, however, one line from the opening stanza becomes central: 'Tyme must be taken in season convenable' (6). And the central stanzas turn on the proper personal uses of time:

> Tyme to be sad, and tyme to play and sporte;
> Tyme to take rest by way of recreacion;
> Tyme to study, and tyme to use comfort;
> Tyme of pleasure, and tyme of consolation … (1–13)

This deals with how one might organize one's life in the area where the social and the personal intersect. In the following stanza the advice offered has more to do with moral behaviour: 'Tyme for to speake, and tyme to holde thy pease', time to put oneself forward 'in prease' and time to 'holde thyselfe abacke' (21–2). The final stanza takes up the idea of 'season' and construes time in terms of the turning of the year and the labours of the months:

> The rotys take theyr sap in tyme of vere;
> In tyme of somer flowers fresh and grene;
> In tyme of harvest men their corne shere;
> In tyme of wynter the north wynde waketh kene … (24–7)

The poem is laconic and non-committal in the sense that most of its assertions are traditional and the author transmits them without comment. But its movement from the power of time, through the use of time, to conformity with the rhythms of the seasons, suggests a moral agenda that, since one cannot control time, the best one can do is seek to come to terms with the passage of time and organize one's life in relation to it. The poem has a refrain, 'every thing must have a tyme' (2) – based on Ecclesiastes 3:1 – and in its bland way this is an apt summary of the poem. No timekeeper is mentioned and the dating, such as appears in the poem, is traditional in the extreme: 'the kalends of Janus' (29), Roman time, appears in the last but one line.

This traditional, conventional poem, stressing the need to come to terms with time and to organize one's life in consonance with its rhythms, is effectively a digest of the conformist mentality of its age. And the impact of the mechanical clock made very little difference, except that the operations of the clock began to be used as an analogy for human behaviour on a more precise level. The mechanical intricacy of the new timekeeper gave impetus to moral allegory on the subject of time.

The clock became a device of moral comparison, an image for the well-regulated behaviour of people: macrocosmic comparisons between the clock and the universe, and the clock and the social organism, begin to be reflected at the microcosmic level of man. As early as 1369 Jean Froissart explored the possibilities of the comparison in *L'Orloge Amoureus*, a long allegorical poem.[36] The poem is frequently referred to by historians of horology because of its astonishing accuracy and detail. The description of the workings of the verge escapement and foliot is one of the earliest that there is.[37] But it also demonstrates the 'virtuousness of technology', valorizing it by making an analogy between the working of the mechanical clock and properly ethical and moral behaviour. It opens with some lines in praise of mechanical clocks:

> L'orloge est, au vrai considerer,
> Un instrument tres bel et tres notable,
> Et s'est aussy plaisant et pourfitable,
> Car nuit et iour les heures nous aprent
> Par la soubtilite qu'elle comprent
> En l'absence meisme dou soleil … (1–6)

> [The clock is, if considered rightly, a very beautiful and remarkable machine, and it is also pleasant and useful, because night and day it tells us the hours by the intricacy of its mechanism, even when there is no sun ...]

Briefly, this reads like a justification of mechanical clocks in terms of their social decorativeness and usefulness (*plaisant et pourfitable*), or in terms of their advantages over sundials. But this is not Froissart's main interest. After commending the man who invented the clock as 'vaillant' and 'sage' (10), he launches into a detailed allegorical anatomy of a lover's emotions in terms of the parts of the clock. The housing of the mechanism – the clockcase – is appropriately the 'coer loyal'. Then he moves to the mechanism itself: the largest cog is 'le vrai desir' (106); the weight which drives the clock is 'la beaute' (113); and the cord by which the weight and the cogwheel are attached is 'plaisance' (114). All of which means that the force of beauty moves part of the lover's heart to thoughts of pleasure, which in turn sets in motion his true desire. But this passion is controlled by reason: 'attemprance' [temperance, moderation] is the escapement mechanism (221) which determines the speed of the clock. Some of the comparisons are truly ingenious, as when the foliot – the oscillating vertical bar which regulates the escapement – is made to stand for 'paours' [fear]:

> Car tout ensi que le foliot branle,
> Droit coers loyaus estre tous jours en branle,
> Et regarder, puis avant, puis arriere ... (251–3)

> [And just as the foliot moves to and fro, loyal hearts must every day be in agitation, and look, sometimes before, sometimes behind ...]

The other parts of the clock are mentioned as the poem develops: the clock face is 'doulc penser' (369), the twenty-four hours each correspond to a virtue, and so on. At times, Froissart appears to be conscious that he is using material which would be appropriate in a technological treatise, and paradoxically an allegory of idealized love. The 'orlogier' (930) or 'governor' of the clock, by whom it is kept in good working order, is initially described at some length as if he were external to the clock: he has to draw up the weights (*plons*) so that the clock will have motive force, order and control the wheels (*roes*), set the foliot so that it will not stop, the spindle (*fuiselet*) and the pins (*brochetes*), and make sure that the striking train will sound the hours (*heures*) in consonance with the figures on the clock-face (*dyal*). But he is not an external entity, but 'souvenirs' (950) – the lover's memory of the lady. The principal virtue which the whole allegory demonstrates is the fairly predictable one of constancy: just as a good clock runs incessantly day and night, never wavering, never stopping, so the loyal heart of the lover should always be moved by thoughts of the lady, which is proposed as an appropriate way for a lover to spend his time. The poet incorporates the clock, making it part of him:

> Tout ensi sui gouvrenés par raison,
> Car je sui la chamber et la maison
> Ou mis est li orloges amoureus ... (1151–3)
>
> [I am completely governed by reason, because I am the room and the house where the clock of love is placed ...]

The intricate interdependence of the parts of a clock, which all move to one end, provides a comforting analogy for the overwhelming nature of love and the proper behaviour of the lover – a fanciful though informed analogy, but one which is worked through rigorously.

This analogy recurs in Sir John Suckling's early seventeenth-century poem *Love's Clock*, which opens

> That none beguiled be by times quick flowing,
> Lovers have in their hearts a clock still going ... (1–2)

As the poem develops, Suckling allegorizes the emotions of lovers, much as Froissart had done, but more briefly, in terms of the parts of a clock – but a more modern clock, driven not by a weight but by a spring and regulated not by a foliot but by a balance wheel:

> Hope is the mainspring which moves desire
> And these do the wheels, fear joy, inspire,
> The balance is thought ... (7–9)

In the final stanza, 'Occasion's the hand which still's moving round', providing an opportunity, when the clock strikes, for 'Kisses ... and what you best like' (13–18) – again, as in Froissart, a comforting conclusion.[38] Whether Suckling knew Froissart's poem is hard to say: Froissart takes the analogy on to himself: 'Je me suis bien comparer à l'orloge ...' (1) [I can well compare myself to the clock ...] but Suckling generalizes the notion to cover all lovers.

However, for those who did not spend their time appropriately, who did not behave with the supposed regularity of the mechanical clock, it could become a threatening or at least a chastening image. Twice in his *Testament*, John Lydgate invokes the clock, self-critically, in relation to his 'gerysh' behaviour, by which he means his 'fickleness' or 'inconsistency':

>   ... Now a good felowe, now all out of ioynte;
>   Now smothe, now stark, now lyke a harde parpoynt;
>   Now as the peys of a diall goth,
>   Now gerysh glad, and anoon after wroth (356–9)
>   ... Fer oute of harre, wilde of condicioun,
>   Ful geryssh, and voyde of all resoun,
>   Lyk a phane, ay turnyng to and fro,
>   Or like an orloge whan the peys is goo (398–401)[39]

Quite what the comparisons 'as the peys of a dial; goth' and 'lyke an orloge whan the peys is goo' mean exactly is difficult to be sure about.[40] If 'goth' and 'goo' mean 'go', 'is working', it is hard to see what can be wrong with the clock. If, on the other hand, they mean 'is gone' or 'is lost' and refer to the weight (*peys*) of the drive-train of the clock, they become fairly meaningless: without the weight the clock would lose all motive power and would stop. But the passages are clearly about inconsistency, and the contrastive juxtaposed phrases and the comparison with the proverbially ever-moving weather-cock (*phane*) 'ay turnyng to and fro' reinforce this.[41] So, perhaps, 'goth' and 'is go' mean 'is gone' or 'is lost' and that Lydgate is referring to the fact that one of the weights (*peys*) balancing the foliot had become detached. In that case the verge and foliot mechanism would not work and the clock would cease to be regulated and keep time poorly, though it would still function, and become a fitting metaphor for his inconsistent behaviour.

For those who wasted time, especially, the clock also became a potentially menacing image. In Shakespeare's *Richard II*, as he languishes in prison in Pomfret Castle after having been forced to give up his throne, the deposed king meditates on the subject. Characteristically, he approaches and leaves the problem in a punning, half-humorous way: a consideration of musical time raises by wordplay the notion of horological time.

>   *Richard*: Music do I hear.
>   Ha, ha; keep time! How sour sweet music is
>   When time is broke and no proportion kept.
>   So is it in the music of men's lives.
>   And here I have the daintiness of ear
>   To check time broke in a disordered string;
>   But for the concord of my state and time
>   Had not an ear to hear my true time broke.
>   I wasted time, and now doth time waste me,
>   For now hath time made me his numb'ring clock.

> My thoughts are minutes, and with sighs they jar
> Their watches on unto mine eyes, the outward watch
> Whereto my finger, like a dial's point,
> Is pointing still in cleansing them from tears.
> Now, sir, the sounds that tell what hour it is
> Are clamorous groans that strike upon my heart,
> Which is the bell. So sighs, and tears, and groans
> Show minutes, hours and times.
> But my time runs posting on in Bolingbroke's proud joy,
> While I stand fooling here, his jack of the clock.
> This music mads me, let it sound no more ... (V. v. 41–61)

To make the man who is hyper-conscious of the passage of time and the way time is his enemy into a clock is bold and imaginative: the passage of time and Richard II's misery, as the allegory unfolds, become co-terminus, 'sighs, and tears, and groans / Show minutes, hours and times' in a one-to-one equivalence. But the passage has resonances beyond the central comparison. The transposed grammatical equivalences of the line 'I wasted time, and now doth time waste me' suggests that he may feel that what has happened to him is part of an unforgiving 'eye for an eye' vengeance. It may also allude to the stories that Richard II was starved to death (*waste*) in Pomfret Castle. But the deposed king is acutely conscious, also, of his lost status as the controller of time, and one recalls his commutation of four years of Bolingbroke's original banishment and Bolingbroke's sardonic comment on it:

> *Bolingbroke*: How long a time lies in one little word!
> Four lagging winters and four wanton springs
> End in a word: such is the breath of kings. (I. iii. 206–8)

But Richard II's time is now controlled by Bolingbroke. When he says it 'runs posting on in Bolingbroke's proud joy' he may intend no more than that while he is imprisoned Bolingbroke is going forever to enjoy kingship. But Shakespeare may also be alluding to the way in which kings had sometimes, following Charles V in 1370, tried to standardize time, or to the way in which noblemen and other dignitaries often had themselves painted with small table-clocks in the background, as status symbols and expensive toys. Richard II clearly feels that in some way he now belongs to Bolingbroke. And by making himself not only into a clock but into a 'jack of the clock' he is enhancing this impression. Clock-jacks were usually dressed as serving-men or labourers, manual workers doing a heavy job with, usually, hammers, and their function in relation to public clocks was, in part at least, to amuse bystanders. The comparison with a clock suggests, not only that the deposed king is conscious, in retrospect, of his wasting of time, but that he feels that he may have become a symbol of Bolingbroke's newly acquired power and a laughing stock, 'fooling' for the amusement of the new king and others.

V

As a model for moral behaviour, however, the timekeeper is best known in the sixteenth and seventeenth centuries because of the use emblem writers made of it. Time was one of the most popular subjects in emblem books, and 'time' as a personified concept appeared in many guises – as an old man with a scythe ('Father Time'), as a winged figure, or as a figure associated with instruments for measuring time. One of the best known of these figures appears in Francis Quarles's *Hieroglyphikes of the Life of Man* (1638) where a lighted candle in an urn, representing human life, is approached by Death and Time: the former is represented as a skeleton holding in his left hand a feathered dart and in his right a snuffer which he is about to place over the candle; the latter appears as an old man with wings holding a sandglass in his left hand. Behind them is a sundial.[42] As a kind of epigraph to the accompanying verses appears the verse from Ecclesiastes 3:1 'To everything there is a time'. And a summary couplet interprets what is going on in the picture:

> The time shall come when all must yield their breath;
> Till then, Time checks th'uplifted hand of Death.

Time is here a preserver as well as a destroyer, because he seeks to restrain the impatience of Death, who wishes immediately to snuff out life's candle. The verses are written as a dialogue, an argument, in the course of which Death complains that the instruments for measuring time run too slowly:

> Time, hold thy peace, and shake thy slow paced Sand;
> Thy idle Minits make no way:
> Thy glasse exceeds her how'r, or else does stand,
> I can not hold, I can not stay ...

The traditional instruments for measuring time appear frequently in emblems – sundials, sandglasses (sometimes with wings), *clepsydrae* – mostly in relation to the swift passing of time, to the course of human life and the ages of man, to the proper and improper uses of time. And, unsurprisingly, mechanical clocks begin to be used in the same contexts.

A fairly simple French example, from Guillaume de la Perriere's *La Morosophie* (1553), shows, in a country landscape with an ominous tree-stump in the foreground, a clock on tall legs. It has a dial with the sun in the middle, roman numerals and a single hand. It is topped by a bell. It is a fairly realistic depiction of a contemporary frame clock, except that, incongruously, wings are attached to each side of it. The going and the striking trains are driven by two weights, on to which a seated man is holding. He is literally doing what the verse recommends – holding on to flying time:

> Advise bien le temps ne t'eschappe:
> Il a bonne aesle, et vole agilement.
> L'homme ruse subitement l'attrappe,
> Et ne le laisse eschapper sottement:
> Donc employer le fault honnestement:
> Car s'il s'enfuyt, l'attaindre est impossible ,
> Et pense aussi qu'il ne t'est pas loysible,
> Le consumer en faisant grosse chere:
> Si tu le perdz, ne te sera possible
> De recouvrer une chose si chere.[43]

[Take good care that time does not escape you, for he has good wings and flies with agility. The skilful man captures him quickly and does not foolishly let him escape. Thus, it is necessary to use him properly, for if he gets away it is impossible to reach him. And consider also that it is not right for you to devour him making great entertainment. If you lose him, it will not be possible for you to recover such a precious thing.]

In another example, from the same source, a young woman, in an idealized spring or summer landscape, sits on a ball, holding in her hands a table clock resting on what looks like a sieve. The subject of the verse is youth, the carelessness of pleasure-seeking youth, and youth's inattention to the passing of time:

> Jeunesse estant sur une boulle ronde,
> Ne pense ailleurs, fors qu'a passer temps;
> Son siege rond, mouable comme l'onde,
> Monstre qu'elle a ses vouloirs inconstantz.
> Les jeunes gens ne sont guieres contents
> De travailler, sinon a leurs desirs:
> Leurs voluptez tournent a desplaisirs,
> Perte de temps, trop grande s'ensuyt,

Jeunesse tasche a tous mondains plaisirs,
Sans adviser que vieillesse la suyt.[44]

[Youth, being on a round ball, does not think about anything else except passing the time. Her round ball, unstable as the wave, demonstrates that she has inconstant wishes. Young people are not very happy to work, except in relation to their desires. Their delights turn to displeasures; too great loss of time follows. Youth tries all worldly pleasures, without considering that old age pursues her.]

A contrast between youth and age is also at the centre of an example from Florentius Schoonhovius's *Emblemata* (1618), but this makes more precise use of the workings of the mechanical clock. The picture shows, in a summer landscape, a man contemplating the inside of a weight-driven clock: it has a dial, a bell on top, and stands on a pedestal framework. The subject of the verse is the contrasts of the world, especially the contrast between speed and caution, and the physics of the mechanical clock provides the starting point. Just as pressure (*nisus*) checks the rapid movement of the wheel (*fervidum motum rotae*) so the far-seeing caution of age restrains (*frenat*) and controls (*regit*) the daring impetuosity of youth. The poem closes by making a point about the operation of these principles in the way a ruler might organize society:

> Idcirco Princeps eligat sibi senes
> Ad consulendum; Iuniores comparet
> Ad exequendum jussa Prudentum senum.[45]

[For that reason, a prince may choose for himself old men for giving counsel; the young are there to execute the orders of prudent elders.]

In an example from Sebastian de Covarrubias Orozco's *Emblemas Morales* (1610), it is again the physics of a clock's movement, this time the weights, which generates the analogy. The poem is in praise of *gravitas* in various punning senses of the word.

> Anda el relox de pesas mas ligero,
> Quando ellas son mas graves y pesadas,
> El hombre quanto mas grave y entero,
> Tanto mas assegura sus pisadas,
> Agil, firme, constante, y verdadero,
> Senalando sus horas compassadas,
> Enfin es un relox, tan regulado,
> Que tarde, o nunca esta desconcertado.[46]

[The clock with weights goes more quickly when the weights are heavier and more substantial. The man, insofar as he is heavier and more robust, is so much more secure in his footsteps, nimble, stable, constant, and true, marking out his measured hours. He is, just like a clock, so regulated that he is never slow or disordered.]

The well-regulated clock is a model for a well-ordered life: the perfection of the machine is something for a human to aspire to and emulate if possible. It is hard to imagine a more complete triumph for the mechanistic view of the world than this little poem.

Finally, I adduce an interesting example of this gnomic and universalising use of the mechanical timekeeper in imaginative literature, in John Webster's *The Duchess of Malfi*, where the Duchess, fearing for the lives of her husband Antonio and their eldest son, counsels flight to Milan – which means they will have to part from her. Antonio moralises this parting in terms of a dismantling of a malfunctioning clock or watch so that it can be put back together 'in better order':

> You counsel safety.
> Best of my life, farewell. Since we must part,
> Heaven hath a hand in't; but no otherwise
> Than as some curious artist takes in sunder
> A clock or watch, when it is out of frame,
> To bring't in better order. (III. v. 59–64)[47]

Antonio's belief that this parting could not be 'otherwise' unless 'Heaven hath a hand in't' suggests that Webster is not only thinking of God – the 'curious artisan' [skilled artificer] – simply as a divine clockmaker, but somebody who, through his providence, can also mend clocks.

VI

The development of the mechanical timekeeper altered the culture of Western Europe. It brought with it a heightened sense of time and privileged virtues such as regularity, constancy, punctuality, exactness. It enhanced the sense – on a spiritual, social and personal level – of the value of time. It suggested ways in which one might organize one's life by dividing it up into compartments – so much time for work, so much time for study, so much time for recreation and rest. And writers reflect about and meditate upon these issues, absorbing the new machine into their literary consciousness.

But the new machine was not universally welcomed. Some writers simply ignored the clock as a means of calculating time. Spenser, as Richard McCabe has pointed out, does not use the word 'clock' in *The Faerie Queene*: 'the precise calibration of time by clocks, calendars and astrological charts is of less importance than the perception of rhythmic correspondences between natural and supernatural sources of renewal'.[48] But Spenser pondered long on topics such as 'mutabilitie', and 'wicked' time does appear in the Garden of Adonis as a destroyer with some features of his traditional form and performing some of his traditional actions. Time 'with his scyth ... Does mow the flowring herbes and goodly things' and later in the same stanza 'He flyes about, and with his flaggy wings / Beates downe both leaves and buds ...'.[49] For others, like Dafydd ap Gwilym, clocks could be ambiguous. In one poem he likens his praise for a girl to 'Gwrle relyn ac orloes' [the sound of the harp or the striking clock], which looks as though he has in mind a striking chamber clock. But in another, a much larger clock with its equinoctial hours, its disregard of the seasons, its imperviousness to day and night, its automatic movement whatever the circumstances, proved irritatingly intrusive. It is a clock which interrupts Dafydd's dream of a beautiful girl:

> Och i'r cloc yn ochr y clawdd
> Du ei ffriw a'm deffroawdd.
> Difwyn fo'i ben a'i dafod
> A'i ddwy raff iddo a'i rod,
> A'i bwysau, pelennau pwl,
> A'i fuarthau a'i fwrthwl,
> A'i hwyaid yn tybiaid dydd,
> A'i felinau aflonydd.
> Cloc anfwyn mal clec ynfyd ... (21–8)[50]

> [Alas, the clock beside the dyke black-countenanced, which awakened me; let its mouth and tongue be vain with its two ropes and its wheel, the stupid balls which are its weights, its four-square case (?) and hammer, with its ducks who think it day, and its restless mill-wheels. Churlish clock with foolish chatter ...]

This must have been written before 1380 when Dafydd is thought to have died. What he refers to is clearly meant to be a mechanical clock, apparently with automata, but none, that I know of, is mentioned in Wales in the fourteenth century. It may have been a monastery clock. But what emerges clearly from this poem is the feeling that it is somehow out of place in what is presented as a rural setting. The sense that the new mechanical timekeeper separates people from the older, more natural rhythm of things – so powerful in the seventeenth century – here gets stated early, and in memorable fashion.

CHAPTER 6

Clocks, order and anxiety in some Renaissance texts

It has been shown earlier that the idea that the universe worked like a clock was current in some writings from the fourteenth century onwards. But not long after Timothy Bright's exposition of the idea in 1591 it became important to both Johannes Kepler (1571–1640) and Robert Boyle (1627–91). As G.J. Whitrow says: early in the seventeenth century 'Kepler specifically rejected the old quasi-animistic conception of the universe and asserted that it was similar to a clock'.[1] Robert Boyle went further and argued that the orderliness and regularity of the universe was an indication of the existence of God, and mentions a specific clock – the Strasbourg clock with its elaborate marionette show:

> ... it is like a rare clock, such as may be that at Strasbourg, when all things are so skilfully contrived, that the engine being once set a-moving, all things proceed according to the artificer's first design, and the motions ... do not require the particular interposing of the artificer, or any intelligent agent employed by him, but perform their functions upon particular occasions, by virtue of the general and primitive contrivance of the whole engine.[2]

The 'mechanical universe' or 'clockwork universe', so enthusiastically espoused by some Enlightenment thinkers of the eighteenth century, was coming into being. Further to this, clocks had come to dominate not only the organization of the church and its services but of daily secular life also: the formal business of the state, the duration of the working day, the precise keeping of appointments, and much else. As Lewis Mumford says: 'The bells of the clock tower almost defined urban existence'.[3] But there was resistance to some of this – not only on a philosophical level – but emanating from lived experience.

One aspect of this doubt had to do with the fact that clocks were not uniformly accurate or reliable. Public clocks were invested with authority in that they dictated the timing of religious and social events. But everybody who lived in a town like London, which had many clocks, knew that they did not strike in unison. And this was complicated by the increasing availability of personalized timekeepers.

For a long time before this, small portable clocks had become status symbols for those who could afford them. In 1481, Louis XI bought from Jehan de Paris 'a clock that has a dial and strikes the hours, complete in all its parts, which clock the king bought to carry with him in all places where he shall go'. In one of his portraits the king had the clock included. And in around 1550, Titian painted a portrait of an unknown Knight of the Order of Malta, whose left hand holds his small table clock, which has a dial and a bell.[4] And, as watches became miniaturized people wore them on their persons. Elizabeth I had one set into a ring, which not only enabled her to tell the time, but also acted as an alarm: it had a small prong which touched her finger to alert her. In 1518 François I had small watches set into the hilts of two of his daggers.[5] A century later, Samuel Pepys takes some pride in owning a watch. His reaction to acquiring it on 12 May 1665 is indicative of the fascination that clocks and watches held in the seventeenth century for those who wished to be fashionable, though he had misgivings about it, because watches were, at this date, notoriously unreliable:

> ... I cannot forbear carrying my watch in my hand in the coach all afternoon, and seeing what a-clock it is a 100 times. And am apt to think with myself: how could I be so long without one – though I remember since, I had one and found it a trouble, and resolved to carry one no more about me while I lived.[6]

His misgivings were not misplaced. On 14 July 1665 he tells us that the watch was back at the clockmakers 'mending'. Nevertheless, Pepys did use his watch for exact timekeeping after it had been repaired. On 13 September 1665 he records that he 'walked to Greenwich, taking pleasure to walk with my minute watch in my hand, by which I am now come to see the distances of my way from Woolwich to Greenwich. And do find myself to come within two minutes constantly to the same place at the end of each quarter of an hour.'[7] But Pepys was interested more generally in clocks and watches and on 22 December 1665 he records how he spent an evening with Viscount William Brouncker 'by my desire seeing his lordship open to pieces and make up again his watch, thereby being taught what I never knew before, and it is a thing very worth while my having seen, and am mightily pleased and satisfied with it.'[8] The skill possessed by Lord Brouncker would have been rare outside professional clockmakers. But Lord Brouncker was a fine scientist, a member of the Royal Society and President in 1662. He is exceptional in all sorts of ways. The possession and intricacies of watches were for the few among whom Pepys felt himself privileged to belong. In general, however, good clocks and watches and good clockmakers were rare at this time, and reliability was difficult to attain. When a reliable watch was to be found, according to Sir John Suckling, others set theirs by it:

> But as when an authentic watch is shown,
> Each man winds up and rectifies his own ...⁹

As now, people tended to set their watches by reference to public clocks, though these among themselves tended to be inconsistent. Even after he acquired a watch Pepys listened to the bells.

But the possession of personalized timekeepers generated literary comment – often sceptical, witty and indirect – but addressing what was perceived to be a problem; the perception of a supposed orderliness that was flawed generated various kinds of anxiety.

II

This could take strangely odd forms, where philosophical ideas are not to the forefront. On the English stage, Berowne's cynical comments on clocks and women in *Love' Labours Lost*, III. i (discussed in the following chapter) appear to have generated a theatrical convention in which unreliable watches were discussed in relation to the unreliability of women in sexual matters.¹⁰ One example, among many, can be found in Thomas Middleton's *Women Beware Women* (?1621) as Bianca converses, in a desultory fashion, with her companions, who all, like the fashionable ladies they are, have watches:

Bianca:	How goes your watches, ladies? What's o'clock now?
First Lady:	By mine full nine.
Second Lady:	By mine a quarter past.
First Lady:	I set mine by St Mark's.
Second Lady:	St Anthony's they say
	Goes truer.
First Lady:	That's but your opinion, madam,
	Because you love a gentleman o' th' name.
Second Lady:	He's a true gentleman then.
First Lady:	So may he be
	That comes to me tonight, for aught you know.
Bianca:	I'll end this strife straight. I set mine by the sun,

>   I love to set by th' best; one shall not then
>   Be troubled to set often.
> *Second Lady*:   You do wisely in't.
> *Bianca*:   If I should set my watch as some girls do
>   By every clock i' th' town 't would ne'er go true;
>   And too much turning of the dial's point,
>   Or tamp'ring with the spring, might in small time
>   Spoil the whole work too ... (IV. i. 1–15)[11]

The passage has to be read carefully: it is important that there is a discrepancy of a quarter of an hour between two of the watches, but not simply so, nor the sentimental attachment associated with a name. But the scene in part depends on wordplay and allusiveness and there is more than a little sexual innuendo in it: 'dial's point' may signify the penis, and 'spring' in the punning sense of 'river' or 'stream' may refer to the female genitalia.[12] It is also set in Florence, though the two churches mentioned are probably not Florentine – though they may be Italian.[13] But the basic issue of the unreliability of watches and of public clocks would have been instantly understood by a London audience, for London clocks were proverbially infamous for their inconsistency.[14] According to Bianca, the only reliable measure of time was the 'sun', that is time as calculated by the sundial – trust that and do not tamper with your pocket watch, a metaphor for being careful with whom you associate as a lover. Here too there is a pun on 'sun' / 'son' signifying her commitment to the ruler, the Duke of Florence. In Thomas Dekker's *The Honest Whore*, III. i. 113, Infelice, wrongly accused of sexual promiscuity, defends herself similarly by the metaphor of the watch: 'mine goes by heaven's Diall (the Sunne) and it goes true'. The ladies' watches here are more-or-less fashion accessories, though they have some use in informing them of the time, especially in relation to meeting their lovers. One suspects that this scene also served to give Middleton, a Londoner, an opportunity to be disparaging about London clocks – which no doubt amused his knowing London audience.

In the fiction of Middleton's play, these ladies are sophisticated people dwellers in a city where public clocks are common and where the possession of a personalized timekeeper is taken for granted and its workings – to a limited degree – understood. But this was not the case everywhere, particularly in provincial England. Clocks, particularly personalized timekeepers, in the seventeenth century were expensive accoutrements and not generally possessed by those who were not wealthy or at least well-to-do and sophisticated. David S. Landes's words still hold generally true about the diffusion of ownership: 'Where once clocks had been the conspicuous consumption and privilege of an exalted few, two centuries of technical advance and production experience had now made them available to a widening circle of bourgeois'.[15] But not everyone was familiar with them and to those who were not they could be disconcerting and disturbing. The famous story about Thomas Allen's watch, in John Aubrey's *Brief lives*, is worth repeating in this context. Thomas Allen was an Oxford university teacher, the owner of many mathematical and scientific instruments – and a watch. Staying with a friend of his on vacation in remote Herefordshire, he left his watch, presumably with a chain or cord ('string') attached, on the windowsill of his bedroom:

> The maydes came in to make the bed, and hearing a thing in a case crying tick, tick, tick, presently concluded that it was the Devill, and took it by the string with the tongues, and threw it out of the windowe into the mote, (to drown the Devill). It so happened that the string hung on the sprig of an elder that grewe out of the mote, and this confirmed them 'twas the Devil.[16]

The contrast here is stark and illuminating despite Aubrey's penchant for the bizarre and the comic. Allen is a sophisticated and learned man, who knows about watches and their use: for him the watch is a scientific instrument which enables him the better to organize his life, and perhaps also the better to decorate his person. For the 'maydes', however, it represents a threat: lower-class girls, presumably, and from provincial backgrounds, they can only understand it in terms of maleficent magic and act accordingly. Aubrey reassures the reader that Thomas Allen got his watch back, but one wonders if he, or Aubrey, ever pondered the implications of the story beyond its comedy, and in Allen's case beyond his relief at not losing his watch.

The clockmakers had invented not only a useful instrument, though it was not always reliable, but one that could be used associatively, like other timekeepers: to the 'maydes' it was unintentionally disturbing and interpreted in a way which made sense to them. But more generally watches could be used to denote transience and the passing of things. In 'Vanitas, Still Life' of 1671, Philippe de Champaigne paints a tulip in a glass vase and an hourglass on either side of a skull. But watches are also to be found in this sort of painting. In one of his many paintings of flowers entitled 'Stilleven met Bloemen en een Horloge', Abraham Mignon (1640–79) depicts a vase of cut flowers, some of which are beginning to droop and lose petals, which is accompanied on the same table by an open silver watch with a blue knotted cord attached to it (see Plate 13).[17] Time here seems to be a destroyer, though evidently a gentle one. Others are more stark. In another 'vanitas' painting by Pieter Claesz of 1630

15 Pierre Moysant's skull watch.

he sets, on a table, a skull on top of some books and papers and in front of it an open pocket watch with a cord attached to it (see Plate 14). In another, this time anonymous, Netherlandish painting of the seventeenth century, the skull and the open watch are accompanied, on what looks like a shelf, by some dice, two rings and various coins. In such contexts watches could be, at best, disconcerting and, at worst, terrifying. And this was recognized by clockmakers themselves. The Prague clock's striking mechanism, as we have seen, is activated by a marionette of a skeleton that pulls a rope. But personalized timekeepers, precisely because they are personalized, more often make the point about time and death usually by way of engravings: they are closer to the individual possessor than any public clock. And they are frequently severely moralistic. A table watch given by Sir William Cooper to Elizabeth Cooper, his daughter-in-law, in 1539 has a coat of arms on the cover and engravings on the dial. The figure of Christ is accompanied by emblems of death and two mottoes: 'Vigilate et orate quia nescitis horam' [Watch and pray for you know not when the time is, Luke 13:33] and 'Quaelibet hora ad mortem vestigium' [Every hour is a step towards death].[18]

'Memento mori' watches in the shape of skulls became fairly common in the sixteenth and seventeenth centuries: people carried reminders of death in their pockets. One such, probably made by Pierre Moysant (*alias* Moyse) of Blois, is very elaborate (see Figure 15).[19] The skull is silver gilt and is generously incised. On the forehead is death as a skeleton with his scythe and sandglass, standing between a cottage and a palace, and around the picture is a text from Horace: 'Pallida mors aequo pulsat pede pauperum tabernas regumque turres' [Pale death visits with impartial foot the cottages of the poor and the towers of the rich], *Odes* I. iv. 13–14. On the back of the skull is Time, again with a scythe, and another text from Horace: 'Tempus edax rerum tuque invidiosa vetustas' [Time and you, envious old age, are devourers of all things] *Metamorphoses*, XV. 234. There is a serpent with its tail in its mouth, an emblem of eternity, incised on this panel too. In the two panels on the top of the skull appear the fall of man, which brought death into the world, and the crucifixion, with an inscription stressing that death has been overcome: 'Sic justiciae satis fecit, mortem superavit, salutem comparavit' [Thus justice was satisfied, death overcome, and salvation obtained]. Emblems of the crucifixion run round the openwork beneath the four panels. Inside the watchcase is the holy family with Jesus in the manger, and on the silver dial appears Saturn eating his children – time the devourer. It can be argued that all clocks stress the inexorable passage of time and the inevitability of death, but watches of this sort make it especially plain.

Many watches were not as censorious as this, but it is probably a watch of this sort that Ciro di Pers (1599–1633) is thinking of when he writes his famous sonnet 'L'Orologio da Ruote':

> Nobile ordigno di dentate rote
> Lacera il giorno e lo divide in ore,
> Ed ha scritto di fuor con fosche note
> A chi legger le sa: SEMPRE SI MORE. (1–4)[20]

> [The excellent instrument with toothed cogs tears the day and divides it into hours, and it has written on the outside with black letters, for whoever can read them, WE ARE DYING ALWAYS.]

The motto on the watch case is perhaps best understood as the continuous present tense, because this is very much a poem not about sudden death but about the inexorable step-by-step journey to death through time, marked out by the movement of the clock: the idea of time the devourer is present here in a very precise way in relation to the toothed (*dentate*) cogs of the clock's movement that chew up the day, and this idea returns later in the sonnet in the phrase 'eta vorace' [voracious age]. But it is the ceaseless sound of the clock that grips his attention, the ticking in the 'hollow metal' (*metallo concavo*) is like a 'funereal voice' (*voce funesta*) which 'echoes' (*risuona*) in his heart. They are like instruments of war, a drum or a trumpet, daring him onwards. And it is with metallic sound that the poem closes:

> E con que' colpi onde 'l metal rimbomba,
> Affretta il corso al secola fugace,
> E perche s'apra, ognor piccia alla tomba. (12–14)
>
> [And with those beats from which the metal resounds, one's progress hastens through flying time, and each hour taps on the tomb so that it will open.]

What desolates the writer of this poem is the sheer mechanical repetitiousness of the time his clock delivers, of which one is reminded in every tick. This feeling became common and could be replicated many times over. But I end this chapter with four examples, from Marlowe, Shakespeare, Donne and Lord Herbert of Cherbury.

III

How it appeared to the original audience is something that one can only speculate about, but the striking of the mechanical clock in the last scene of *Dr Faustus* retains its ability to shock at once by its surprise and by the inevitability of its logic. The coming of death is a traditional feature of morality drama, but what gave Marlowe the idea of using the clock can only be guessed at. Perhaps because the story is set in Germany and that German clocks were imported into England in the latter part of the sixteenth century suggested it. Or perhaps the twenty-four years' contract with the devil, which Marlowe inherited from the traditional story, suggested an analogy with the hours of the day. Or perhaps the fact that Faustus is a scholar and that the play begins and ends with him in his study had something to do with it, for clocks and other instruments for measuring time were often found in Renaissance libraries and studies. But this is a scholar's tragedy. Faustus's study is also a library and his tragedy is initially generated by books, and later by writing. At the opening of the play Faustus, in his study, contemplates his books and expresses dissatisfaction with four canonical authors – Aristotle, Galen, Justinian and even Jerome's Bible – preferring instead the 'metaphysics of magicians / And necromantic books' (I. 48–9) which, at the end of the play, he recognizes (too late) have been his undoing: 'I'll burn my books' he says as the devils take him (XIX. 190).

In the intervening period, Faustus has been given control over many things, including time, for twenty-four years: it has enabled him to make present figures from the past, though 'these are but shadows not substantial' (Alexander and his concubine, XII. 54; Helen of Troy, XVIII. 28, 99), as well as seemingly disturbing the natural order of the seasons by producing grapes in January (XVII. 21) for the Duke of Vanholt and his Duchess.[21] But he has scarcely done anything important with this ability. Thomas a Kempis had written: 'It is sad that you do not employ your time better, when you may win eternal life hereafter. The time will come when you will long for one day or one hour in which to mend, and who knows whether it will be granted.'[22] It is this process of wishing for more time, too late, that Faustus goes through on his last night as the clock strikes eleven:

> Now hast thou but one bare hour to live
> And then thou must be damn'd perpetually.
> Stand still, you ever-moving spheres of heaven,
> That time may cease, and midnight never come;
> Fair nature's eye, rise, rise, again and make
> Perpetual day; or let this hour be but
> A year, a month, a week, a natural day,
> That Faustus may repent and save his soul. (XIX. 134–41)

He quotes a version of a line from Ovid's *Amores*, I. xii. 40, 'O lente, lente currite noctis equi' [O run slowly, slowly, horses of the night!] where Ovid tries to prolong a pleasurable night he has spent with his lover – unavailingly. It could be done – but only if you were a god: in *Amores* I. xiii. 45–6 Jove artificially extended the night he spent with Alcmena, when Hercules was conceived, by ordering the chariot of the moon make three circuits of the heavens. Faustus had thought that his pact with the devil and his abilities at the magical arts might make him at least into a demigod:

> A sound magician is a demi-god;
> Here tire, my brains, to get a deity! (I. 61–2)

But Faustus is neither a deity nor a demigod. Nor does he exist in the mythological world of Ovidian time. His time is organized by the striking of the clock, the contemporary mechanical timekeeper which had its own scientific momentum. The time of the clock is not reversible, or extendable, or stoppable. 'The stars move still, time runs, the clock will strike.' (XIX. 143). No evasion is possible for Faustus, no escape, and the 'watch' strikes, in turn, the half hour (163) and finally 'The clock striketh twelve':

> O, it strikes, it strikes! Now, body, turn to air,
> Or Lucifer will bear thee quick to hell! (183–4).

It may be tempting, at this point, to imagine that there is something superstitious being implied here – the belief that evil was particularly powerful and effective at midnight[23] – but midnight here is simply important because it is the end of the day, the final day of Faustus's twenty-four years.

He had earlier made a written agreement couched in legalistic terms, very like a promissory note, which he signs:

> I, John Faustus of Wittenberg, doctor, by these presents so give both body and soul to Lucifer, prince of the east, and his minister Mephistophilis, and furthermore grant unto them that, four-and-twenty years being expired, the articles above written inviolate, full power to fetch and carry the said John Faustus, body and soul, flesh, blood, or goods into their habitation wheresoever. By me John Faustus' (V. 105–12)

In the following line Mephistophilis refers to the document as 'your deed'.

The transaction in which Faustus has engaged with the devil is formulated rather like a business agreement. As he explains to the scholars earlier in the scene: 'I writ him a bill with mine own blood: the date is expired; the time will come and he will fetch me' (XIX. 66–8). So it is perhaps appropriate that the mechanical clock, which had come to regulate business, should be the instrument by means of which Faustus is held to account.

But it is clear that Marlowe had also been thinking seriously about clocks and closure, perhaps on a more metaphysical or philosophical level, from the laconic signing off formula for the play: 'Terminat hora diem, terminat auctor opus' [the hour ends the day, the author ends his work] – though this again is rendered in terms of the workers being released from toil at a predetermined moment, timed by the clock.

IV

Shakespeare 'conceded, more readily than Spenser or any of his great contemporaries, the mechanical origins of his anxiety', writes John Kerrigan, in relation to the appearance and importance of the clock in the *Sonnets*.[24] In fact, a whole range of systems relating to the passing of time is invoked – the turning of the seasons, the labours of the months, the lunar cycle, the course of the sun through the day, the ages of man. And other sorts of timekeepers are referred to, particularly the sundial and the sandglass. But, especially in the sequence of sonnets 1–126, the clock is a powerful presence, as Shakespeare tries to persuade the 'fair young man' to recognize the aging process, to marry and have children as a way, along with others, of overcoming time and achieving for himself some sort of immortality. When the clock appears it is, significantly enough, in Sonnet 12, and its opening line stresses counting, the striking of a clock which registers the 24-hour cycle in two sets of twelve: 'When I do count the clock that tells the time ... (1).' And there follow, as the sonnet is developed, reference to the alternation between 'brave day and hideous night' (2), the human aging process in 'sable curls all silvered o'er with white' (4), the natural seasonal cycle in 'lofty trees ... barren of leaves' (5) and two punning lines which elide the natural cycle and the human – harvest time with a funeral:

> ... summer's green all girded up in sheaves
> Borne on the bier with white and bristly beard. (7–8)

Appropriately, 'Time's scythe' appears in the penultimate line. The mechanical clock appears again, significantly in Sonnet 60, which deals with 'minutes':

> Like as the waves make towards the pebbled shore,
> So do our minutes hasten to their end ... (1–2)

The first clocks with minute hands appeared in the sixteenth century and it is one of these that Shakespeare has in mind, the contemplation of which, with the number of the sonnet, generates the opening.[25] Time is here broken down into ever smaller segments, but some of the images and themes of the earlier sonnet reappear. There are allusions to the 'labours of the months' in the phrase 'sequent toil' (4) and the human aging process as 'nativity ... crawls to maturity' and 'delves the parallels in beauty's brow' (5–8). In this sonnet time gives and then takes away: 'nothing stands but for his scythe to mow' (12).

None of the other sonnets begins with the clock, but the clock, nevertheless, haunts the sequence. In Sonnet 115, for example, 'reckoning Time', that is, time that counts and is counted, and also time that holds one to account in a legal and mercantile sense, appears and it is a destructive figure:

> ... reckoning Time, whose millioned accidents
> Creep in 'twixt vows and change decrees of kings,
> Tan sacred beauty, blunt the sharp'st intents,
> Divert strong minds to th'course of alt'ring things ... (115. 5–7)

The word 'creep' alludes to the saying 'Time creeps', and 'tan' suggests the aging process. All this appears again, in a slightly altered form, in the sestet of Sonnet 104, another text about aging and the passage of time:

> ... yet doth beauty, like a dial hand,
> Steal from his figure, and no pace perceived;
> So your sweet hue, which methinks still doth stand,
> Hath motion, and mine eye may be deceived;
> For fear of which, hear this, thou age unbred:
> Ere you were born was beauty's summer dead. (9–14)

The idea of seasonal time is obviously present in the last phrase, but much of this relates to timekeeping. The 'dial hand' is the hand of the mechanical clock, which 'steals', in the proverbial sense,[26] because it is difficult to perceive its slow but unstoppable movement ('no pace perceived'), just as it is difficult to perceive, in the short term, the aging process: it may appear that the young man's beauty 'still doth stand' but that is an illusion – the poet may be 'deceived' – because actually the process of aging 'hath motion', and continues whether one can register it in the short term or not. It is the constant ticking away of time which cannot be reversed which proved to be the most disturbing aspect of the mechanical clock.

This theme may even appear, in an etiolated form, in the last poem of this sequence, Sonnet 126, which pulls together many of the ideas and images about time[27] which run through the whole work:

> O thou, my lovely boy, who in thy power
> Dost hold Time's fickle glass, his sickle hour,
> Who hast by waning grown, and therein show'st
> Thy lovers withering, as thy sweet self grow'st;
> If Nature, sovereign mistress over wrack,
> As thou goest onwards, still will pluck thee back,
> She keeps thee to this purpose, that her skill
> May Time disgrace and wretched minutes kill.
> Yet fear her, O thou minion of her pleasure;
> She may detain, but not still keep her treasure.
> Her audit, though delayed, answered must be,
> And her quietus is to render thee.

By a bold metaphorical transference Shakespeare makes the 'lovely boy' into a figure of time: he holds the hourglass and the sickle. He has grown older, more impressive, as time has passed and as his lovers have been 'withering' –

ostensibly a seasonal metaphor which is picked up later. But 'sickle' and 'waning' also suggest movement through time by way of the lunar cycle, and 'waning' and growing here have been read at one level as referring back to the hourglass: as the top compartment gets emptier, the pile of material in the bottom compartment grows. The clock is suggested by 'minutes', and the argument, briefly, seems to allow that 'Nature', who keeps the boy looking young may be intending in this case to 'kill' time, reversing the normal processes. But the last four lines recognize the inevitability of the process of aging: Nature can 'detain', in the sense of 'slow down', but not keep him 'still', that is, 'in a static state' as well as 'constantly'. In the last couplet 'audit' and 'quietus' are accounting words and the idea of paying one's debt to nature, that is, 'dying' is present by implication. Though it concludes a sequence of sonnets, this poem is not in the conventional fourteen-line form: it consists of twelve lines in couplets. Thomas Thorpe, in 1609, printed it with two sets of brackets where lines 13 and 14 might have been, as if something was missing. But the poem makes complete sense as it is, and it may well be, since he had used the number 12 earlier to generate a poem on a clock, that Shakespeare wanted this numerical association in the final poem of this sequence.

V

On 27 February 1614, John Harrington, 2nd baron of Exton, died of smallpox at the age of twenty-two. John Donne, who was a friend of his sister Lucy, countess of Bedford, wrote an elegy for him,[28] which uses some of the same ideas as the passage quoted from Middleton's play. The dead young man was said to have been 'the most complete young gentleman of his age this kingdom could afford for religion, learning and courteous behaviour',[29] and in one place Donne compares him to a pocket watch and regrets that the small compass of his life did not allow him to become like a public clock:

> Though as small pocket-clocks, whose every wheel
> Doth each mismotion and distemper feel,
> Whose hand gets shaking palsies, and whose string
> (His sinews) slackens, and whose soul, the spring,
> Expires, or languishes, whose pulse, the fly,
> Either beats not, or beats unevenly,
> Whose voice, the bell, doth rattle, or grow dumb,
> Or idle, as men, which to their last hours come,
> If these clocks be not wound, or be wound still,
> Or be not set, or set at every will;

> So youth is easiest to destruction,
> If then we follow all, we follow none.
> Yet, as in great clocks, which in steeples chime,
> Placed to inform whole towns, to employ their time,
> An error doth more harm, being general,
> When, small clocks' faults, only on the wearer fall;
> So work the faults of age, on which the eye
> Of children, servants, or the state rely.
> Why wouldst not thou then, which hadst such a soul,
> A clock so true, as might the sun control,
> And daily hadst from him, who gave it thee,
> Instructions, such as it could never be
> Disordered, stay here, as a general
> And great sundial, to have set us all? (131–54)

The comparison is on one level the vehicle for what Donne is trying to say here – which is that Harrington's life was so exemplary that it was a pity that it should have been so short, for, had he lived longer, he would have provided a model of behaviour for others, just as an accurate public clock regulates the behaviour of whole towns, whereas a good pocket watch is a personalized timekeeper and regulates the behaviour of its owner only.

Nevertheless, what the passage says or suggests about clocks, and particularly about pocket watches, is interesting. It is clear that Donne knew about the mechanics of pocket watches: we know that he possessed one, for he bequeathed to his brother-in-law Sir Thomas Grymes 'that striking clock which I ordinarily wear'.[30] All early clocks and the large public clocks of Donne's day were powered by falling weights, but in watches the 'spring' provided the motive force and it is a spring-driven watch that Donne has in mind here. One of the problems with early spring-driven watches was the equalization of motive force as the mainspring wound down. This was addressed first by a stack-feed mechanism, and later by the device of the fusee wheel, conical in shape, which acted as an intermediary wheel between the mainspring and the wheel-train of the watch, and around which a cord (later a chain) passed.[31] This is the 'string' Donne mentions here and he explains its function in one of his sermons: 'In a watch, the string moves nothing, but yet, it conserves the regularity of the motion of all'.[32] Since this watch has a 'bell' it must have had a striking train, and the 'fly' is the device that regulates the speed of the stroke. The singular 'hand' is interesting, because it suggests that Donne had in mind a watch with only an hour hand – which was the case with most early watches.³³ This is the reading of most of the manuscripts. But some of the manuscripts and the 1633 print of Donne's *Poems* read 'hands', so clearly there were those who thought that watches normally at this time had a minute hand as well.³⁴

Donne, as the possessor of a watch and the possessor of knowledge as to how it worked, was also among the privileged. But apart from his familiarity with the mechanics of clockwork what is notable about Donne's passage is that, for him, clocks and watches had important social functions: they exist to tell the people how to 'employ their time'. It is true that the clock enabled people to measure time more accurately, but it did not enable them to control it any the better. Quite the reverse in fact. The regular and incessant ticking of the clock, measuring the time in exact pulses without reference to anything except its own constructed mechanism, brought a new sense of anxiety into ideas about the passage of time: the clock not only measured out the progress of a human life but, minute by minute, ticked it on to death: despite Harrington's abilities and virtue 'all is at once sunk in the whirlpool death' (162). The pocket watch is here a vehicle for Donne to address, elegantly and appropriately, the question of unrealized hopes and unfulfilled potential in relation to the young man's death.

VI

Equally disconcerting, but in a different way, is my final text. As clock-makers' skills developed timepieces became increasingly accurate, and it became possible to divide time into ever smaller units: clocks with second hands became increasingly available in the seventeenth century. And it is the small divisions of time, as well as the sleeplessness and the dark thoughts attendant on that condition, which generate the anxiety behind Lord Herbert of Cherbury's poem *To his Watch when he could not Sleep*. Like the 'maydes' he was technically a provincial: his holdings were mainly in the adjacent county of Shropshire. But Lord Herbert was a different kind of provincial – a diplomat, politician, scholar, poet, an habitué of the court, and a possessor of a watch, which, unlike the 'maydes' in Aubrey's provincial story, he understands only too well:

> Uncessant minutes, whil'st you move you tell
> The time that tells our life, which though it run
> Never so fast or farr, your new begun
> Short steps shall overtake; for though life well

> May scape his own account, it shall not yours,
> You are Death's auditors, that both divide
> And summ what ere that life inspir'd endures
> Past a beginning, and through you we bide
>
> The doom of Fate, whose unrecall'd decree
> You date, bring, execute; making what's new,
> Ill and good, old, for as we die in you
> You die in Time, Time in Eternity.[35]

The phrase 'new begun' perhaps recognizes the recent emergence of the watch, or perhaps that he purchased this one recently. But much of this is traditional. It is again about counting and accounting, as in Sonnet 126, the final sonnet of Shakespeare's first sequence: 'tell' again here means 'communicate' as well as 'count out', and the idea of death as the closing of a financial account is again present throughout. For the rest the language is simple and deliberately very specific. It is the prefixes in words like 'uncessant' and 'unrecall'd' denoting the nature of mechanical time, the 'minutes' steadily ticking by, which cannot be recovered, which seize Lord Herbert's attention. They are 'Death's auditors' because they both 'divide' and add up ('summ') the course of a life. And they operate without any moral distinction, counting out whatever is 'ill and good' in the same mechanical way. The end of the poem alludes to a problem – the relationship of time to eternity – which had puzzled thinkers from Plato onwards, but it is not further pursued here at any philosophical level. The lines may be intended to be consolatory: 'minutes' disappear in the more general flux of time, and time itself may be subsumed in eternity, which is different from time. But all this does not cancel the disturbing paradox that the 'short steps' of time have the ability to 'overtake' life 'though it run / Never so fast or farr'.

Mechanical time had its own momentum and nothing demonstrated this more insistently than the personalized timekeeper that became an ever-present accoutrement for the better-off: when it was not in their pockets it was on their bedside tables. On 24 June 1664 Samuel Pepys mentions seeing in the Queen's bedchamber 'a clock by her bedside wherein a lamp burns that tells her the time of the night at any time'.[36] The mechanical timekeeper had become domesticated, familiarized, but it did not make it any the less disconcerting for all that. The beautifully articulated syntax of the poem, though it is of three rhymed stanzas, constitutes (in the interpretation of modern editors, with which I agree) a single sentence. It never hesitates or deviates, never wavers into self-pity or sentimentality, but follows its own inexorable, partly linguistic and syntactic, logic. There is no flinching about what the poem asserts, but formally and artistically, there is also a simple, but intelligent and clear-eyed, endorsement of the inevitability and truth of what it says. The poem recognizes the new mechanistic world of time, and, perhaps reluctantly, in understanding what his watch tells him, the sophisticated Lord Herbert accepts it. He adjusts to modern time – the time of the mechanical clock – and recognizes the adjustment, as we all have to.

CHAPTER 7

Some conclusions

As CLOCKS BECAME MORE USED in the sixteenth century, and as their production and types proliferated, there appear to have emerged differences and rivalries between various kinds of clockmakers. It can be established that blacksmiths continued to be the major makers and repairers of large public clocks – whether they were urban or ecclesiastical: R.W. Symonds quotes an entry in the farm accounts of the Lancashire family of Shuttlecocks in 1597 for '... the smith of Lostoke for working one day at the cloke at Smithelles vj d'.[1] But this situation was largely though not entirely confined to the villages and towns of the shires. Matters changed substantially for clockmakers in the sixteenth and seventeenth centuries as smaller timepieces – domestic clocks and watches – became more in demand. As Carlo Cipolla trenchantly and accurately states it: 'The craftsmen who had to satisfy the new vogue now needed the skills of the goldsmiths rather than those of the blacksmiths and locksmiths. In England, France, Germany, Italy, and in many other places, a clear-cut distinction developed between "makers of big public clocks" and "makers of little clocks and watches".' And he goes on to demonstrate that 'after the middle of the fifteenth century, at least in the more developed areas, the great majority of clockmakers came from the large social stratum of artisans that was characteristic of European towns'.[2]

But, he writes, thinking particularly of watches, 'In matters of horology English backwardness was conspicuous until the last decades of the sixteenth century': clockmakers tended to produce 'unimaginative but diligent replicas of French and German models'.[3] Earlier, in England, for finer work, usually on smaller, domestic clocks, patrons had recourse to foreign workers, particularly those from Germany: when Henry VIII got interested in astronomy and timekeeping he appointed the Bavarian Nicholas Kratzer, 'Nicholas the astronomer', as the 'deviser of the kings horlogeries' (see Plate 15). He was essentially a mathematician, so 'deviser' may mean that he planned the make-up and structure of the clocks, but he is also recorded as having been paid six shillings for 'mending of a clok', so he may have had more practical skills: this is also suggested by the portrait of him after Holbein in which he holds a clock on which he is working and on the table before him are the tools of his trade.⁴ Henry VIII's Privy Purse expenses for 1529 to 1532 record many purchases of 'clokkes and dialles', mainly from foreign clockmakers resident in England. From an inventory of the king's wardrobe in British Library MS Harley 1519 come some contemporary descriptions of some royal clocks, which were elaborate and highly decorated: 'one clocke of iron with a larum to the same with the Kinges arms crowned vppon the same with three counter bases of copper, two of them wreathen and gilte and the third playne and with small counter bases of like copper and gilte'. Then there is another iron clock 'haveinge doors of copper and not gilte, with three belles and two men that striketh the hours on top of the bell'. It also had 'an egle gilte set vppon a case of iron' and defined the changes of the moon. This looks as though it was a lantern clock with clock-jacks. Then there is another iron striking clock 'in a case of glass', set in 'iron gilte' and painted. The quite reasonable deduction follows that 'the royal clocks in Henry's palaces were not the product of the English blacksmith's forge, but the work of alien handicraftsmen'.⁵ This is borne out by F.J. Britten who points out that in August 1530, fifteen pounds was paid 'to a Frenchman called Drulardy, for iij dyalls and a clokk'. He also notes that in December of that year money was paid to 'Vincent Keney clok maker for xj clokkes and dialls', who sounds as though he was English or Irish. 'So many payments within a brief period', writes Britten, 'warrant the assumption that the clocks were a form of present favoured by his majesty'. Henry VIII is said to have given an ornate bracket clock as a wedding present to Anne Boleyn. It was later bought by Queen Victoria and is now in Windsor Castle, but who made it is not known.⁶

This situation persisted for a long time: many makers of clocks and watches, attracted by the prosperity of Britain, particularly London, came from south Germany and the Low Countries, fleeing religious persecution, and there were Huguenot craftsmen from France. Many made outstanding small clocks and watches – people like Francis and Michael Nouwen from Brabant and Nicholas Vallin from Flanders. They sometimes bought their way into one of the craft guilds or City Companies, principally in order to legitimize their trade and have access to markets, sometimes into the Blacksmiths Company, or any other guild which would admit them. But some operated on the margins of the law, in the 'liberties' where guild rules were more difficult to enforce.⁷ There were outstanding English makers, particularly of domestic clocks, like Bartholomew Newsom, and later a number who operated in London – but this situation could not go on indefinitely, and English clockmakers increasingly felt themselves to be under-appreciated, their skills disparaged and their livelihoods threatened. It is perhaps a sign of the times that Berowne in *Love's Labours Lost* targets what he perceives as the unreliability of women, with a series of horological puns comparing them to German clocks:

> What? I love, I sue, I seek a wife?
> A woman, that is like a German clock,
> Still a-repairing, ever out of frame,
> And never going aright, being a watch,
> But being watched that it may still go right. (III. i. 184–87)

The last line appears to mean that women, like clocks, need constant vigilance if they are to be made to behave properly. Berowne's disparagement of women is deliberately unfair – it is part of his self-fashioning – but he is also unfair to 'German' clocks and watches, of which many were imported into England: the products of German manufacture were not notably more unreliable than those of English makers. Moreover, he is totally contradicted by the opinion of Fynes Morison, in about 1600, who had travelled widely in Europe. In his *Itinerary* he writes that 'touching manuall arts, the Dutch are a people more industrious then the Germans and excell them in all arts and trades' but makes an exception of 'the Germans of Nuremberg' who are regarded as 'the best workmen for clockes and some like thinges'.[8] He also says later that the English 'prefer strangers as well physitians as other like professors then their own countrymen as more learned and skilful then they are …'.[9] But this generalization did not hold – at least not for long – as far as clockmakers were concerned, because in 1622, as there had been earlier in 1618 and 1620, there was a formal registration of discontent by some of the native populace. Sixteen clockmakers, citizens and householders of the city of London petitioned the king that they were 'much aggrieved both in their astates credittes and trading through the multiplicitie of forreiners using their profession in London'.[10]

In 1631 the trade became more formalized and regulated, with the establishment of the Worshipful Company of Clockmakers of London by means of a charter granted by Charles I (see Plate 16). This embodied, as is the case with most charters of this kind, a restrictive and protective attitude to the trade and its practitioners, and was not good news for those clockmakers who belonged to the Blacksmiths Company, or to some other guilds, or for those who chose to work within the 'liberties'. Its structure resembled the structure of the earlier London companies. The governing body comprised of fourteen 'assistants' chosen from the 'freedom' to serve, three 'wardens' who were to serve the Master, all elected by a simple majority vote (as is apparently the situation today). The first master appointed was David Ramsey, a

Scotsman, but he scarcely attended meetings, and Henry Archer, one of the wardens, usually acted in his stead.

The charter (some of whose items I paraphrase) sets out criteria for membership: the company was to include all English clockmakers, whether freemen of the city or not, who lived within the city or within a radius of ten miles around it. In addition, no foreigner should attempt to work within the area covered by the charter, unless he was naturalized or was working with a recognized professional clockmaker. But the company's reach could extend outside London and the ten-mile radius: it was allowed by the charter to regulate all present and future trade throughout the whole of England. According to the charter, the stated object of the foundation of the company was the protection of the public interest and the company was allowed to punish and reform abuses, which included the making and offering for sale of badly made or deceitful goods. To this end it was stipulated that no Englishman or foreigner who had imported horological artefacts, or parts of them, into England or Wales, should attempt to market them before they had been brought to the Clockmakers' Hall or meeting place and inspected by the court and duly approved and marked. Officers of the Clockmakers' Company were also permitted to enter any kind of ship or land-based premises where they suspected horological items to be present and, if they were found to be faulty, to destroy them if they were found to be incapable of being improved so as to make them saleable. This charter, London, Guildhall MS 6430, is highly protective of clockmakers, particularly English clockmakers, but it does have the more general virtue of insisting on higher standards in the trade.[11]

Basic to the continuity of any company of this sort is its attention to its future, particularly to its apprentices. In some ordinances, subsequently enacted,

> it is ordained that no person or persons whatsoever, which hereafter shall not have served seven years at the least as an apprentice to the said trade and art and mystery of a clockmaker, graver, case-maker, or anything otherwise peculiarly belonging to the same trade ... shall use the said trade art and mystery of a clock maker...

Masters were enjoined to teach their apprentices the basic physics and mechanics of making clocks but also a whole range of other skills such as '... the making of cases or boxes of silver or brass, and likewise the several springs belonging to a watch, clock or larum, and likewise all other particular and peculiar things belonging to such watches, clocks, larums, mathematical instruments and sun-dials ...'. This is so that trained apprentices would 'truly understand both the beginning and ending of their work …'. The ordinance also forbids the buying in of these things from outside the company.[12] Again this is protective and implicitly an insistence on high standards in the continuity of the profession. What is evident from stipulations such as this is that the profession was accommodating a wide range of skills ancillary to the making of clockwork, and specializations within the profession grew up. It is doubtful if there were many people who made every part of a finished product, from the clockwork to the ornamentation. But it is questionable as to how well this specialization worked. It may have improved the quality of shoddy workmanship, but, evidently, it did not improve immediately the accuracy of the timekeepers that were produced.

Clockmakers and especially watchmakers became justifiably proud of their productions. From 1661 comes a text pointing out that '… many carry watches about them that do little heed the fabrick and the contrivance, or the wit and skill of workmanship; as there be many that dwell in this habitable world that do little consider or regard the wheel work of this great machine, and the fabric of the house they dwell in.'[13] A little later, in 1675, the invaluable *Horological Dialogues* of John Smith appeared. In his opening section he addresses 'the use, right management of clocks and watches'. He substantiates this in the traditional manner:

> … Clocks, in that perfection in which the age enjoys them, excel all other instruments in [their] officiousness in all times, and in all places, as well in the nights as in the day, as well in cloudy skies or in clear weather, as well in close roomes as in the open air, which no other horological instrument besides this is able to perform …[14]

He follows this by explaining the mechanics of clockwork, the various types of clock and how they differ from each other, and how to choose a good clock and how to set it up. He also considers their 'regularity' and what factors can cause them to go wrong. He is particularly specific about the care with which intricate watches need to be treated. Even when they are functioning properly he is not impressed by their accuracy: 'Observe also to set your watch continually by one sun-dial, because it is seldom known that two sundials go true together; so that, if you set it sometimes by one, and sometimes by another, you will never know when your watch or clock goeth right.' Watches and clocks needed to be set by sundials, but sundials themselves did not always give time consistently with one another. He goes on to advise: 'set it (if possible) always to one hour on the same dial, because many times the hour-lines give not true time alike'.[15] All this a far cry from the confidence in sundials expressed by

Middleton and Donne. But all this was also improved upon by the invention and development of the pendulum.

The history of the invention and development of the pendulum is highly disputed, but it seems clear that Galileo Galilei (1564–1642) and Christaan Huygens were important to it.[16] There is a legend that in 1582 Galileo was in Pisa Cathedral and observed a chandelier as it moved in the wind and noted that a suspended weight, whatever the arc, took the same time to swing from one side to the other. He did not immediately explore the horological possibilities of the pendulum, but in 1641, a year before he died, he began to think about how a pendulum might be used to regulate a clock. Later, his son Vincenzo Galilei tried to make a clock based on his father's design, but did not complete it before he died: an unfinished pendulum clock is mentioned among his possessions. In 1659 a drawing by Viviani, Galileo's biographer, of a clock incorporating some of Galileo's ideas, was sent by Leopold dei Medici to Ishmael Boulliau, a prominent French astronomer, and to his friend Huygens, who got it in January 1660. But Huygens was also thinking about the pendulum: he was not a clockmaker, but an astronomer and mathematician and, conscious of the importance of what he had designed, turned over the practicalities of its application to others. In June 1657 Huygens commissioned Saloman Coster, a clockmaker in The Hague, to manufacture clocks based on his principles. Later that year, Ahasuerus Fromenteeel, a Dutchman but a member of the Worshipful Clockmakers Company of London, sent his son to work for Coster to build clocks – for a salary and expenses. With Coster's permission, in May 1558, John Fromenteel returned to his father's workshop in London and naturally brought with him the theoretical knowledge of the pendulum and techniques of applying the physics of it to the making of clocks.[17] There is scarcely a better example of the generous camaraderie of the clockmakers of Europe. But this is how ideas travelled.

The invention and development of the pendulum, important though it was, did not solve all things immediately. There were, in any case, differences in the way it was applied: in the words of G.J. Whitrow, 'Galileo's clock involved a new type of escapement which was superior to the verge type retained by Huygens. Each swing of the pendulum pushes the top [toothed] wheel from one projecting pin to the next.'[18] But it was the Huygens design which initially persisted and became standard, but only for a short time. There emerged serious problems: it used the verge escapement and a short pendulum that oscillated rapidly and could be affected by the drive train mechanism of the clock. A few years later, perhaps in 1666, Robert Hooke, a London-based scientist rather than a clockmaker, began to experiment with a longer pendulum which had a slower swing and a more restricted arc. This, as John Smith later recognized, was a considerable improvement in terms of the accuracy of clocks:

> ... clocks who have their motion regulated by a pendulum arc are more excellent than those who are regulated by a ballance, and those that are regulated by a long pendulum are far more excellent that those regulated by a short one ...[19]

There also emerged, at about the same time, a design for an escapement mechanism which worked better with the long pendulum: this may have been the invention of Robert Hooke, but Joseph Knibb (1640–1711) and William Clement (1638–1704), makers of clocks and members of the Worshipful Clockmakers Company of London, both have claims.[20] In this system the escape wheel was positioned vertically and above it, engaging and releasing the teeth, was an arm, shaped like an anchor, with two flukes, which was slowly oscillated by the long pendulum – the 'anchor escapement' still in use today.

This device needed to be housed in a tall clock and there emerged in the latter part of the seventeenth century clocks with an upper dial showing the hours and minutes, weight-driven, and regulated by the long pendulum and anchor escapement, often housed in wooden cases, sometimes ornately decorated and brightly painted – the long-case clock or grandfather clock of today. The disadvantage of the anchor escapement was that it needed to be placed on a level surface and needed not to be moved – or else the mechanism, which was gravity based, would be disturbed and the clock would stop. The perceptive John Smith again puts the matter clearly, this time in his *Horological Disquisitions Concerning the Nature of Time* (1694), which deals principally with pendulum clocks. Smith opens his address to the reader with the assurance that he does not wish to 'cover the clock-makers' imperfections' but to demonstrate 'those unavoidable variations between the time given by the sun and that of a good and well-adjusted clock and to give such directions as may yet reduce them to nearer agreement in time'. And the greater part of the book is devoted to this, with various charts detailing the suggested adjustments which could be made to give a better alignment. But there are also some perceptive sociological insights – particularly the contrast he draws between the London specialists and the provincial buyers of clocks:

> The difficulty in setting up pendulum clocks rightly in such places where the help of the clock maker cannot be had, is the reason that many gentlemen who live far off from London, are as yet unfurnished

with them; and it also too often happens, that clocks who at first have been set up well as to matter of going, have bi accident been misplac'd or jumble'd awry, and so are made to stand still and become useless meerly for want of skill in the owner to put them to rights.

And he follows this by a series of suggestions for how pendulum clocks should be set up: when it stands well with a regular beat of the pendulum, 'you must make him fast to the place he stands against'.[21]

But it is possible that some of the more learned and sophisticated of those living in provincial contexts liked to think of themselves as independent of mechanical timekeepers. In one of the earliest poems that he wrote – *A Country Life*: 'To His Brother Master Thomas Herrick', who had left London in about 1610 to become a farmer – Robert Herrick (1591–1674) signals, by means of an allusion to the cock in Chaucer's *Nun's Priest's Tale* and a pun on 'watch', a preference for natural over mechanical timekeeping. His brother, he says, will readily interrupt his pleasant dreams, and begin work in the traditional way from daybreak:

> ... to rise when Chanticleer
> Warns the last watch, but with the dawn dost rise
> To work ... (56–8)

In his later poem, *The Grange, or Private Wealth*, he extrapolates on this, in a literary fashion – in a kind of idyll – and characterizes his vicarage of Dean Prior (Devon) as a limited, but self-sufficient, bucolic entity. He talks of being served by a single maid ('Prew', 5), of his hen, goose and lamb, of his 'fat' mousing cat, his dog ('Trasy', 26), and how he has no need of a clock:

> Though clock,
> To tell how night draws hence, I've none,
> A cock
> I have, to sing how day draws on. (1–4)[22]

Here, perhaps unsurprisingly in this sort of poem, he sets aside the mechanical clock in favour of the traditional 'natural' timekeeper. It is difficult to know how serious and realistic this is, and how far it depends on literary gesture and convention. In practical terms, it would be inherently unlikely that his stock would have been singular: to be viable, his lifestyle would have needed hens, geese and sheep in the plural. On the other hand, it is known that his servant 'Prew' was Prudence Baldwin, and that his dog 'Trasy' was a spaniel – so to this extent it is accurate. There is here, perhaps, some wry recognition of his marginalized and provincial lifestyle, what he calls his 'rural privacy' (28), and this coheres with the distantly Stoic ideal of 'contentment with little': '... toys to give my heart ease: / Where care / None is, slight things do lightly please' (30–2). But, the quasi-ironic, deliberately diminishing language of this ('toys', 'slight', 'lightly') suggests that Herrick felt that this was not a position which was stable and could be adhered to in the long-term. The 'quietist', separatist, country-based agenda, assumed by some seventeenth-century poets, was rendered untenable not only by political developments (Herrick was deprived of his living in Dean Prior in 1647 but restored to it in 1662), but also by technological advances.

For portable clocks – chamber clocks, the popular lantern clocks and the like – clockmakers continued, well into the eighteenth century, to use the verge escapement and the short pendulum and these clocks continued to be purchased over the whole of England – in London and in the provinces. One could not confidently say that clocks were everywhere in England at this point, but they were available in most places.

These developments in relation to the pendulum and the invention and development of the balance spring (claimed by both Huygens and Hooke) in watches – still used in mechanical watches – brought clockmaking, particularly that as practised in London, up to a new standard. This period was what Sir George White called the 'Golden Age of English clockmaking'.[23] This moment in the late seventeenth century did not constitute by any means the end of speculation about the measurement of time, nor of clockmaking. It is as well to be reminded of A.J. Turner's judgment:

> The pendulum clock thus changed the nature of the time by which men lived, it did not change the standard of comparison. No clock was yet reliable enough to act as a standard for others nor was there any practical way in which its time could have been transmitted to more than a few other clocks. Clocks still had to be regulated against the sun and the stars, and for the majority of clock-owners this meant by a sun-dial ... [24]

Nevertheless, this was an important moment, and since this book was never meant to go beyond this period it is perhaps as good a place as any to end. Many writers, including Samuel Butler, have said that a work of art, or more specifically a poem, is never completed or finished, but abandoned, and though this study cannot claim the status specified here, it can legitimately cease to explore further.

After about 1670 the trade developed quickly, particularly in London, and many clocks and watches, in increasingly ornate and intricate designs, were produced – particularly for use in domestic contexts. And clockmakers continued to experiment, in order to enhance the use and attractiveness of clocks, with increasingly intricate striking clocks, 'repeater' clocks, clocks showing lunar as well as solar movement, equation clocks and much more. Numerous examples of these have survived and have been preserved and catalogued and can be seen in the museums of the world – where it is best to see them. They have also been extensively and elaborately photographed. Though readers may derive something new from my descriptions of relatively early timekeeping devices and clocks seen *in situ*, they do not need to read my, or anybody else's, descriptions for these later clocks: they can look at them for themselves. But though they had achieved much, the scientists and clockmakers of this period, including Huygens, had hopes of being able to construct a reliable maritime chronometer, but this, at this period, was beyond them, though a lot of thought was expended on the problem.[25] A solution had to wait for the ingenuity and persistence of John Harrison (1693–1776), the son of a carpenter, in the next century. After a number of failures – Samuel Beckett's words 'fail again, fail better' were never more relevant – he managed to produce a clock, significantly in the form of a large watch, which served the purpose.[26] This not only successfully addressed the problem of calculating the spatial concept of longitude in terms of time and accurate timekeeping, but it probably also resulted in the saving of countless numbers of seafarers' lives.

II

It is difficult to know not only where to end a work like this, but also how to end it. However, some attempt at summarizing what has been a temporally and spatially extensive exploration may be appropriate. Towards the end of the seventeenth century time obviously did not stop and nor did the development of the mechanical clock. But it can be said that in this period the mechanical clock had progressed from its hesitant beginnings in the 1270s and had become an object which had materially altered the culture of Europe. It had displaced other methods of calculating diurnal time, by means of sundials, candle clocks, hourglasses and water-clocks – though decorative sundials and hourglasses in various forms were (and are) still in use in specific contexts. The concept of equal hours had been established, both for day and night, as had the trust in calculation based on the physics of force – through the falling weight or the spring – and resistance through the foliot, the balance wheel and various types of pendulum. And all this had been described, interpreted and moralized by the makers and decorators of mechanical clocks, by artists and extensively and imaginatively by writers.

But the practical dimension of the development of the mechanical clock is also important and crucial. To give actuality to these theoretical advances demanded a body of trained craftsmen who could make these instruments. In relation to early clocks, blacksmiths, locksmiths and gun-makers were important and, as has been shown, blacksmiths remained important into the sixteenth and seventeenth centuries for the making and maintaining of larger public clocks, usually clocks for town or village churches. But, as the mechanical clock's importance increased, so more sophisticated makers became involved. The case of the Oxford-trained Richard of Wallingford is worth recalling here: he was the son of a blacksmith, but the clock he fashioned for the monastery of St Albans far exceeded in its ambitious intricacy anything that his father might have conceived or produced. And gradually specialized clockmakers emerged, capable of producing more sophisticated instruments, working on smaller scales, fashioning domestic clocks and watches, often of intricate design, without compromising the increasing accuracy of their timekeeping. In England the regulation of the trade through the establishment of the Royal Clockmakers' Company of London, described earlier in this chapter, cannot be overestimated.

Though the development of the mechanical clock did not lead to a solution of any of the profound philosophical problems relating to the study of time,[27] it did for some thinkers – from the later Middle Ages onwards – provide an image of the way in which the universe may have been conceived as working, how God may have set it up: the constant depiction of the zodiac on early clocks, together with other celestial imagery, served to give force to this idea. The clock also served to sharpen the cultural awareness of time in its own more practical levels: the mechanical clock, displacing the *clepsydra*, provided a means by which religious institutions could organize their operations, particularly their services, and not long afterwards a means by which secular institutions – from entities as big as a state – might conduct their business. In towns and cities, the public clock – often highly valued – provided a means of identity and a focus for how their ways of life might be organized: whether it was a large and elaborate astrological clock like that on the town hall in Prague, or a simpler version such as that in the small Lombard town of Clusone (both described earlier), mechanical clocks were preserved and carefully maintained in their localities over the years. They increasingly defined the ways in which employers and the trade guilds negotiated standards of workmanship, the length of the working day, holidays, and the appropriate payment of wages. Quantifiable time came to have a monetary value. 'Time is money' became proverbial: in Francis Bacon's terms 'time is the measure of business, as money is of wares, and business is bought at a dear hand where there is small dispatch'.[28] Here 'dispatch' means promptness, and using time, with punctuality, and not wasting it gave rise to another cautionary seventeenth-century proverb: 'If you lose your time you cannot get money or gain'.[29]

But early mechanical clocks – usually through their marionette shows – claimed not only to display instruction on religious matters for the secular public, but also to enjoin certain ideas in relation to other sorts of behaviour in both social and moral contexts. The routine inclusion of 'the labours of the months' on many early clocks were not only demonstrations of the orderliness of the world set in time, but a reminder of the responsibilities expected of mankind, not only to support themselves economically, but to live well in consonance with the passage of time. And as early as the Prague clock of the fifteenth century, the vain man with his mirror and the miser with his money bags, both appearing in the context of the deathly skeleton who pulls the rope which strikes the hours, are constant reminders of the strain of moral admonition that is often part of the clocks of these centuries – particularly in relation to the personalized timekeepers of the sixteenth and seventeenth centuries. These strictures are usually expressed in terms of traditional biblical or classical commonplaces, reminding one that time passes and has to be used for the social good or for the salvation of one's soul. They are conventional and often trite, but because they are located on personalized timekeepers – on watch-cases usually – they are for the eyes of the individual and are implicitly coercive in that they imply that the responsibility for moral action rests on that particular individual. Possibly more than any other development, the emergence and spread of the watch have enhanced the individual's awareness of time. According to the fourteenth-century author of *The Cloud of Unknowing*, echoing St Augustine, 'tyme is maad for man, & not man for tyme'.[30] But after the development of the mechanical clock this proposition has become somewhat problematic.

Notes

PREFACE

1 This essay first appeared in *The European Review*, 11:4 (2003), pp 453–74. It was subsequently reprinted with some corrections in my *Occasions for writing: essays on medieval literature, politics and society* (Dublin, 2010), pp 62–82.
2 This essay appeared in *On literature and science: essays, reflections, provocations*, ed. Philip Coleman (Dublin, 2007), pp 43–61.

INTRODUCTION

1 See G.J. Whitrow, *History*, p. 50. Antiphon's fragmentary writings contain the earliest references to time that we have.
2 See *Revolution*, pp 10–11.
3 See *Medieval machine*, pp 147–70.
4 See *Time, work and culture*, p. 52.
5 See *Technics and civilization* (New York, 1939), pp 14–15.
6 See H.K.F. Eden and Eleanor Lloyd, *The book of sun-dials* (London, 1900), p. 303 (No. 545).
7 See *Time*, p. 19.
8 All of the scholars mentioned in the foregoing pages have, quite properly in my view, used discursive literary texts, both in prose and in poetry, as material evidence for the existence and use of clocks in the later Middle Ages and the Renaissance. In addition, there have been more specific studies relating to this relationship. I have found the following both inspiring and useful: A.J. Gurevich, 'Time as a problem of cultural history' in Louis Gardet et al. (eds), *Cultures and time* (Paris, 1976), pp 229–45; Linne Mooney, 'The cock and the clock: telling time in Chaucer's day', *Studies in the Age of Chaucer*, 15 (1993), pp 91–108; Nancy Mason Bradbury and Carolyn P. Collette. 'Changing times: the mechanical clock in late medieval literature', *Chaucer Review*, 43:4 (2009), pp 351–73; and more specifically to Chaucer, Scott Lightsey, *Manmade marvels: medieval culture and literature* (New York, 2007), though this is not exclusively devoted to clocks.

CHAPTER 1. *The shape of time: history and the life of man*

1 The *Enneads* are quoted from *Plotinus* with an English translation by A.H. Armstong, 6 vols (Cambridge MA and London, 1967), III. 297.
2 The *Confessions* are quoted from the translation by R.S. Pine-Coffin (London, 1961).
3 The *Physics* are quoted from *Aristotle, The Physics* with an English translation by Philip H. Wicksteed and Francis M. Cornford, 2 vols (London and New York, 1929).
4 See *Plato* with an English translation by R.G. Bury, 12 vols (Cambridge MA and London, 1975), IX. p. 77.
5 On this issue see the fine article by Anne Higgins, 'Medieval notions of the structure of time', *Journal of Medieval and Renaissance Studies*, 19 (1989), pp 227–50.
6 See Cicero, *De Natura Deorum*, edited with an English translation by H. Rackham (Loeb: Cambridge MA and London, 1979), p. 173.
7 See *History*, p. 43.

8   See *Hesiod, the Homeric hymns and Homerica*, ed. and trans. by H.G. Evelyn-White (Loeb, 57: Cambridge, MA, 1936).
9   *The City of God* is quoted from the translation by Henry Bettenson (London, 1984).
10 For much of the material in this section I am dependent on David Ewing Duncan's *Calendar*, pp 29–51 and G.J. Whitrow, *History*, especially pp 56–70.
11 See Robbins, *Secular lyrics*, p. 62 (No. 68).
12 For the version I was taught see *The Oxford dictionary of nursery rhymes*, ed. Iona and Peter Opie (Oxford, 1951), pp 380–1 (No. 469).
13 For the various time schemes that developed in the Middle Ages I am much indebted to David Ewing Duncan, *Calendar*, especially pp 52–126, G.J. Whitrow, *History*, especially pp 71–86, and R.L. Poole, *Medieval reckonings of time* (London, 1918) and his *Studies in chronology and history* ed. A.L. Poole (Oxford, 1969).
14 Quotations are from and references are to *Bede, Ecclesiastical history of the English people with Bede's Letter to Egbert and Cuthbert's Letter on the death of Bede*, translated by Leo Shirley-Price, revised by R.E. Latham and with translation of the minor works and a new Introduction and Notes by D.H. Farmer (rev. edn London, 1990).
15 See *Studies in chronology and history*, p. 9.
16 Ibid., pp 12–13.
17 Ibid., pp 13–20.
18 Ibid., pp 23–4.
19 See R.L. Poole, *Medieval reckonings of time*, pp 46–7.
20 See my *John Skelton: the career of an early Tudor poet* (Dublin, 2014), pp 356–75 for a study of the poem.
21 See Skelton, *English poems*, p. 312.
22 See *Edmund Spenser, the shorter poems*, ed. Richard A. McCabe (London, 1999), pp 32–4 and p. 40.
23 See *From memory to written record: England 1066–1307*, 2nd ed. (Oxford, 1993), pp 299–304. I am much indebted to Clanchy's section 'Dating documents' for much of the material in this paragraph.
24 See *The Domesday of St Paul's*, ed. W.H. Hale, Camden Society 69 (1857), p. 109.
25 For Skelton's calendar see Scattergood, *John Skelton*, p. 56. For the poems see *The complete English poems of John Skelton*, ed. John Scattergood, rev. ed. (Liverpool, 2015), pp 96–7, 208–9.
26 See *Historians of the Middle Ages* (London, 1974), p. 30.
27 See John Williams, *Early Spanish manuscript illumination* (New York, 1997), pp 110–27 and plates 36–40, but there is an extensive bibliography on this unusual and important manuscript. For a digitized version see www.bl.uk/manuscripts.
28 A number of the topics addressed in this and subsequent paragraphs are discussed in Werner Vebeke, Daniel Verhelst and Andries Welkenhuysen (eds), *The use and abuse of eschatology in the Middle Ages* (Leuven, 1988). See particularly Richard Landes, 'Lest the millenium be fulfilled: apocalyptic expectations and the pattern of Western chronography, 100–800', pp 137–211.
29 For much of what follows in this section I have relied extensively on Norman Cohn's *The pursuit of the millennium: revolutionary millenarians and mystical anarchists of the Middle Ages* (London, 1957) and Bernard McGinn's *Visions of the end: apocalyptic traditions in the Middle Ages* (Columbia, 1979). See also the brief but pertinent comments by Anne Higgins, 'Medieval notions of the structure of time', *Journal of Medieval and Renaissance Studies*, 19 (1989), especially pp 240–4.

30 For Adso's *Libellus Antichristi* see McGinn, *Visions of the end*, pp 82–7.
31 For the *Pseudo-Methodius* see McGinn, *Visions of the end*, pp 70–5.
32 See particularly the comprehensive overview of Simon MacLean, 'Reform, queenship and the end of the world in tenth-century France: Adso's "Letter on the Origin and Time of Antichrist" reconsidered', *Revue Belge de Philologie at d'Histoire*, 86:3/4 (2008), pp 645–75.
33 On Augustine on the 'six ages' scheme see Burrow, *Ages of man*, especially pp 80–92 and 198–200. See also Whitrow, *History*, p. 80.
34 On the importance of Isidore of Seville see Burrow, *Ages of man*, especially pp 82–8.
35 For a digitized version see www.bl.uk/manuscripts.
36 For a facsimile with an informative introduction, see A. Derolez, *The making and meaning of the Liber Floridus* (Turnhout, 2015).
37 See *The homilies of Wulfstan*, ed. Dorothy Bethurum (Oxford, 1971), No. Ia, Ib, II, III, IV, V.
38 See *The homilies of Wulfstan*, XX. 7–15. But the quotation is taken from the text in *Sermo Lupi ad Anglos*, ed. Dorothy Whitelock (London, 1963), lines 1–12.
39 See *Anglo-Saxon poetic records III: The Exeter Book*, eds George Philip Krapp and Elliott Van Kirk Dobbie (New York and London, 1936), pp 227–9.
40 See *The Seafarer*, ed. Ida L. Gordon (London, 1960).
41 On Joachim see Bernard McGinn, *Visions of the end*, pp 126–41; Cohn, *The pursuit of the millennium*, pp 108–13; Burrow, *The ages of man*, p. 111; Whitrow, *Time in history*, pp 81–2; and two books by Marjorie Reeves, *Joachim of Fiore and the prophetic future* (London, 1976) and *The influence of prophecy in the later Middle Ages* (Oxford, 1969).
42 See Marjorie Reeves and Beatrice Hirsch-Reich, *The Figurae of Joachim of Fiore* (Oxford, 1972), especially pp 24–38.
43 For a comprehensive overview of the shapes that Antichrist could assume see Bernard McGinn's essay 'Portraying Antichrist in the Middle Ages' in Vebeke (ed.), *The use and abuse of eschatology in the Middle Ages*, pp 1–48 with copious illustrations.
44 See *The pursuit of the millennium*, p. 111.
45 *Martin Chuzzlewit* (1842), Chapter 11.
46 *A Shropshire lad* (1896), II 'Loveliest of trees …'
47 See *The metaphysical poets* ed. Helen Gardner (London, 1979), pp 108–11 for the text and p. 312 for Henry King's life.
48 *A stanzaic Life of Christ*, ed. F.A. Foster (EETS OS 116, 1926), lines 101–4.
49 See *Ages of man*, pp 5–11 for three age schemes.
50 See Burrow, *Ages of man*, the portraits on Frontispiece, p. 84 (Titian) and p. 180.
51 See *Ages of man*, p. 194.
52 On this see the fine study by Mary Dove, *The perfect age of a man's life* (Cambridge, 1986), and for an illustration see on p. 97 the 'ages of man' frescoes from the Palazzo Trinci, Foligno, dating from about 1400. See also the illustrations of this scheme in Burrow, *Ages of man*, frontispiece, and facing pp 64 and 180.
53 The text is taken from *The vision of Piers Plowman: a critical edition of the B-Text based on Trinity College Cambridge MS B. 15. 17*, ed. A.V.C. Schmidt (London, 1997).
54 On the importance of the *vigilia* in this scheme see Burrow, *The ages of man*, pp 60–71 and Mary Dove, *The perfect age of a man's life*, pp 107–8.
55 Whiting O 29.
56 See Carleton Brown (ed.), *Religious lyrics of the fifteenth century* (Oxford, 1967), No. 151, lines 64–70 (pp 238–4).
57 See Brown (ed.), *Religious lyrics of the fifteenth century*, No. 147, lines 9–16 (pp 230–3).

58 Quotations are from *The Parlement of the Thre Ages*, ed. M.Y. Offord (EETS OS 246, 1967). See my study of the poem in *The lost tradition: essays on Middle English alliterative poetry* (Dublin, 2000), pp 86–99.
59 See *Metamorphoses*, ed. and trans. by F.J. Miller, 2 vols (Loeb: New York and London, 1916), Book XV, lines 199–200.
60 On the 'four age' scheme see Burrow, *Ages of man*, pp 12–36. His exposition is illustrated by Byrhthferth's diagrams between pp 21 and 22. For an illustration of this scheme from the Holkham Bible picture book see Dove, *The perfect age of a man's life*, 69. Here it is adduced in relation to the Wheel of Fortune.
61 See *Edmund Spenser, the shorter poems*, ed. Richard A. McCabe (London, 1999), pp 41 and 152.
62 See R. Klibansky, Erwin Panofsky and Fritz Saxl, *Saturn and melancholy* (London, 1964), p. 114.
63 See *Minor poems*, I, pp 329–62.
64 See John Lydgate and Benedict Burgh, *Secrees of the Old Philisoffres*, ed. R. Steele (EETS ES 88, 1894).
65 On the influence of Ptolemy see particularly Burrow, *Ages of man*, pp 36–45. On pp 197–8 he prints the relevant section of *Tetrabiblos* IV, Chapter 10, in the translation of F.E. Robbins (Loeb: Cambridge MA and London, 1940).
66 On the use of this scheme by Fortescue and Raleigh see Burrow, *Ages of man*, pp 50–2. For other uses of the scheme by Renaissance writers see Dove, *The perfect age of a man's life*, pp 10–13.
67 For Burrow's account of these paintings see *The ages of man*, pp 44–6 and for an illustration see facing p. 85.
68 See *The perfect age of a man's life*, pp 98–100 and the two illustrations on p. 99.
69 For Burrow's reading of this speech see *Ages of man*, pp 52–4.
70 On the meaning of 'dial' here see A.G. Rigg, 'Clocks, dials and other terms' in Douglas Gray and E.G. Stanley (eds), *Middle English studies presented to Norman Davis in honour of his seventieth birthday* (Oxford, 1983), pp 255–74 especially pp 266–8.

CHAPTER 2. *Living in time: years, months, weeks and days*

1 The text is taken from *The works of the Gawain poet: Pearl, Cleanness, Patience, Sir Gawain and the Green Knight*, ed. Ad Putter and Myra Stokes (London, 2014). All subsequent quotations from *Sir Gawain and the Green Knight* are taken from this text.
2 See John Scattergood and Myra Stokes, 'Travelling in November', *Medium Aevum*, 53 (1984), pp 78–83.
3 For overviews of this tradition see Rosamund Tuve, *Seasons and months: studies in a tradition of Middle English poetry* (Cambridge, 1975), Derek Pearsall and Elizabeth Salter, *Landscapes and seasons of the medieval world* (London, 1973), and Bridget Ann Henisch, *The medieval calendar year* (University Park, PA, 1999). See also Barbara Hanawalt, *The ties that bound: peasant families in medieval England* (Oxford, 1986), pp 124–40.
4 See Robbins, *Secular lyrics*, p. 62 (No. 67).
5 See *Secular lyrics*, p. 246.
6 For a text see *Reliqiae Antiquae*, ed. Thomas Wright and James O. Halliwell-Phillipps, vol. I (1841), pp 43–7.
7 The text is taken from *Sonnetti Burleschi e Realistici dei Primi Due Secoli*, ed. Francesco Massera (Scrittori d'Italia: Bari, 1920). There is a spirited verse translation by Thomas C. Chubb in *Medieval age: specimens of European poetry from the ninth to the fifteenth century*, ed. Angel Flores (London, 1963), pp 166–71.

8   See Enrico Castelnuovo, *Il Ciclo dei Mesi di Torre Aquila a Trento* (Museo Provinciale d'Arte, Trento, 1987), which has fine illustrations not only of the individual months, but also of detailed sections of the paintings. Enrico Castelnuovo interestingly invokes both the 'turning of the seasons' passage from *Sir Gawain and the Green Knight* and the *Très Riches Hueres du Duc de Berry* for comparison, see p. 11.

9   I take the following information from *Les Très Riches Heures du Duc de Berry: Musée Condé, Chantilly*, Introduction and Legends by Jean Longnon and Raymond Cazelles, Preface by Millard Meiss (London, 1969).

10 See his essay 'Social history and the Book of Hours' in Roger S. Wieck, *The Book of Hours in medieval art and life* (London, 1988), p. 35.

11 See Eamon Duffy, *Marking the hours: English people and their prayers, 1240–1570* (London, 2006). For what follows I am much indebted to this highly informative book. Though the secondary literature on this type of book is, unsurprisingly, extensive.

12 For their popularity in the later Middle Ages and on into the world of print, see Eamon Duffy, *The stripping of the altars: traditional religion in England, 1400–1580* (London, 1973), pp 209–98.

13 See Nigel Rogers, 'Patrons and purchasers: the original owners of Books of Hours produced in the Low Countries for the English market' in *Corpus of Illuminated Manuscripts*, XI, XII: Low Countries, series 8, ed. B. Cardon (Louvain, 2002), pp 1165–81.

14 In Christopher de Hamel's *Meetings with remarkable manuscripts* (London, 2018), two of the manuscripts studied are 'books of hours': see pp 376–425 and 508–63. One is from France and the second from Flanders.

15 For this manuscript see L.L. Williams, 'A French Book of Hours in the Royal Irish Academy', *The Arts in Ireland*, 2:3 (1974), pp 32–9, and for a more detailed treatment 'A Rouen Book of Hours for Sarum Use, *c.*1444 belonging to Thomas, Lord Hoo, Chancellor of Normandy and France', *Proceedings of the Royal Irish Academy*, 75 C9 (1975), pp 189–212. I am much indebted to these articles. My attention was first drawn to this manuscript by Dr Catherine Yvard, to whom I am immensely grateful. For her comments on it see 'Minute masterpieces: study of a late fifteenth-century Book of Hours (Chester Beatty Library Western MS 89)' (PhD, Trinity College Dublin, 2004), 4 vols, IV, pp 83–92. For the not very accurate copying of the English see my chapter 'Dublin, Royal Irish Academy MS 12 R 31: A French scribe copies English' in John Scattergood, *Manuscripts and ghosts: essays on the transmission of medieval and Renaissance literature* (Dublin, 2000), pp 198–214.

16 See Duffy, *Marking the hours*, p. 4.

17 See 'Richard of York: books and the man' in Erik Kooper (ed.), *Current research in Dutch universities and polytechnics on Old English, Middle English and historical linguistics: papers read at the Twenty-Seventh Research Symposium held in Utrecht on 16 December 2005* (Utrecht, 2006), pp 37–48, especially pp 42–4.

18 See Duffy, *Marking the hours*, p. 23.

19 See for this manuscript Anne F. Sutton and Livia Visser-Fuchs, *The Hours of Richard III* (Stroud, 1990).

20 See Duffy, *Marking the hours*, p. 43.

21 See Robbins, *Secular lyrics*, p. 63 (No. 70).

22 Lydgate, *Minor poems*, I, pp 363–77 (No. 69).

23 See Greene, *Carols*, p. 190 (No. 311.1) for the text, and p. 418 for the comment.

24 See *The great household in late medieval England* (London, 1999), p. 84. I am much indebted to this informative and detailed book.

25 See Woolgar, *The great household*, p. 86.

26 Quoted from *Wynnere and Wastoure*, ed. Stephanie Trigg (EEtS 297, 1990), p. 11.
27 See Greene, *Carols*, p. 6 (No. 11).
28 See *Fast and feast: food in medieval society* (University Park, PA, 1976), p. 221. I am much indebted to this book for much of what follows in this paragraph.
29 See Glynne Wickham, *Early English stages, 1399–1600*, 2 vols (London, 1959), I, p. 188.
30 See Wickham, *Early English stages*, I, pp 197–8.
31 See *Minor poems*, II, Nos. 41, 42, 44.
32 See *Minor poems*, II, Nos. 45, 46.
33 See Greene, *Carols*, p. 80 (No. 132B).
34 See John Russell's *Boke of Nurture* in *The Babees Book*, ed. F.J. Furnivall (EETS OS 32, 1868), lines 719–94. For Burrow's account see *Ages of man*, pp 29–30. For Whitrow's account see *History*, pp 74–5.
35 See *Two early Tudor lives: the life and death of Cardinal Wolsey, by George Cavendish and the life of Sir Thomas More by William Roper*, edited by Richard S. Sylvester and David P. Harding (London, 1969), pp 73–4.
36 See *English moral interludes*, ed. Glynne Wickham (London, 1976), p. ix.
37 For Henry Percy, fifth earl of Northumberland, as a patron of the arts see Mervyn James, *Society, politics and culture: studies in early modern England* (Cambridge, 1986), pp 83–90. In his *Household Book* it is specified that the earl's almoner should be 'a maker of Interludys' (p. 22).
38 See *The Macro plays: The Castle of Perseverance, Wisdom, Mankind*, ed. Mark Eccles (EETS 262, 1969), p. 164.
39 *The great household*, p. 95.
40 *Minor poems*, II, pp 649–51 (No. 33).
41 See *The poems of William Dunbar*, ed. James Kinsley (Oxford, 1979), p. 69.
42 See *Pepys's Diary*, III, p. 267.
43 *The great household*, p. 93.
44 See *A collection of ordinances and regulations for the government of the royal household made in divers reigns, from King Edward III to King William and Queen Mary ...* (London, 1790), p. 121.
45 See *The Cely letters, 1472–1488*, ed. Alison Hanham (EETS 273, 1975), p. 156 (No. 169).
46 For these poems see Greene, *Carols*, Nos. 451–8 (pp 275–9). See also Robbins, *Secular lyrics*, Nos. 23–9 (pp 17–25).
47 The text is taken from Greene, *Carols*, No. 453.
48 For the sermon extract see Greene, *Carols*, p. 490 (my translation).
49 Ibid., pp 324–5.
50 See her essay 'English almanacks from script to print' in John Scattergood and Julia Boffey (eds), *Texts and their contexts: papers from the Early Book Society* (Dublin, 1997), p. 11. This essay provides an authoritative but concise overview of the subject. For a more general account see Bernard Capp, *English almanacks, 1500–1800: astrology and the popular press* (Ithaca, NY, 1977).
51 For a similar weather prediction relating to St Paul's Day (29 June) see Robbins, *Secular lyrics*, p. 63 (No. 71).
52 See Robbins, *Secular lyrics*, pp 63–7 (No. 72, lines 113–20).
53 Ibid., pp 67–70 (No. 73, lines 7–22).
54 See Keith Thomas, *Religion and the decline of magic: studies in popular beliefs in sixteenth- and seventeenth-century England* (London, 1991), p. 736.
55 See D.W. Robertson, *English literary history*, 19 (1952), 9.

56 See *The Boke of Cupide*, lines 46–50, 55, 86–100 in *The works of Sir John Clanvowe*, ed. V.J. Scattergood (Cambridge and Totowa NJ, 1975).
57 Both use the phrase 'good fellow' ironically in a pejorative sense. See my essay '*Goodfellas*, Sir John Clanvowe and Chaucer's *Friar's Tale*: "occasions of sin"' in Cliodhna Carney and Frances McCormack (eds), *Chaucer's poetry: words, authority and ethics* (Dublin, 2013), pp 15–36.
58 See *Early Irish lyrics: eighth to twelfth century*, edited and translated by Gerard Murphy (Oxford, 1956), pp 140–7.
59 See *Early Irish lyrics*, pp 148–51.
60 Compare *Romeo and Juliet*, III. vv. 8–9.

CHAPTER 3. *Measuring time in the Middle Ages and Renaissance*

1 See *Feudal society*, trans. L.A. Manyon, 2 vols (Chicago, 1962), I. p. 74.
2 As Landes points out, the 'stop watch' can identify a particular moment at which something happens, can attempt to 'seize it in flight', but that does not stop time, which is 'logically impossible': see *Revolution*, pp 108–9.
3 For a comparison see *The Romaunt of the Rose and Le Roman de la Rose: a parallel text edition*, ed. Ronald Sutherland (Oxford, 1968), p. 8.
4 See *Anglo-Saxon poetic records I: The Junius Manuscript*, ed. G.P. Ktapp (New York and London, 1931), p. 14.
5 This description is based partly on personal observation. But I am grateful to Dr Daniel Mc Carthy of Trinity College Dublin, for pointing out this interesting clock to me and, through getting closer to the clock-face than I was allowed to, telling me about the unequal hours.
6 See his essay 'The origins of modern time' in *Time*, ed. A.J. Turner (The Hague: Tijd voor Tijd Foundation Amsterdam, 1990), p. 21. This is the catalogue of the 'Images of Time' Exhibition held in the Nieuwe Kirke, Amsterdam in 1990.
7 See *John Donne, The complete English poems*, ed. A.J. Smith (London, 1971), pp 72–3.
8 See 'The origins of modern time', p. 19.
9 See Claudia Kren, 'The traveller's dial in the late Middle Ages: the Chilinder', *Technology and Culture*, 18 (1977), pp 419–35.
10 See Susan Foister, Ashok Roy and Martin Wyld, *Making and meaning: Holbein's Ambassadors* (London, 1997), especially pp 30–43.
11 See ibid., p. 35.
12 For a good summary of the history and the various kinds of sundial see Britten, *Old clocks*, pp 16–25.
13 This is from personal observation.
14 See Evelyn Edson, *Mapping time and space: how medieval mapmakers viewed their world* (London, 1997), pp 135–7. The map is reproduced as Figure 7.1 on p. 136.
15 See *Time reckoning in the medieval world: a study in Anglo-Saxon and Norman sundials* (British Sunial Society, 2010), p. 46.
16 This is based partly on personal observation, but I have also been substantially informed by S.A.J. Bradley's *Orm Gamalson's sundial: the lily's bloom and the rose's fragrance* (The Kirkdale Lecture 1997), (Kirkdale, 2002).
17 On this, and on the sundial on St Gregory's Minster, see Guy A. Points, *An introduction to Anglo-Saxon church architecture and Anglo-Saxon and Anglo-Scandinavian sculpture* (West Byfleet, 2015), pp 69–70, where there are some good photographs.
18 There are, unsurprisingly, many collections of these mottoes, usually in older books: see, for example, A.H. Hyatt, *A book of sundial mottoes* (New York, 1903).

19 For a text see *The poems of Andrew Marvell*, ed. Hugh MacDonald (London, 1952), pp 51–3.
20 The famous botanist Carl Linnaeus, in the eighteenth century, hypothesized a Horologe or Watch of Flowers, based on the 'chronobiology' of 46 species of flowers and herbs, and a number of Victorian gardeners attempted to give this actual form.
21 See Tilley B 202.
22 See Whiting T 325 and T 309.
23 For a comprehensive overview see A.J. Turner, *The Time Museum catalogue of the collection, Vol. 1, Time measuring instruments, Part 1: Astrolabes, astrolabe-related instruments* (Time Museum, 1986). See also W. Hartner, 'The principle and use of the astrolabe', *Oriens-Occidens* (Hildesheim, 1968), pp 287–318 and J.D. North, 'The astrolabe', *Scientific American*, 230 (1974), pp 96–106.
24 On this sort of timekeeper see Britten, *Old clocks*, pp 31–2.
25 See Britten, *Old clocks*, pp 31–2.
26 *Asser's Life of King Alfred*, translated from the edition of Stevenson, by A.S. Cook (Boston, MA, 1906), pp 104–5.
27 See R.T. Balmer, 'The operation of sand-clocks and their medieval development', *Technology and Culture*, 19 (1978), pp 615–32. For examples see also F.J. Britten, *Old clocks*, pp 32–3.
28 This is the form it takes in what is probably the earliest depiction in Ambrogio Lorenzetti's *Allegory of Good Government*, painted in 1338, in the Palazzo Pubblico, Siena. Tenperantia (Temperance) holds an hourglass. For a reproduction see Frederick Hartt, *A history of Italian Renaissance art*, rev. ed. (London, 1980), colour plate 14 and figures 119 and 120.
29 Quoted from Turner, *The Time Museum catalogue of the collection*.
30 See Ben Jonson, *Poems*, ed. Ian Donaldson (Oxford, 1975), p. 144.
31 See *Cavalier poets*, ed. Thomas Clayton (Oxford, 1978), p. 25.
32 For various examples of this instrument see Britten, *Old clocks*, pp 25–31. See also Cipolla, *Clocks*, pp 29–31; Whitrow, *History*, pp 101–2; Landes, *Revolution*, pp 21–2, 51–2.
33 For this and for other water-clocks from the Islamic world see D.R. Hill, *Arabic water-clocks* (Aleppo, 1981). I owe this reference to my friend John Comiskey, who has seen the water-clock in Fez.
34 See *Apocolocyntosis*, ii. 2–3 (quoted by Whitrow, *History*, p. 66).
35 For a study of this and the previous methods of timekeeping addressed here and some stunning illustrations see *Time*, ed. A.J. Turner (The Hague: Tijd voor Tijd Foundation Amsterdam, 1990), especially pp 18–23, 94–109. This is the catalogue of the 'Images of Time' Exhibition held in the Nieuwe Kirke, Amsterdam in 1990.
36 See the brief but authoritative essay by J.D. North, 'Monasticism and the first mechanical clocks' in J.T. Fraser and N. Lawrence (eds), *The study of time II: Proceedings of the Second Conference of the International Society for the Study of Time, Lake Yamanaka, Japan* (Berlin, 1975), pp 381–93. On the Cistercian Rule and its relation to water-clocks see C.B. Drover, 'A medieval monastic water-clock', *Antiquarian Horology*, 1 (1953–6), pp 54–8, 63.
37 See *The Chronicle of Jocelin of Brakelond*, ed. with a parallel translation by H.E. Butler (Edinburgh, 1949), p. 107.
38 See Silvio A. Bedini, 'Clocks and the reckoning of time' in *The encyclopaedia of the Middle Ages*, pp 457–64 (458–9). This, however, is doubted by Landes, *Revolution*, p. 70.
39 On this see Cipolla, *Clocks and culture*, pp 38–40; Landes, *Revolution*, pp 53–78. For the interaction between religious and secular timekeeping see especially Jacques le Goff's classic essay 'Merchant's time and church's time in the Middle Ages' in *Time, work and culture*, pp 29–42.
40 I have sometimes modified Sinclair's translations.

41 See François Villon, *Oeuvres: Edition Critique avec Notices et Glossaire*, ed. Louis Thuasne, 3 vols (Paris, 1923), vol. I, pp 171–2. For the Sorbonne bell see Pierre Champion, *François Villon: Sa Vie et Son Temps*, 2 vols (Paris, 1913), vol. I, pp 142–3.
42 See *The Cely letters, 1472–1488*, ed. Alison Hanham, (EETS 273, 1975), p. 151 (Letter No. 165).
43 See *The Cely letters*, p. 35 (Letter No. 39). See also a letter dated 12 August from Richard Cely the Elder reporting on a battle near Courtrai which 'begane on Saterday at iiij of the cloke at afternoon, and laste tyll nyghi' (p. 55. Letter No. 59).
44 See the wonderfully informative and discursive treatment of *The Millar's Tale* and the *The Reeve's Tale* in J.A.W. Bennett's *Chaucer at Oxford and at Cambridge* (Oxford, 1974), particularly pp 27–57.
45 Quoted by R.W. Symonds, *English clocks*, p. 15. He also includes similar wills.
46 The etymology is from John of Garland's *Dictionarius* (quoted by Jacques le Goff, *Time, work and culture*, p. 36).

CHAPTER 4. *The development of the mechanical clock*

1 See Reginald Pecock, *The Repressor of Over Much Blaming of the Clergy*, ed. Churchill Babington, 2 vols, Rolls Series 19 (London, 1860), vol. I, p. 118.
2 See 'Clocks, dials and other terms' in Douglas Gray and E.G. Stanley (eds), *Middle English studies presented to Norman Davis in honour of his seventieth birthday* (Oxford, 1983), pp 255–74 (258).
3 See Anthony J. Duley, *The medieval clock of Salisbury Cathedral* (Friends of Salisbury Cathedral Publications, 1977).
4 See his *Time in history*, p. 101.
5 For studies of the development of early clocks see particularly Cipolla, *Clocks and culture*, pp 1–75; Landes, *Revolution*, pp 53–84; Jean Gimpel, *Medieval machine*, pp 147–70.
6 See *Clocks and culture*, p. 30.
7 Quoted by Jean Gimpel, *Medieval machine*, p. 153.
8 For the contested implications of this passage see Lynn Thorndike, 'The invention of the mechanical clock about 1271 AD', *Speculum*, 16 (1941), pp 242–3.
9 According to Whitrow, this was the 'crucial invention that made the mechanical clock possible': *History*, p. 103. For his description of how this mechanism worked see pp 103–5. My explanation relies heavily on his more detailed account, which has helpful diagrams.
10 For other useful explanations of the verge escapement mechanism see Cipolla, *Clocks and culture*, pp 121–2; Robertson, *Evolution*, pp 14–19; R.W. Symonds, *English clocks*, pp 16–19; Landes, *Revolution*, pp 198–9; and Hugh Tait, *Clocks and watches*, pp 5–8. See also E.J. Tyler, *European clocks* (London, 1968), pp 7–9. All of these books have helpful diagrams and illustrations of early examples of this clockwork. Cipolla explains the workings of the balance wheel (again with a useful diagram) on pp 122–3.
11 These details are from Cipolla, *clocks and culture*, pp 41–2.
12 See *Calendar of patent rolls*, Edward III, 4 May 1368.
13 See R. Allen Brown, 'King Edward's clocks', *The Antiquaries Journal*, 29 (1959), pp 83–8. For other royal clocks see G.M. Woolgar, *The great household* pp 83–4.
14 See *English church clocks: their history and classification* (Ashford, Kent, 1977), pp 4–6.
15 For details about these metalworkers see Cipolla, *Clocks and culture*, pp 50–1.
16 Quoted by R.W. Symonds, *English clocks*, p. 16.
17 See Gimpel, *Medieval machine*, p. 160.

18 This passage is discussed both by Robertson, *Evolution*, pp 43–4 and Landes, *Revolution*, p. 84.
19 For details see Cipolla, *Clocks and culture*, pp 47–50; and more generally on the development of personal timekeepers see Landes, *Revolution*, pp 85–97.
20 See *Cambridge Middle English lyrics*, ed. Henry A. Person (Seattle, 1962), pp 53–4 (No. 62).
21 For examples of lantern clocks see A.J. Turner, *Time*, pp 86–7.
22 On this clock see J.D. North, 'Monasticism and the first mechanical clocks', p. 385.
23 For Richard of Wallingford see the definitive edition of his work by J.D. North, *Richard of Wallingford*, 3 vols (Oxford, 1974), especially I, pp 441–526. See also his later *God's clockmaker: Richard of Wallingford and the invention of time* (London, 2005). See also E. Watson, 'The St Albans clock', *Antiquarian Horology*, 11 (1979), pp 576–84.
24 De Mézières's description is quoted from Cipolla, *Clocks and culture*, pp 45–6.
25 On de' Dondi's astrarium see Gimpel, *Medieval machine*, pp 159–65; and for a more detailed account see S.A. Bedini and F. R. Maddison, 'Mechanical universe: the astrarium of Giovanni di Dondi', *Transactions of the American Philosophical Society*, 56, part 5 (1966).
26 On this clock see F.J. Britten, *Old clocks*, pp 63–5.
27 See Clive Ponsford, *Time in Exeter* (Ponsford, 1978), pp 31–4.
28 See Cipolla, *Clocks and culture*, p. 42.
29 For an interesting account of clock-jacks see F.J. Britten, *Old clocks*, pp 36–58, where are to be found descriptions of these various clocks. The accounts of the clocks in Wells and Prague are taken from personal observation. There is, however, an excellent account by Robert Dunning, *Wells Cathedral clock* (The Chapter of Wells Cathedral, 2011), with close-up photographs of much of the detail. For an earlier account see R.P. Howgrave-Graham and L.S. Colchester, *The Wells clock* (Friends of Wells Cathedral, 1971), which again has good illustrations.
30 For an excellent account, with illustrations, of the Strasbourg clocks and their importance see F.C. Haber, 'The cathedral clock and the cosmological metaphor' in *The study of time II*, pp 399–416. For a magnificent and detailed photographic record of the clock as it is see Roger Lehni, trans. R. Beaumont-Craggs, *Strasbourg Cathedral's astronomical clock* (Editions 'La Goélette, 2002).
31 For the various modifications to the Strasburg clock see F.J. Britten, *Old clocks*, pp 54–7.
32 This is from personal observation. For a detailed account of Jean Fusoris as a constructor of clocks see Emmanuel Poulle, *Un Constructeur D'Instruments Astronomique au XVe Siècle: Jean Fusoris* (Paris, 1963), pp 27–40.
33 See Cipolla, *Clocks and culture*, p. 34 for an account of this clock.
34 On this see the interesting article by Linne Mooney, 'The cock and the clock: telling time in Chaucer's day', *Studies in the Age of Chaucer*, 15 (1993), pp 91–109.
35 For this rhyme and its interpretation see Cipolla, *Clocks and culture*, p. 41 and Landes, *Revolution*, p. 75. But the criticism may be otherwise: one might translate this as 'The clock on the palace goes as he (the king) pleases' and refer more generally to his wish to control time.
36 See J. Viellard, 'Horloges et Horlogers Catalans a la Fin du Moyen Age', *Bulletin Hispanique*, 63 (1961), pp 161–8; C.F.C. Beeson, 'Perpignan 1356 and the earliest clocks', *Antiquarian Horology*, 7 (1970), pp 408–14, and the same author's more comprehensive treatment *Perpignan 1356: the making of a tower clock and bell for the king's castle* (London: Antiquarian Horological Society, 1983).
37 See *Paston letters and papers of the fifteenth century*, ed. Norman Davis, Part I (Oxford, 1971), p. 413 (Letter 248) and p. 554 (Letter 339).

38 See *Kingsford's Stonor letters and papers, 1290–1483*, edited and introduced by Christine Carpenter, two volumes in one (Cambridge, 1996), vol. II, pp 6–8 (Letter No. 166).
39 See Tilley, C 426.
40 See Cipolla, *Clocks and culture*, pp 45–6; Gimpel, *Medieval machine*, p. 165.
41 See F.C. Haber's fine essay 'The cathedral clock and the cosmological clock metaphor' in J.T. Fraser and N. Lawrence (eds), *The study of time II*, pp 399–416.
42 See Landes, *Revolution*, pp 82–3.
43 For a description of this treatise and the illustration which accompanies it see Eleanor P. Spencer, 'L'Orloge de Sapience, Bruxelles, Bibliotheque Royale MS IV.iii', *Scriptorium*, 17 (1963), pp 277–99. I have taken much information on Suso from this fine article. See also H. Michel, '*L'Horloge de Sapeince* et l'Histoire de l'Horlogerie', *Physis*, 2 (1960), pp 291–8, where the clocks are discussed in great detail. See also Henry Suso, *Wisdom's Watch on the Hours*, trans. Edmund Colledge (Washington, DC, 1994).
44 See K. Horstmann, 'The Orlogium Sapientiae or The Seven Points of True Wisdom', *Anglia*, 10 (1888), pp 323–89. The quotation is from p. 325.
45 See Nicole Oresme, *Le Livre du Ciel et du Monde*, ed. Albert D. Menut and Alexander J. Denomy. Translated with an introduction by Albert D. Menut (Madison, WN, 1968), pp 288–9. I have used Menut's translation.
46 *Revolution*, p. 57.
47 I owe this point to my colleague Professor Corinna Salvadori Lonergan, to whom I am also generally indebted for much advice on Dante.
48 See Eleanor P. Spencer, 'L'Orloge de Sapience: Bruxelles, Bibliotheque Royale MS IV. 111', p. 279. For a study see Charity Cannon Willard, 'Christine de Pison's "Clock of Temperance"', *L'Esprit Créatur*, 2 (1962), pp 149–54.
49 See Nancy Bradbury and Carolyn Colette, 'Changing times: the mechanical clock in late medieval literature', *Chaucer Review*, 43 (2009), pp 351–73, especially p. 362 for a somewhat different reading of this passage. They stress very firmly the political and social implications: '… de Mézières links governance, *attemprance*, justice and political stability. *Attemprance* as restraint is central to a clock's steady movement and to the stability of a realm: power and energy must be harnessed and flow in predictable patterns'.
50 See Cipolla, *Clocks and culture*, p. 46.
51 *A Treatise of Melancholie*, with an introduction by Hardin Craig. The Facsimile Text Society No. 50 (New York, 1940), pp 67–8, 80. I owe this reference to Dr Andrew Power.
52 For a discussion of these issues see chapters 6 and 7 of this book.

CHAPTER 5. *The use of time: some social and moral implications of the mechanical clock*

1 See, *Time, work and culture*, pp 49–50.
2 See C.F.C. Beeson, *English church clocks, 1280–1850* (Antiquarian Horological Society London, 1971), p. 16.
3 *Summa de Vitiis et Virtutibus* (Antwerp, 1587), Tractatus V, Caput I, p. 77, cols a and b.
4 See R. de l'Espinasse, *Les Metiers et Corporations de Paris* (1886), Part 1, p. 52. For an excellent account of these labour regulations and disputes see Jacques le Goff, *Time, work and culture in the Middle Ages*, pp 44–9.
5 See John Scattergood, 'A note on the moral framework of Donne's "The Sunne Rising"', *Neuphilologische Mitteilungen*, 92 (1981), pp 307–14.
6 See Donne's *Poems*, pp 80–1.
7 See 'The Hours of the Day in medieval French', *French Studies*, 13 (1959), p. 243. For these and other examples see Landes, *Revolution*, pp 77–8.

8   See A. Thierry, *Receuil de Monuments Inedits de l'Histoire du Tiers Etat* (Paris, 1850), pp 456–7.
9   See G. Espinas and H. Pirenne, *Receuil de Documents Relatifs a l'Histoire de l'Industrie Drapere en Flandre*, I (1906), p. 6.
10 See Drummond Robertson, *The evolution of clockwork* (London, 1931), p. 34.
11 For details about the bridge-clock in Caen and the clock in Milan see David S. Landes, *Revolution in time*, p. 73.
12 See Carlo Cipolla, *Clocks and culture*, p. 39 for these details.
13 See David S. Landes, *Revolution in time*, p. 79 for this story.
14 The bell of this clock was broken as it was transported to Dijon and had to be replaced. I have seen this clock and it appears to me that there have been other modifications over the years. For another illustration see F.J. Britten, *Old clocks and watches and their makers*, p. 37.
15 For details about these labour disputes, and full references, see Jacques le Goff, *Time, work and culture*, pp 45–8; David S. Landes, *Revolution*, pp 73–5.
16 See L.F. Salzman, *Building in England down to 1540* (Oxford, 1952), pp 61–2.
17 On this interesting text see Jacques le Goff, *Time, work and culture*, pp 50–1.
18 This complaint appears in the London Merchant Tailors' Minutes 1488–93, 60v–61r, and is quoted from Sylvia Thrupp, *The merchant class of medieval London, 1300–1500* (Ann Arbor, MI, 1962), p. 169.
19 *The Cloud of Unknowing and the Book of Privy Counselling*, ed. Phyllis Hodgson (EETS OS 218, 1944), p. 20.
20 See *Les Romans de Chrétien de Troyes IV: Le Chevalier au Lyon (Yvain)*, ed. Mario Roques (Paris: Champion, 1971), lines 5211–15.
21 Roger Fenton, *A Treatise of Usurie* (1611), p. 2. Many thanks to Dr Peter Smith for this reference.
22 On this whole subject see Jacques le Goff's entertaining monograph *Your money or your life: economy and religion in the Middle Ages*, translated by Patricia Ranum (New York, 1988), especially pp 33–45, from which much of the material in this paragraph is taken.
23 Quoted from Diana Wood, '"Lesyng of Tyme": perceptions of idleness and usury in late medieval England' in R.N. Swanson (ed.), *The use and abuse of time in Christian history* (Published for the Ecclesiastical History Society by the Boydell Press, 2002), pp 107–16 (the quotation is from p. 111). I am much indebted to this fine article.
24 See *Essays*, ed. Michael J. Hawkins (London, 1994), pp 107–9.
25 See *Historical poems of the fourteenth and fifteenth centuries*, ed. R.H. Robbins (New York, 1959), No. 51, lines 33–6.
26 Quoted from G.R. Owst, *Literature and pulpit in medieval England* (Cambridge, 1933), p. 352.
27 Quoted from Iris Origo, *The merchant of Prato: Francesco di Marco Datini* (London, 1963), p. 335.
28 See J.A.W. Bennett, *Chaucer at Oxford and at Cambridge* (Oxford, 1974), pp 40–2.
29 See *Calendar of early Mayor's Court Rolls of the City of London AD 1208–1307*, ed. A.H. Thomas (Cambridge, 1924), p. 52. There is an interesting discussion of issues of this sort in R.H. Tawney, *Religion and the rise of capitalism; a historical study* (London, 1929), pp 50–5.
30 See H. Riley, *Memorials of London and of London life* (London, 1886), pp 226–7 for the spurriers' articles and pp 537–8 for the proposals from the smiths.
31 The text is from Robbins, *Secular lyrics*, pp 106–7 (No. 118).
32 My translation. For J.D. North's line-by-line translation see *God's clockmaker*, pp 21–2.

33 For an excellent account of the legal and social background to this poem, and for some highly informed ideas about its provenance, see Elizabeth Salter, 'A Complaint against Blacksmiths', *Literature and History*, 5 (1979), pp 194–215.
34 For a study of all the known texts see A.S.G. Edwards, *Notes and Queries*, 59 (2012), pp 494–6.
35 For a text see *The poetical works of John Skelton*, ed. Alexander Dyce, 3 vols (Boston, 1864), I, pp 160–1. Many of the ideas appear to have been suggested by Ecclesiastes 3:1–12.
36 Quotations are from Jean Froissart, *Le Paradis d'Amour, L'Orloge Amoureus*, ed. Peter F. Dembrowski (Geneva, 1986). For interesting treatments of this poem see Dembrowski's article 'L'Orloge Amoureus de Froissart', *L'Esprit Createur*, 18, I (1978), 19–31; Francoise Pathau, 'Scientific allusions and intertextuality in Jean Froissart's *L'Orloge Amoureus*', *Medieval and Renaissance Studies*, 20:2 (1990), pp 151–72; Michel Zink, 'L'Orloge Amoureus de Froissart ou la Machine a Tuer le Temps', in *Le Temps, sa Mesure et sa Perception au Moyen Age*, ed. Bernard Ribemont, Actes du Colloque Orleans, Avril 1991 (Caen, 1992), pp 269–77.
37 See Robertson, *Evolution*, pp 552–61; Cipolla, *Clocks and culture*, pp 34, 118, 129; Whitrow, *History*, p. 121; Landes, *Revolution*, pp 85–6.
38 See *Cavalier lyrics*, ed. Thomas Clayton (Oxford, 1978), p. 235.
39 See *Minor poems*, I, No. 68, pp 329–62.
40 See A.G. Rigg, 'Clocks, dials and other terms' in Douglas Gray and E.G. Stanley (eds), *Middle English studies, presented to Norman Davis in honour of his seventieth birthday* (Oxford, 1983), pp 255–74 for a discussion.
41 See Whiting W 157–61 and Tilley W 423: 'As wavering' (variable) as the weathercock.
42 For an account of this emblem see Rosemary Freeman, *English emblem nooks* (New York, 1978), pp 122–3. This emblem is reproduced as a frontispiece to the book.
43 For the emblem and the verse see *Emblemata: Handbuch Zur Sinnbildkunst des XVI. Und XVII Jahrhunderts*, ed. Arthur Henkel and Albrecht Schoe (Stuttgart, 1976), col. 1340.
44 *Emblemata*, col. 1535.
45 *Emblemata*, col. 1341. The motto is 'Sat cito, si sat bene'.
46 *Emblemata*, col. 1340. The motto is 'Pondere levior'.
47 See *Six plays by contemporaries of Shakespearre*, ed. C.B. Wheeler (1955), p. 456.
48 See Richard McCabe, *The pillars of eternity: time and providence in* The Faerie Queene (Dublin, 1989), pp 36 and 88.
49 See *The Faerie Queene Books I–III*, ed. Douglas Brooks-Davies (London, 1993), III. vi. 39, p. 430.
50 See Dafydd ap Gwilym, *Poems*, ed. and translated by Rachel Bromwich (Llandysul, Dyfyd, 1982), pp 30 and 110–13.

CHAPTER 6. *Clocks, order and anxiety in some Renaissance texts*
1 See *Time in history*, p. 122.
2 See *The works of the Honourable Robert Boyle* ed. T. Birch (London, 1772), vol. V, p. 163.
3 See *Technics and civilization* (New York, 1939), p. 14.
4 See Cipolla, *Clocks and culture*, p. 47 for an account of this Louis XI's clock. Titian's Knight of Malta is illustrated on p. 90. For English examples see Julia Faraday, 'Tudor time machines: clocks and watches in English portraits c.1530–1630', *Renaissance Studies*, 33 (2019), pp 239–66.
5 See Landes, *Revolution*, p. 91 for these two examples.
6 See *Pepys's Diary*, II. 153, 166.
7 Ibid., II. 188.

8 See *Pepys's Diary*, II. 226.
9 From the epilogue to *Aglaura*: quoted from Landes, *Revolution*, p. 92.
10 See the extensive note in *Love's Labours Lost*, ed. Richard David (London, 1991), pp 56–7.
11 Quoted from *Thomas Middleton, Women Beware Women*, ed. J.R. Mulryne (Manchester, 1986).
12 See Eric Partridge, *Shakespeare's bawdry* (London, 2001), under 'dial', 'point', 'peculiar river'.
13 J.R. Mulryne thinks that St Mark's in Venice and St Anthony's in Padua are what is probably behind these references, though St Mark's in Florence (opposite which the historical Bianca lived) is mentioned at I. iii. 84: see *Thomas Middleton: Women Beware Women*, p. 119. There is no church of this period in Florence dedicated to St Anthony.
14 See Tilley, C426.
15 See Landes, *Revolution*, p. 91.
16 See *Brief lives and other selected writings*, ed. J. Powell (London, 1949), p. 133. G.J. Whitrow, *History*, p. 113 tells the story with a slightly different emphasis.
17 In the Rijksmuseum, Amsterdam.
18 For an account of this clock see Britten, *Old clocks*, p. 103.
19 For the details of this macabre object, and illustrations, see Britten, *Old clocks*, pp 109–11. For another illustration see Landes, *Revolution*, Figure 19.
20 See *Lirici Marinisti*, ed. Benedetto Croce (Bari, 1910), p. 372. For John Kerrigan's translation to this famous poem see Shakespeare, *Sonnets*, p. 35.
21 Reference is to *Dr Faustus*, ed. John D. Jump (London, 1962).
22 *The Imitation of Christ*, translated by Leo Shirley-Price (London, 1952), Chapter 23, pp 57–8. The passage is based on II Corinthians 6:2.
23 For a comic version of this belief see the *Towneley Second Shepherds' Play* where Mak's wife seeks to explain away the presence of a stolen sheep hidden in a cradle as her child who has been magically transformed: 'he was takyn with an elfe, / I saw it myself. / when the clok stroke twelf / was he forshapyn' (616–19). See *The Towneley Plays*, ed. Geeorge England and Alfred W. Pollard (EETS ES 71, 1966), p. 136.
24 See *William Shakespeare: The Sonnets and A Lover's Complaint*, ed. John Kerrigan, p. 38. I am much indebted to John Kerrigan's excellent account of time in the *Sonnets* on pp 33–41.
25 See René Gratiani, 'The numbering of Shakespeare's Sonnets: 12, 60, and 126', *Shakespeare Quarterly*, 35 (1984), pp 79–82.
26 Compare Whiting, T 325.
27 See Jon R. Russ, 'Time's attributes in Shakespeare's Sonnet 126', *English Studies*, 52 (1971), pp 318–23.
28 See Donne's *Poems*, pp 256–63.
29 The words are those of Sir James Whitelocke in *Liber Famelicus*, p. 39 (quoted in *John Donne: the Epithalamions, Anniversaries and Epicedes*, ed. W. Milgate [Oxford, 1978], p. 197).
30 See R.C. Bald, *John Donne: a life* (Oxford, 1970), p. 563.
31 For an elegant and brief explanation of the stackfeed and the fusee wheel in relation to early watches see Symonds, *English clocks*, pp 20–6. See also Hugh Tait, *Clocks and watches*, pp 20–3, especially Diagram 16. There is also a brief explanation of the way the fusee worked in Cipolla, *Clocks and culture*, pp 122–3, with Figure 3, a diagram. See also E.J. Tyler, *European clocks* (London, 1968), pp 23–4.
32 See *The sermons of John Donne* ed. G.R. Potter and Evelyn M. Simpson, 10 vols (Berkeley, CA, 1953–62), VII, p. 430.
33 See Landes, *Revolution*, pp 87–97 for the development of watches. For illustrations of some watches with a single hand see Britten, *Old clocks*, pp 107–8.

34 See Landes, *Revolution*, pp 128–9 for the development of minute hands.
35 See *The Metaphysical poets*, ed. Helen Gardner (London, 1957), p. 92. For a concise account of his life see pp 320–1.
36 See *Pepys's Diary*, II. 61.

CHAPTER 7. *Some conclusions*

1 See R.W. Symonds, *English clocks*, p. 18.
2 See *Clocks and culture*, pp 53–4.
3 Ibid., p. 69.
4 See Sir George White, *The clockmakers of London* (London, 1998), p. 6, and Susan Foister, Ashok Roy and Martin Wyld, *Making and meaning: Holbein's Ambassadors* (London, 1997), p. 38, Plate 31.
5 See R.W. Symonds, *English clocks*, p. 27.
6 See *Old clocks and watches*, pp 60–1.
7 On this see Sir George White, *Clockmakers*, pp 7–8.
8 See *Itinerary*, ed. C. Hughes (London, 1903), p. 372.
9 See *Itinerary*, p. 475.
10 See R.W. Symonds, *English clocks*, p. 31.
11 For the foundation and early history of the Worshipful Company of the Clockmakers of London see Sir George White, *Clockmakers*, pp 9–12 and R.W. Symonds, *English clocks*, pp 30–3. The opening of the beautiful charter, for which Mr John Chappell in 1634 was paid 4 pounds, for 'flourishing and finishing', is reproduced by Sir George White, p. 11. I take the quotations from the digitized facsimile.
12 On this see particularly Sir George White, pp 10–11.
13 Quoted by Sir George White, from *Humane industry* (1661), on p. 2.
14 *Horological Dialogues*, Part 1, Dialogue 1 (p. 3).
15 *Horological Dialogues*, Part 2, Dialogue 2 (pp 56–7).
16 For accounts, from which I have derived much information, of this invention and its development see R.W. Symonds, pp 330–33, Sir George White, pp 14–15, and especially Whitrow, *History*, pp 123–7. For the rivalries involved see the detailed and circumstantial account of Robertson, *Evolution*, pp 75–129.
17 See Symonds, *English clocks*, pp 34–5.
18 See *History*, p. 124 where Whitrow reproduces the drawing and offers a highly informed commentary on it.
19 *Horological Dialogues*, Part 1, Dialogue 3 (p. 18).
20 See Sir George White, *Clockmakers*, pp 20–1.
21 For these quotations see pp 49 and 51.
22 For the texts see *Cavalier poets*, ed. Thomas Clayton (Oxford, 1978), pp 117–21 and 135–6.
23 See *Clockmakers*, pp 20–3.
24 See 'The origins of modern time', p. 22.
25 See Robertson, *Evolution* pp 143–74.
26 See Dava Sobel, *Longitude: the true story of a lone genius who solved the greatest scientific problem of his time* (London, 1996); Landes, *Revolution*, pp 156–73.
27 For a study of some of these ideas see G.J. Whitrow, *What is time?* (Oxford, 2003).
28 See *Essays*, ed. Michael J. Hawkins (London, 1994), p. 64.
29 See M.P. Tilley, *The proverbs of England in the sixteenth and seventeenth centuries* (Ann Arbor, MI, 1950), T 295. For 'Time is money' see T 320.
30 See *The Cloud of Unknowing*, p. 20.

Further reading

I have found the following books particularly useful in understanding timekeeping instruments and charting the development and spread of early clocks.

C.F.C. Beeson, *English church clocks: their history and classification* (Ashford, Kent, 1977)

F.J. Britten, *Old clocks and watches & their makers* (Antique Collectors Club, 1994)

Carlo M. Cipolla, *Clocks and culture, 1300–1700* (New York and London, 2003)

David Ewing Duncan, *The calendar: the 5000-year struggle to align the heavens – and what happened to the ten missing days* (London, 1998)

H.K.F. Eden and Eleanor Lloyd, *The book of sun-dials* (London, 1900)

Evelyn Edson, *Mapping time and space: how medieval mapmakers viewed their world* (London, 1997)

Jean Gimpel, *The medieval machine: the industrial revolution of the Middle Ages* (London, 1977)

David S. Landes, *Revolution in time: clocks and the making of the modern world*, rev. and enlarged edn (Cambridge, MA, 2000)

Jacques Le Goff, *Time, work and culture in the Middle Ages*, translated by Arthur Goldhammer (Chicago, 1980)

John North, *God's clockmaker: Richard of Wallingford and the invention of time* (London, 2005)

J. Drummond Robertson, *The evolution of clockwork* (London, 1931)

David Scott and Mike Cowham, *Time reckoning in the medieval world: a study in Anglo-Saxon and Norman sundials* (British Sunial Society, 2010)

Dava Sobel, *Longitude: the story of a lone genius who solved the greatest scientific problem of his times* (London, 1996)

R.W. Symonds, *A book of English clocks*, rev. edn (London, 1950)

Hugh Tait, *Clocks and watches* (London, 1990)

Time, edited by A.J. Turner (The Hague: Tijd voor Tijd Foundation Amsterdam, 1990). This is the catalogue of the 'Images of Time' Exhibition held in the Nieuwe Kirke, Amsterdam in 1990.

Time in the medieval world, edited by Chris Humphreys and W.M. Ormrod (York, 2001)

Sir George White, *The clockmakers of London* (London, 1998)

G.J. Whitrow, *Time in history: views of time from prehistory to the present day* (Oxford, 1989)

Index of manuscripts

BRUXELLES
Bibliothèque Royale MS IV. 111, 114–15, **Plate 12**

CAMBRIDGE
University Library MS Dd. 5. 76, 104
    Ff. 6. 8, 63
Fitzwilliam Museum MS 54, 63
Gonville and Caius College MS 353, 73

DUBLIN
Royal Irish Academy MS 12. R. 31, 61–2, 64–5, **Plate 6**
Trinity College Library MS 661, 136–7

EXETER
Cathedral MS 3501, 33–4

GHENT
University Library MS 02, 31–2

LONDON
British Library MS Additional 11695, 29, **Plate 1**
   MS Additional 2398, 130
   MS Additional 18851, 63–4, **Plate 7**
   MS Additional 22720, 52
   MS Additional 28681, 84–5
   MS Arundel 92, 133–4
   MS Cotton Julius C. viii, 105
   MS Cotton Nero D vii, **Plate 9**
   MS Harley 1519, 165
   MS Harley 2341, 23
   MS Yates Thompson 31, 31
Guildhall MS 6430, 166–8, **Plate 16**

OXFORD
Bodleian Library MS Ashmole 328, 43, **Figure 1**
  MS Ashmole 1796, 106
  MS Digby 88, 51–2, **Figure 3**
Corpus Christi College MS 255A, 34, **Plate 2**

USHAW
  College MS 43, 62

General Index

Though there are a number of general entries about concepts such as the 'ages of man' or the 'ages of the world', this is essentially an index of names, mainly of places, people, works of literature and some paintings. It does not include the names of characters in works of literature except in the case of Chaucer, where individual stories in the *Canterbury Tales* are identified by their tellers. It includes the names of scholars mentioned in the text, but not those referred to only in the Notes. The arrangement of items is alphabetical, as generally is the arrangement within items, except in the case of the Bible where the arrangement follows the order of the books in the Authorised Version. There are several general headings, which are then subdivided, such as 'battles' (where the arrangement is chronological) and 'London' (where the arrangement is alphabetical, though 'Companies and Guilds' have their own sub-section). The arrangement under 'clocks and watches' deals alphabetically only with the technical workings of mechanical timekeepers: individual medieval and Renaissance clocks are listed under the places where they are (or were) situated. Chronology is important in a study such as this, so I have added dates where I feel reasonably confident about them (mainly for writers, artists and clockmakers) and where I think they may be useful. I have also tried to situate some of the lesser known places listed in their broader geographical localities. Index entries in **bold** refer to images.

'a gest of Robyn hode', 54
Adso, abbot of Montier-en-Der
    (*c*.910–92), 32
    Libellus Antichristi, 30–1
'ages of man', 35–49
'ages of the world', 29–35
Aix-sur-Lys (Pas de Calais), 124
Aldbrough (Yorkshire), 86
Alexander the Great (356–325 BC), 30
Alfred the Great, king (849–99), 92–3
Alighieri, Dante (1265–1321), 115–17
    Inferno: I. 1–6, 37
        I. 37–40, 36

Paradiso X. 39–48, 115–17
    XII. 139–40, 35
    XV. 97–9, 96
    XXI. 10–18, 115–17
Allen, Thomas, 151
almanac(k)s, 73–9
Amaltei, Girolamo:
    'Horologium Pulverum', 93
Amiens, 123–4
Angoulême, 26
Antiphon (*c*.480–401 BC), 15
Aquinas, St Thomas (1225–74):
    Summa Theologica, 128–9

Archer, Henry (d. 1642), 166–7
Aristotle (384–322 BC), 154
    De Anima III. 12, 39
    Physics IV. x–xii, 18
    Rhethoric II. 12–14, 39
Arras (Artois), 123
Arundel, Thomas, bishop of Ely (1333–1414), 72
'As I went out on my playng…', 140–1
Asser, bishop of Sherborne (d. c.909):
    Life of Alfred, 91–2
astrolabes, 88–91
Aubrey, John (1626–97):
    Brief Lives, 151, 161
Augustine of Canterbury (d. 604), 24
Augustine of Hippo, Saint (354–430), 19, 32, 38, 175
    Confessions: XI. 14, 18
    De Civitate Dei (City of God): XI. 6, 21
    XII. 14, 22
    De Diversis Quaestionibus LXXX III, 31–2
    De Genesi contra Manichaeos, 31
Augustus Caesar (63 BC–AD 14), 23

Bacon, Francis (1563–1626):
    'Of Usury', 129, 174–5
Baldwin, Prudence, 171
Baret, John, 98
Bath (Somerset), 33
battles:
    Hastings (1066), 85
    Roosebeke (1382), 125
    Shrewsbury (1403), 135–6
    Agincourt (1415), 65
    Bosworth (1485), 62, 77
    Flodden (1513), 72
Beaufort, Lady Margaret, 62
Beckett, Samuel, 165

Beckford, Captain, 72
Bede, the Venerable (673–735), 63
    De Tempore Ratione, 24–5, 63
    Historia Ecclesiastica Gentis Anglorum, 24–5
Beeson, C.F.C., 102–3
bells, 96–8
Berkeley, Anne, 37–8
Betson, Thomas, 112
Beverley (Yorkshire), 70
Bible:
    Genesis 3:19, 129
        49:17, 30
    Exodus 20:9, 79
    Psalms 11:9, 22
        90:10, 35–6, 38
    Ecclesiastes 1:2, 40
        1:19, 22
        2:11, 86
        12:8, 40
    Daniel 2:32–3, 29
        2:37–41, 29
        7:3–8, 29
    Matthew 24:6–8, 24–30
    Luke 6:35, 128
        12:36–8, 40
        13:35, 152
    Romans 6:9, 22
        13:11, 23
    I Thessalonians 4:17, 22
    II Thessalonians 2: 1–3, 30
    Revelations 11:3, 34
        13:1, 30
        13:5, 30–5
        13:6, 34
        14:6, 34
Blacksmiths, 132–4
Bloch, Marc, 80
Blois, 153
Boleyn, Anne (1507–36), 165

Bologna, 102
'books of hours', 60–5
Boulliau, Ishmael (1605–94), 169
Bourges:
   Cathedral of St Etienne, 109–10, **110**
Boyle, Robert (1627–91), 113–14, 147
Bright, Timothy (c.1549–1615), 147
   Treatise of Melancholie (1591), 118–19
Britten, F.J., 91, 165
Bromyard, John (d. 1352):
   Summa Praedicantium 129
Brouncker, Viscount William (1626–84), 148–9
Burgh, Benedict (with John Lydgate) (1413–83):
   Secrees of the Old Philisoffres, 45
Burrow, John, 39, 46
Bury St Edmunds, monastery of, 74, 94–6, 98
Butler, Samuel (1612–80), 172
Byrhtferth, 42–3
   Manual, 42–3, **43**
   Ramsey Computus, 42

Caen, 124
'Caeser Masrer', 62
Cahors (Lot), 26
Calais, 97, 112
calendars, 15, 23, 27, 51–77
Calva, Domenico:
   Disciplina degli Spirituali, 26–7
Cambridge, 70
Canterbury, 88
Casamari, Cistercian monastery of (Lazio), 34–5
Castello Toblino, 59

Cavendish, George (1494–1562), 69
Cecil, Henry, Lord Burghley (1520–96), 75
Cely, George, 72–3, 97–8
   Richard, 72–3, 97–8
Charles I, king of England, 166
Charles V, king of France, 92–3, 102, 104, 111–12, 141
Charles VII, king of France, 104, 109
Charles d'Orleans (1394–1465), 60
Chartres Cathedral, 102
Château de Lusignan, 59
Chaucer, Geoffrey (c.1343–1400):
   Book of the Duchess, 98
   Franklin's Tale, 55–6
   Knight's Tale, 75
   Merchant's Tale, 25
   Miller's Tale, 98, 131
   Nun's Priest's Tale, 25, 111, 171
   Parson's Tale, 69, 127
   Prologue to the Man of Law's Tale, 87–8
   Prologue to the Parson's Tale, 88
   Romaunt of the Rose, 98
   Shipman's Tale, 83
   Treatise on the Astrolabe, 88–91
   Troilus and Criseyde, 75
Chester, 70
China, 14. 101
Chobham, Thomas (c.1160–c.1236), 125
Chrétien de Troyes (d. c.1183):
   Yvain, 127–8
Cicero, Marcus Tullius (106–43 BC):
   De Natura Deorum II. xx. 51–2, 19
Cipolla, Carlo M., 101, 124, 164
Clanvowe, Sir John (c.1341–91), 75–6
   The Boke of Cupide, 75
Claesz, Pieter (1597–1661):
   'Vanitas' (1630), 131–2, **Plate 14**

Claudius Ptolemy (90–c.168):
  Tetrabiblos IV, 45–6
Clement, William (1638–1704), 170
Clanchy, Michael, 28
clocks and watches:
  anchor escapement, 170–1
  balance wheel, 173
  jacquemarts (clock-jacks), 106–9, 141–2
  springs, 119, 139, 173
  verge and foliot escapement mechanism, **101**, 102, 137–8, 140, 169, 173
  weights, 102, 104, 106, 140, 144–5, 173
Cloud of Unknowing, The, 127, 175
Cluny, 102, 109
Clusone (Lombardy), 81–2, 174, **82**
Cohn, Norman, 35
Cologne, 96
Colombe, Jean (1430–96), 59–60, **Plate 5**
Commines (Hainault), 126
'Consona sunt aer, sanguis, puericia verque …', 44
Cooper, William, 152
  Elizabeth (his daughter), 152
Coppinghall (Staffordshire), 103
Corazzo, Benedictine monastery of (Calabria), 34
Cosenza (Calabria), 34
Coster, Saloman (1620–59), 169
Courtrai (West Flanders), 125
Cowham, Mike, 85

Dafydd ap Gwilym (d. 1380), 146
Dar-al-Magana, Fez (Morocco), 94, **95**
Datini, Francesco (1335–1410), 130–1
de Champaigne, Philippe (1602–74):
  'Vanitas', still-life (1671), 151

de Dinteville, Jean (1504–55) French ambassador, 83–4
de Lorris, Guillaume (1200–38):
  Le Roman de la Rose, 80
de Meung, Jean (c.1240):
  Le Roman de la Rose, 103–4
de Mezières, Philippe (1327–1405), 103, 106
  Le Songe du Vieil Pèlerin, 117–18
de Picquigny, governor of Artois, 124
de Pisan, Christine (1364–c.1430):
  L'Epistre d'Othea, 117
de Selve, Georges, bishop of Latour (1508–41), 83–4
de la Perrière, Guillaume (c.1499–1565):
  La Morosophie (1553), 143–4
de' Dondi, Giovanni (1330–86) 103, **105**, 106, 112
dei Medici, Leopoldo (1617–75), 169
Dekker, Thomas (1572–1632):
  The Honest Whore, III. i. 113, 150
di Bartolo, Christofano, 130–1
di Pers, Ciro (1599–1633):
  'L'Orologio da Ruote', 153–4
Dickens, Charles (1812–70):
  Martin Chuzzlewit, 36
Dijon:
  Cathedral of Notre Dame, **125**, 125–6
Dionysius Exiguus (c.500–60), 24
'disguisings', 68
Donne, John (1592–1631):
  'Nocturnal on St Lucy's Day', 82
  'Obsequies on the Lord Harrington', 159–61, 169
  'The Sunne Rising', 121–2
Dove, Mary, 46
Drulardy (French clockmaker), 165
Duffy, Eamon, 62

Dunbar, William (c.1460–c.1520):
  'My prince in god, gif the guid grace …', 71–2
Dunstable (Bedfordshire):
  Priory of the Austin Canons, 105

Edward I, king of England, 131
Edward III, king of England, 68, 102, 106
Edward the Confessor, king, 85
Egypt, Valley of the Kings, 84
Elizabeth I, queen of England, 14
emblems, 142–5
England, 61, 83, 102, 112, 150, 164–7, 172
  Cotswold Hills, 131
  East Anglia, 131
Exeter:
  Cathedral, 103
  St Mary Steps (Matthew the Miller clock), 107

Fenton, Roger (1565–1616):
  A Treatise on Usury (1611), 128
Ferrara (Emilia Romagna), 102
Ferrers, Anneis de, 28
  William de, 28
Ferzango, Pietro, 81
Finn Cycle, 76–7
Flamma, Galvano (1283–1344), 124
'flame-clocks', 92–3
Flanders, 61, 63
Florence, 26, 150
  Badia (church of the Benedictines), 96
Folgore di San Gimigniano (1270–1332):
  Sonnetti dei Mesi, 56–8
Fortesque, Thomas (1534–1611), 46

France, 25–6, 31, 103, 164
  Auvergne, 26
  Poitou, 26
François I, king of France, 148
Froissart, Jean (1357–1405):
  L'Orloge Amourouse, 137–9
Fromenteel, Ahasuarus (1607–93), 169
  John (his son, 169
Fusoris, Jean (1365–1436), 103
  Astrolabe, 89, **89**
  Bourges Cathedral clock, 109–10, **110**

Gad's Hill (Kent), 136
Galen (b. AD 129), 154
Galilei, Galileo (1564–1642), 169
  Vicenzo (his son), 169
Genesis B, 81
Genoa, 102
George of Liechtenstein, Prince Bishop (1390–1419), 58
Gervase of Canterbury (d. 1170), 25–6
Germany, 164–6
Ghent, 126
  Cathedral, 107
  work-bell, 123, 126
Gimpel, Jean, 17
Giorgione (1477–1510):
  Three Ages of Man, 39, **Plate 3**
Greece, 84
Greene, R.L., 65, 73
Gregory XIII, Pope (1502–65), 24, 27
Gressham, James (fl. 1626), 112
Grymes, Sir Thomas (1574–1644), 160
Guildford (Surrey), 68

Hague, The, 169
Hall, Thomas, 'blacksmythe', 103

Harold, king of England, 85
Harrington, John, second baron of Exton (1592–1614), 159–61
Harrison, John (1695–1776), 92, 173
Harvey, Gabriel (1545–1630), 27
Hatfield (Hertfordshire), 72
Henisch, Bridget Anne, 68
Henry VI, king of England, 71
Henry VII, king of England, 62–3, 70, 72
Henry VIII, king of England, 106, 164–5
Henry of Asti (d. 1345), 28
Herbert of Cherbury, Lord (1593–1633):
    'To his Watch when he could not Sleep', 161–3
Herefordshire, 151
Herrick, Robert (1591–1674):
    'The Hour-Glass', 93–4
    'A Country Life', 171
    'The Grange', 171–2
    Thomas Herrick (brother), 171
Hesiod (d. ? 750–650 BC):
    Works and Days, 20
Hill, Richard (London grocer), 67
Holbien, Hans (d. 1545), 164–5
    The Ambassadors, 83–4
Hoo, Sir Thomas, Chancellor of Normandy (1396–1455), 61–2, 65
    Eleanor Welles (wife) 61–2, **Plate 6**
Hooke, Robert (1635–1703), 169–70
Horace (Quintus Horatius Flaccus (65–8 BC):
    Odes IV. vii, 86
Houseman, A.E. (1859–1936), 36
How the Plowman Lerned his Pater Noster, 52–3
Hull, Agnes (of York), 62

Humphrey, duke of Gloucester (1390–1447), 69
Humphreys, Chris, 122–3
Huygens, Christian (1627–95), 169, 172

Innocent III, Pope (1160–1216), 35
Isabella of Castile (1451–1504), 63
Isidore of Seville (*c*.560–636):
    Etymologiae, 31
Italy, 102–3, 130–1

James IV, king of Scotland, 71–2
'Januar: By thys fyre I warme my handys …,' 51–2, **53**
Jean II, king of France, 59
Jean, duc de Berry, 59–60
    Bonne de Berry, 60
Jehan de Paris, 148
Jerome (Eusebius Hieronymus) (*c*.342–420), 29–30, 154
Jerusalem, 34
Joachim da Fiore (*c*.1135–1202), 34–5
Jocelin of Brakelond (d. 1211), 94–6
Johannes de Sacrobosco (1195–1256):
    De Sphaera, 88–9, 101–2
John of Aragon, King (1350–96), 111
John of Garland (1195–1272), 98
Jonson, Ben (1532–1637):
    'The Hour-Glass', 93
Julius Caesar (*c*.101–44 BC), 23
Justinian (*c*.482–565), 154

Keney, Vincent, 'clok maker', 165
Kepler, Johannes (1571–1640), 117, 147
Kerrigan, John, 156
King, Henry (1592–1669):
    'The Exequy', 37–8
King's Langley (Hertfordshire), 102

Kirkdale (Yorkshire):
    St Gregory's Minster, **85**, 85–6
Kirke, Edward (1553–1613), 27
Knibb, Joseph (1646–1711), 170
Kratzer, Nicholas (?1487–1550) 106,
    164–5, **Plate 15**

'labours of the months', 51–60, 109,
    156–7, 175
'Ladd y the daunce a mysssomer
    day …', 73
Lambert of St Omer (d. c.1125):
    Liber Floridus, 31–2
Landes, David S., 15–16, 113–14, 117,
    136, 150
Langland, William:
    Piers Plowman B XII. 3–9, 39–40
Langthorpe Tower
    (Northamptonshire), 46–7, **47**
le Goff, Jacques, 16, 120, 129
Leland, John (1503–52), 106
'Let no man cum in to this hall …', 67
'… l'horloge du palais …', 111
Limbourg brothers, Herman, John
    and Paul (fl. 1385–1416), 59–60,
    Plate 5
Limrick or Lymeryke, Thomas (MP
    for Gloucestershire), 97
    Elizabeth (his daughter), 97
London, 68, 84, 97, 112, 147–8, 150,
    165–6, 171–2
    Eastcheap, 136
    Greenwich, 148
    Guilds and Companies:
        Blacksmiths, 132, 165
        Clockmakers, 166–70, 174
        Goldsmiths, 68
        Mercers, 68
        Merchant Tailors, 127
        Spurriers, 131–2

Hampton Court, 69
    Hampton Court clock, 106, **107**
Kennington, 68
London Bridge, 206
St Paul's Cathedral, 28, 103
Woolwich, 148
Lorenzetti, Ambrogio (1280–1348):
    Allegory of Good Government, 92–3,
    Plate 8
Louis IV, king of France, 30–1
    Gerberga (his wife), 30–1
Louis XI, king of France, 109, 148
Lucca (Tuscany), 25
Lucius III, Pope (1097–1185), 34
Lucy, countess of Bedford, 159
Lydgate, John (1370–1451):
    'Kalendare', 64
    'mummings' (Eltham, Hertford,
        Windsor), 68
    'Testament', 44–5, 139–40
Lyon, 124

Mankind, 70
Mantua, 111
Manfredi, Bartolomeo (Manuan
    clockmaker), 110–11
Marlowe, Christopher (1564–93):
    Dr Faustus, 154–6
Martial (Valerius Martialis, c.40–
    c.104):
    Epigrams V. xx, 86
Marvell, Andrew (1618–78):
    'The Garden', 86–7
Maryon, William (Merchant of the
    Staple), 97
'Master Wenceslas', 58
McCabe, Richard, 145–6
Meath, 93
Mecca, 89
merchants, 129–31

Merton (London), 68
Middleton, Thomas (1580–1627):
   Women Beware Women IV. i,
     149–50, 159, 169
Mignon, Abraham (1640–79):
   Stilleven met Bloemen en een Horloge,
     151, **Plate 13**
Midwinter, William (wool merchant),
   97
Milan:
   Church of St Eustorgio, 102
   Church of St Gothard, 102
Monasterboice (Co. Louth), 84
Mooney, Linne, 73–4
Moryson, Fynes (1556–1630):
   Itinerary, 166
Montélimar (Drome), 124
Moysant or Moyse, Pierre:
   skull watch, 153, **152**
Mumford, Lewis, 16, 147
'mummings', 68

Nemesius, bishop of Emesa (fl. *c*.390),
   19–20
Newgrange (Co. Meath), 78
Newsom, Bartholemew (d. 1682),
   165
Nicholas of Lynn (b.?1330–1360):
   Kalendrium (1386), 87–8
North, John, 108
North Stoke (Oxfordshire):
   St Mary the Virgin, 84–5
Northleach (Gloucestershire):
   Church of St Peter and St Paul,
     97–8
Norwich:
   Cathedral, 103–4, 133
Nouwen, Francis (1571–93), 165
   Martin (1545–1616), 165
Nuremburg, 166

'O vanyte off vanytes & all is
   vanite ... ', 40
Oresme, Nicole (1323–82):
   Livre du Ciel et du Monde, 114–15
Orm, son of Gamal, 85
Otford (Kent), 45
Ovid (Publius Ovidius Naso,
   43 BC–*c*.AD 17–18):
   Amores I. xiii, 155
   Metamorphoses XV. 199–200, 41–2
     XV. 234, 153
   Odes I, 12, 153
     IV. vii, 86
Oxford, 90, 105, 131, 174
   Merton College, 103

Palermo (Sicily), 34
Paris, 61, 96, 111, 120, 122
   Château de Vincennes, 102
   Hotel St Paul, 102
   Notre Dame, 122
   Royal Palace, 120
   Sainte Marie-des-Champs, 122
   Sorbonne, 96–7
Parlement of the Thre Ages, The, 41
Paston, John II, 111–12
   John III, 111–12
Pavia (Lombardy), 112
Pecock, Reginald, bishop of
   Chichester (1395–1461):
   *Repressor of Overmuch Blaming of
     the Clergy*, 99–100
Pepys, Samuel (1633–1703):
   Diary, 72, 148–9, 162
Peraldus, Gulielmus (*c*.1190–1271):
   De Vitiis et Virtutibus, 120–1
Percy, Henry, fifth earl of
   Northumberland, 65–6, 70
Perpignan, 111
Philo Judeus (*c*.20 BC–*c*. AD 50)

Philip IV (le Bel), king of France, 123–4
Philip the Bold, duke of Burgundy, 124–5
Pisa, 26, 126
    Cathedral, 169
Plato, 21–2
    Timaeus 37A, 18
    38B, 19
    39D, 19
'plays and dramatic performances', 69–71
Plotinus (d. AD 270):
    Enneads III. vii. 1, 18
Poole, R.L., 24–6
Poos, Laurence R., 60
Prague:
    town hall clock, 109–10, 152, 174–5, **Plate 11**
Prato (Tuscany) 130–1
'Puisque la ville me loge …', 124

Quarles, Francis (1692–1744):
    Hieroglyphikes of the Life of Man, 142
Queenborough (Kent), 102

Raleigh, Sir Walter (1552–1618):
    History of the World, 46
Ralph de Diceto, dean of St Paul's, London (1120–1202), 28
Ramsey Abbey (Cambridgeshire), 42
Ramsey, David (1580–1659), 166–7
Ranulph, earl of Chester (1094–1155), 28
Richard II, king of England, 68
Richard III, king of England, 62–3
Richard, third duke of York, 62
Richmond Castle (Yorkshire), 98
Rigg, A.G., 99

Robertus Anglicus (fl. 1271), 101–2
Rodez (Averyon), 26
Romans (Drôme), 124
Rome, 34, 94
Rouen, 61
Ruin, The, 33
Russell, John:
    Boke of Nurture, 69
Ryche, Katheryne, 112

Salisbury:
    Cathedral clock, 99–100, **100**, 120
    'sand-clocks', 92–4, 142, 156, 174
Seafarer, The, 33–4
Schoonhovius, Florentinus (1594–1648):
    Emblemata (1618), 144
Scott, David, 65
Sebastian de Covarrubias Orozsco (1539–1613):
    Emblemas Morales (1610), 144–5
Seneca, Lucius Annaeus (4 BC–AD 65), 94
Siena, 25
    Palazzo Pubblico, 92–3
Sir Gawain and the Green Knight, 50–1, 66, 70–1
Shakespeare, William (1564–1616) 154
    As You Like It: II. vii, 47–9
    1 Henry IV: II. ii, 134–6
    2 Henry IV: I. iii, 15, 136
    Henry V: IV. i, 122
    Love's Labours Lost: III. i, 149, 165
    Macbeth: II. i, 78
    Richard II: I. iii, 141
        V. v, 140–2
    Richard III: V. vi, 76–7
    Romeo and Juliet: III. v, 91
    Sonnets, 1–126, 156–9, 162

Shropshire, 161
Shuttlecocks family of Lancashire, 164
Skelton, John (? 1460–1529):
   'A Lawde and Prayse Made for Our Sovereigne Lond the Kyng', 28
   The Garlande of Laurell, 27–8
   ? 'On Tyme', 136–7
Smalley, Beryl, 29
Smith, John (fl. 1675–94):
   Disquisirion Concerning the Nature of Time (1694) 170–1
   Horological Dialogues (1675), 168–70
Sosigenes (astronomer, fl. 45 BC), 23
Southwold (Suffolk), 106
Spain, 89, 130–1
Spenser, Edmund (1552–99):
   The Faerie Queene, 145–6
   The Shepheardes Calender, 27, 43–4
Spiritual Franciscans, 35
St Albans (Hertfordshire), 104–5, 174
   Abbey clock, 104–5, **Plate 9**
St Bunyan's Church (Cornwall), 86
St George, 65
'St Swithuns day if thou dost rain ...', 73
Stanzaic Life of Christ, A, 38–9
Stonehenge (Wiltshire) 78
Stonor, Sir William, 112
Strasbourg:
   Cathedral clock, 108, **108**, 113–14, 147
Suckling, Sir John (1609–42) 149
   'Love's Clock', 139
sundials, 16, 83–8, 111, 142, 156, 167–9, 173

Suso, Heinrich (d. 1366):
   Horologium Sapientiae (*The Seven Poyntes of Trewe Wisdome*) 114, **Plate 12**
Symonds, R.W., 164

Tabula Exemplorum, 129
'tempus donum dei est ...', 126
'The bores heed in hande bring I ...', 68–9
Théruanne (Pas de Calais), 126
Thomas a Kempis (1380–1471), 155
Thorpe, Thomas (1569–1625), 159
Tiberius, Emperor (42 BC– AD 37), 24
Titian, Tiziano Vedellio (1488–1576), 39, 148
Tostig, earl of Northumberland, 85–6
Tours (Cher et Loire), 61
Trento (Trentino Alto Agige):
   Torre dell' Aquila, 'ciclo dei mesi', 58–9, **Plates 4a, 4b**
Très Riches Heures du Duc de Berry, 59–60, **Plate 5**
Turner, A.J., 16–7, 81–2, 172
'Two stones yt hath or els yt is wrong ...', 104

Ulf Thoraldson, Prince, 86
usurers, 128–9

Vallin, Nicholas (1563–1603), 165
'vanitas' paintings, 151–2
Venice, 26
Victoria, queen of England, 165
Villon, François (1401–c.1463):
   Le Lais, 96–7
Viollet le Duc, Eugène (1814–79), 109

Virgil (Publius Virgilius Maro,
    70 BC–AD 19):
    Eclogues IV. 4–7, 34–6, 20–1
    Georgics III. 284, 86
Visconti family, 112
Visser Fuchs, Livia, 82

Wales, 146, 167
Wallingford, Richard, abbot of St
    Albans (1292–1336), 103–6, 174,
    Plate 9
Warwickshire, 74, 100
'water-clocks' (*clepsydrae*), 94–6, 113,
    142, 173–4
Webster, John (*c.*1580–1632):
    The Duchess of Malfi, III. v, 145
Wells (Somerset), 106–7
    Cathedral clock, 107–9,
    Plates 10a, 10b
White, Sir George, 172
Whitrow, G.J., 19–20, 100, 147, 169

William of Kerkeby, prior of
    Wallingford (d. 1302), 106
William of Moerbeke, 39
Windsor Castle (Berkshire), 165
Wolsey, Cardinal Thomas
    (1473–1530), 69
Woolgar, G.A., 65, 71
Wulfstan, bishop of Worcester
    (d. 1023):
    Sermo Lupi ad Anglos, 32–3
Wyclif, John (*c.*1330–84), 99
Wynkyn de Worde (d. 1534), 52
Wynnere and Wastoure, 66–7

Yolande of Aragon, 98
York, 70
    Girdlers' Guild, 123
    Minster, 107, 122, 126
    Ouse Bridge, 123
    work-bell, 126
Yorkshire, 131